Audiovisual Script Writing

NORTON S. PARKER

RUTGERS UNIVERSITY PRESS
New Brunswick, New Jersey

Copyright © 1968 by Rutgers, The State University of New Jersey
Library of Congress Catalogue Card Number: 68-18693

ISBN: 0-8135-0797-9 Paper

Manufactured in the United States of America

Second printing

Grateful acknowledgment is made to the University
of California Press for access to glossary material from
Raymond Spottiswoode, *Film and Its Techniques*, 1966.

Preface

Many people think of the motion picture film only as a source of entertainment; the general public has little reason to know that the nontheatrical film field has mushroomed into an immense industry; in some respects it is now a broader field for writers than Hollywood ever was. The nontheatrical film field now presents broader areas for creativity; it presents stimulating challenges; and it presents enormously attractive money-making opportunities.

Since millions of Americans go to the movies every week, it is obvious that the production of motion pictures is a giant industry. In addition to the steady output of feature films for release to motion picture houses, Hollywood also produces nearly nine hundred films a year for television.

It is estimated that in 1963 more than ninety-six hundred nontheatrical films (including filmstrips) were produced, an increase of eleven hundred over 1961. In 1964 the ten thousand mark was passed, and in 1967 more than twelve thousand nontheatrical films were produced. The total investment in the nontheatrical audiovisual industry was six hundred and thirty-eight million dollars in 1963, six hundred and sixty-seven millions in 1964, seven hundred and thirty-nine millions in 1965, and close to one billion in 1967.

This phenomenal increase in the use of audiovisuals in mass communication by business firms, educators, community groups, and federal, state, and local government agencies has occurred since World War II. Religious groups have their own film programs for release over television and other means of exhibition.

More than six thousand industrial firms and business corporations now use film as part of their programs and presentations to stockholders, customers, salesmen, and employees. The broad field of public-relations and public-service films is an enormous one. The United States Army, Navy, and Air Force have large continuing programs for training, orientation, education, information, and documentary films. Among other government agencies, the Department of Agriculture has its own film unit for domestic distribution, and the United States Information Agency has one for overseas distribution.

As a result of this expansion, a great many people have found themselves engaged in the production of motion picture films, television films, and video tapes, without previous experience in basic audiovisual writing and production techniques.

Various people in various jobs in audiovisual production can profit by understanding the genesis of all production—the writing phase. For the beginning film writer, a fundamental knowledge of the audiovisual medium is essential. All forms of writing demand solid construction, unity and form, proper continuity, and economy of expression.

Entertainment films are usually based on original stories or are adaptations of novels or plays. They are produced primarily as a commodity. Few nontheatrical films are made in anticipation of direct monetary returns, yet many demand as much imagination, creativity, and craftsmanship as the entertainment film. As a matter of fact, the nontheatrical film often poses difficult problems—giving a dull subject an imaginative cinematic presentation, one that will compel audience interest.

Most nontheatrical films employ the same basic techniques as films made for entertainment. There is a very close relationship between the fundamentals of the two fields, since the same principles of organization of material, of unity and form, and of script format and presentation apply to each. Training and experience in one field can open the door to the other. The nontheatrical film industry is much less difficult to break into than the more highly competitive entertainment field. For those writers with exceptional talent and drive it can be a stepping-stone to the entertainment world.

This book presents only fundamental principles and techniques, as basic guidelines for the beginner and the serious student—practical applications rather than abstract discussions of creativity and artistic expression. The student and the beginner must learn the rudiments, if his natural aptitude or talent is to express itself through professional craftsmanship. He must find the answers to three basic questions: What is a motion picture production script? In what form must it be written? Why must it be written in that form?

The sole purpose of this book is to give the beginning writer the basic tools with which to launch a satisfying and rewarding career.

Norton S. Parker

Contents

Audiovisual Script Writing

Part I: The Importance of the Visual in Action

1 Thinking Visually

In writing for the motion picture screen or for films for television, the writer must learn first to think in terms of moving visual presentation. This kind of writing is comparable to learning to speak a foreign language; if you are to learn a new language fluently, you must learn to *think* in that language. The heart of the matter is: How successfully can the scene described in the script be transferred to the screen? How will that scene *play?*

Obviously, the ability to think in the language of moving visual presentation, and to judge objectively that presentation prior to filming, varies with each writer. Some writers have a talent for visualization which can be developed; they think in terms of picture and action. Other writers are bound by the way words and phrases look to the eye or sound to the ear. Again, the importance of the visual cannot be overstressed. How often have you heard a sudden sound and said, "What was that?" If you had *seen* what created that sound you would have known what it was.

Retention of the Visual

The sense of hearing is not nearly as reliable for immediate identification, understanding, and memory retention as the sense of sight. U.S. Navy tests have shown that an audience understands much more of what it sees than what it hears, and remembers for a longer period what it has seen rather than what it has heard.

Active "Silents" and Static "Talkies"

The motion picture film, in the early years of its existence as a form of major entertainment, relied almost entirely on the moving visual. The subtitles had to be read and were therefore visual. But the actors relied on pantomime to tell the story taking place on the screen. Some of the old silent films are, of course, recognized today as great cinematic art.

In the era of the silent film, subtitles were held to a minimum, used only to explain what the action could not convey. The telling of the

5

story was left to the skill of the moving visual. Then came the "talkies," and for a time they did little else but talk. Temporarily, the eloquence of pantomime and action were forgotten. *This* was the stage transferred to film! Actors read their lines and, at long last, could be heard by their audience. And the lines were pages long, read in static situations against static backgrounds.

Hollywood entrepreneurs raided Broadway, looking for directing and writing talent. New York stage directors were imported by the dozen. Famous motion picture directors of the silent film were dropped on the assumption that they were not qualified to direct dialogue. In time, this attitude proved invalid, and the action picture recovered its rightful character. The essence of the motion picture— that is, *primacy of the visual in action*—returned. Some of the silent film directors, experts in visual action techniques, were rehired and dialogue gradually ceased to dominate the visual.

The Film in Audiovisual Communications

The motion picture film is the parent medium of audiovisual communications. It includes the fundamentals of writing which are basic

On the set, with actors at left, camera crew at lower right, and technicians in surrounding areas. U.S. Army Photo.

to television and tape recording. Having mastered script writing principles and techniques of motion pictures, the writer should be able to adjust himself to the demands of a script format. These demands vary, because the mechanical means of photography and methods of production vary. With the motion picture film in widespread use on television, it is vital that the audiovisual writer be trained in script writing.

Today, segments of motion picture film are being integrated with television film and tapes during the recording phase or production phase. The combination of previously shot film footage with television and tape recording gives these closely related media greater scope in subject matter. This integration during the recording phase is accomplished by an electronic photographic process, with the camera rephotographing the previously shot film footage as it is projected through the film camera chain.

Pictures That Move

Whatever the different mechanical means used in photographing or recording—motion picture film, TV film, or tape—the end product is a sequence of moving pictures to the audience. This is why the fundamentals of audiovisual writing must apply to all three methods of production.

Blueprint for the Film

A shooting script or scenario is the blueprint of the picture prepared by the writer, the architect of the picture. The director becomes the builder when he converts the script to action on film. In the same sense, the film editor or cutter also becomes a builder when he puts the film together.

You, the writer, must ask yourself, "How will the action described in my script look when it is on the screen?" How do you want it to look? Have you visualized it realistically? Have you fully communicated your thoughts to the director in scene description and camera angle? Does each scene have continuity with the scene immediately preceding and immediately following it? Has your script unity and form?

Unity and Form

A script with unity and form is one in which ideas are organized in proper relationship in time, place, and mood to form a coherent, integrated whole. Unity and form are synonymous with proper continuity and good construction in the organization of material—the right thing in its right place at the right time.

2 Essentials of Film Writing

Before going into a detailed study and analysis of actual production scripts and their treatments, the student and the beginning writer should be briefed on a few essentials. Even a cursory review of these essentials should help the student to gain a better understanding of the example scripts and of the practical application of the basic principles and techniques they reflect.

What, Why, and Who

When a writer is assigned to write any type of film, certain aspects should be spelled out for him at that time:

What—the subject matter, its scope, and its limitations;
Why—the purpose of the film clearly defined;
Who—the audience for whom the film is intended.

After the writer has a reasonably clear idea of what his job will be, he will start his research.

Research

The worth and effectiveness of your production script (whether non-theatrical or theatrical) can only be measured by the quality of your research—your knowledge of the subject. Research cannot be accomplished by superficial reading, brief observations, or reliance on a single authority.

To the three categories of authorities or technical advisors—good, bad, or indifferent—should be added a fourth—the person who is the master of his subject but who cannot communicate what he knows; he may be expert in his field but he is inarticulate. And, being an expert on his subject, he may be inclined to say to himself, "Oh, any damn fool should know *that!*" Consequently, what he does *not* tell the writer may be one of the most important things for the writer to know. The writer in the nontheatrical script field must be a good reporter and skillful in extracting information from source material,

8

technical advisors, and other authorities. He must know how to search out in detail and then how to organize his material.

Organization of Material

The writer works toward achievement of unity and form in his script for audiovisual presentation. Again, the right thing in the right place at the right time will pave a smooth and orderly way to the final script.

The writer must ask himself: What is the most logical and at the same time most imaginative approach I can make to introduce the subject and capture immediate audience interest? How must I develop my material so that my audience will clearly understand what I have to show and say? How must I present it to gain audience empathy and to sustain audience interest? How must I pull together the many threads to bring the presentation to its most effective ending?

The one thing to avoid is overcrowding the script with more major points than your audience can easily absorb.

Running Time

Experience has shown that in most categories of nontheatrical films a running time of 30 minutes or less is the best length for the most effective teaching, orientation, or selling job. In these types of film it becomes increasingly difficult to hold audience interest and to insure its retention longer than half an hour at one sitting. An instructional film which requires more than 30 minutes to project should be broken up into two or more parts, each part to be given a separate showing. There are, of course, exceptions to all rules, such as a documentary with strong human interest that can hold the close attention of the audience for an hour or more.

The arbitrary length or running time of most nontheatrical films demands that the contents be tailored to fit the particular length of running time. You cannot write a script for four or five reels if the assignment calls for three reels—27 to 28 minutes of running time. Thus there must be a general guideline to go by.

Ideally, a shooting script, in final form and proper format, written for approximately 27 to 28 minutes of running time, should be about 30 pages in length, approximately a page for each minute of running time. It should comprise about 120 to 150 script scenes—10 pages and 40 to 50 scenes per reel. This is a standard that works out with surprising accuracy. However, the rule must remain flexible, for there are exceptions depending on the nature of the subject matter, the manner of presentation, the extent of individual scene description, the running time of individual scenes, the bulk of page content, and the amount of spacing in setting up the format.

It is possible that a script written for approximately 30 minutes of running time might run less or more than 35 pages and have more or less than 160 script scenes. But experience shows that it is safe to stick as close as possible to the rule of 10 pages and 40 to 50 scenes to the reel. In shooting the average production script involving all-original shooting, the experienced director may shoot from 15 per cent to 25 per cent of added scenes for maximum coverage.

The preliminary organization and evaluation of your research material has a direct bearing on the length of the film. A given running time of 28 minutes may be accomplished without difficulty. On the other hand, if the material is extensive, and if first analysis seems to indicate that it cannot be fitted into less than 40 to 45 minutes of running time, you must decide what to eliminate and what to use. You must evaluate the relative importance of the various major and minor informational, selling, or instructional points, as well as the more plainly superfluous — employing the art of effective condensation.

The Treatment

The experienced writer can arrive at a rough estimate of film running time before he has written his screen treatment. The inexperienced writer may not be able to make such an estimate until he has organized his material into a first-draft shooting script. In any event, a detailed treatment is necessary for an estimation of running time and to be able to see, on paper, a detailed outline of the subject matter, organized in proper continuity and with an indication of the style of presentation.

The term "Treatment," used in motion picture terminology, is frequently confused with "Concept," "Outline," or "Synopsis." A synopsis, in the usual sense of the word, is a condensed statement. A concept, in ordinary usage, is an idea — a more or less abstract idea. An outline is a brief presentation of the principal features of a proposal.

A treatment is a detailed narrative, sequence by sequence, of what your shooting script or scene and narration script will substantially become.* It is a narrative account of all events and happenings in proper continuity, which you will develop in greater detail in your shooting script as a master guide for the director, cameraman, and film editor.

Do not permit yourself to write too briefly or loosely in preparing your treatment. It carries your story line and should be a well-developed, informative, and polished narrative. It must also win the approval of your producer or sponsor, as well as others who may have a critical interest in the film. Therefore, it is important that you spell out

---

* See pp. 22 and 193 for complete examples.

what you intend to do in the development of the shooting or production script. Do not leave the critical reader of your treatment in doubt, puzzled or misled about what you propose to show in the film and how you will show it.

Often, the inexperienced writer fails to put down on paper *all* that is in his mind about his subject. He knows what he wants to see on the screen; yet he may fail to convey to his reader all that he himself can plainly visualize. In omitting detail he endows the reader with clairvoyant powers which the reader does not possess. Do not rely on your reader to guess what you mean or what you intend to do. Tell him plainly what you mean, so that *he* can clearly see all that *you* see. Remember, too, that the well-developed treatment provides a clue to production costs. If excessive costs become apparent upon reading the treatment, revisions can be made to meet the financial limitations of the production budget before the shooting script is written. Such a control factor saves time and money and is one of the practical purposes for writing the treatment.

When you write your production script, develop the visual first. That is an essential step in the organization of the work. Then write the narration to match, to explain and/or to complement the visual.

Audiovisual Writing — "Lean" Writing

Audiovisual writing is "lean" writing. In scene description, do not indulge in the use of words and phrases which may make beautiful reading but do not describe action and cannot be photographed. Since your treatment is in detailed narrative form, with possible key narration or dialogue inserted, it may have a certain flow. But your shooting script is a scene-by-scene, sequence-by-sequence layout of specific instructions for the director and his production staff to follow as closely as the actual shooting problems will permit.

The director (in nontheatrical production he may be a cameraman-director) has only one use for a script. He must have a script which clearly describes *what* he is to shoot and substantially *how* he is to shoot it. Your script must be written so that the film can be photographed effectively and economically.

Center of Interest

A standard rule in shooting a motion picture is to keep the camera focused on the center of interest and its closely related aspects at all times. The focus must be as close as possible on that center of interest. Even though the director or cameraman-director assumes that this is one of his chief responsibilities, the writer must think and write in the same terms. That is why camera angles are specified in the script—the Extreme Close Up, Close Up, Close Shot, Medium Close, Medium

Shot, Medium Long Shot, Long Shot, Full Shot, and so on. The experienced director will try to choose the best possible angle from which to photograph an object or an action. Even so, he still must have a fairly accurate blueprint to follow. The script is that blueprint. The use of camera angles will be discussed later in detail.

Limbo Technique

In focusing attention on the center of interest, the Limbo Shot or Limbo Technique can be very useful. The Limbo Shot is made against a neutral or blacked-out background. It excludes everything except the principal object or objects to be photographed, with only the essential furnishings or props.

Certain types of production lend themselves to variations of Limbo Technique, either throughout the entire film or in a portion of it. Many educational and instructional films restricted to low budgets can be made effectively by employing the Limbo Technique. It can be used as an economical means of telling a more dramatic type of story where expensive set construction and elaborate sets are not necessary. It is particularly effective when used to focus maximum audience attention on an object or action, or a series of actions, either for greater impact or to eliminate distracting clutter.

One example of a Limbo setting against a blacked-out background would be a businessman at his desk. The only furnishings and props would be the desk, chair, desk pad and pen set, an ashtray, and a telephone. All walls, pictures, windows, doors, other furnishings, and props normally found in such an office would be eliminated.*

Limbo does not limit the imagination of the audience to the confines of a detailed set. When used in the strictest sense of the term it does not necessarily limit the action to an exact location or specific time. It is an impressionistic technique.

Limbo has been used on occasion in entertainment films since the 1920's, in certain instances for greater dramatic impact or to create the world of fantasy. It is closely related to the cameo type of shooting technique, in which people and the action are held in the immediate foreground in "tight" shooting, to the exclusion of everything not essential to the action.

However, Limbo is a stylized type of production, and its use must be considered with care. Does the subject matter lend itself to Limbo Technique? If it does, will Limbo Technique be the most effective means of presentation? Any special effect or technique should be used only when it increases the film's effectiveness, or makes feasible

*See Scenes 1 and 147 on pp. 42 and 80 for other illustrations.

the production of a film whose budget restrictions would prohibit its production by more elaborate means.

Scripts for Previously Shot Film

Many nontheatrical films, such as film progress reports, coverage of technical research and development projects, and certain types of documentaries, are made from film that has been shot before a writer is brought in. The film may have been shot in newsreel fashion and must be put together in proper continuity. The writer may be assigned either before or after a film editor has put the scenes together in a rough cut version.

If a writer takes on the job prior to a rough cut, he will have to screen all the footage to familiarize himself with the material available on which to build his story line. He will then prepare a cutting outline, indicating by brief description the scenes he has selected to tell his story in continuity. This cutting outline is then followed by the film editor in making his first rough assembly of the footage. The writer can then start writing his first draft narration. It is here that a knowledge of running time and of the ratio of words of narration to feet of film is necessary. (The majority of nontheatrical films carry narration instead of live dialogue.)

Again, in timing narration, no mathematical rule can be applied. One type of narration requires slower reading on the part of the narrator while another may require faster reading. Allowance must be made for natural pauses. Changes of mood in a film may influence the pacing of narration. Don't try to time your narration by reading it silently to yourself. Silent reading is usually twice as fast as reading aloud by the same person.

Film Running Time and Narration

There are 16 frames per foot of 35 mm film, and 40 frames per foot of 16 mm film.

35 mm sound speed is 24 frames per second, or 1½ feet of film per second, which is a projection speed of 90 feet per minute. 16 mm sound speed is 36 feet per minute.

One 1000-foot reel of 35 mm is equivalent to one 400-foot reel of 16 mm. The ratio is 10 to 4. Each requires the same running time — about 11 minutes.

For printed titles allow about a word to the foot of 35 mm film, and about 2½ words per foot of 16 mm film.

Average narration is about 1½ words per foot. Based on these ratios, a 10-foot scene in 35 mm would accommodate about 15 words of narration, and a 10-foot scene in 16 mm about 37 words.

Progression of camera angles from a FULL SHOT or ESTABLISHING
SHOT of a group, through a MEDIUM CLOSE TWO SHOT and a CLOSE
TWO SHOT, to an individual CLOSE SHOT, in a Limbo setting.

FULL SHOT or ESTABLISHING SHOT of a group in Limbo.   U.S.
Army Photo.

MEDIUM CLOSE TWO SHOT in Limbo.   U.S. Army Photo.

CLOSE TWO SHOT in Limbo. U.S. Army Photo.

Individual CLOSE SHOT in Limbo. U.S. Army Photo.

This does not mean that it is necessary or desirable to crowd every scene with the maximum number of words it can support. The above figures are given only to show maximum capacity at the rate of 1½ words per foot of 35 mm film.

An extreme is about 2 words per foot, or 180 words per minute. This has been referred to as a "newsreel" type of narration, and is about the rapid-fire rate of delivery in certain TV spot commercials. Such a deluge of fast talk could not be tolerated by the listener for more than a minute or two.

If you have a scene on 10 feet of 35 mm film, you know that you will be limited to about 15 words of narration to cover that scene. For 10 feet of 16 mm, the limit is about 37 words. But give your audience a chance to absorb what they hear over one scene before going on to the next. Let the visual carry as much of the message as possible.

There are some subjects, particularly technical or mechanical ones, for which the narration must be suitably slow and deliberate. Such narration would run about one word to the foot of 35 mm film. So, between two extremes, we find an average approximation of 1½ words to a foot of 35 mm film.

When you are working with stock film, or film previously shot, you will be able to apply these ratios to determine more exactly the overall running time in both film and narration.

A fair estimate in advance timing of scene length in a production script for original shooting comes only through experience. But you can generally count on approximately 30 pages and about 120 to 150 script scenes for a film to run 30 minutes — one minute to the page.

The conventional or standard film used by major producers in the motion picture industry is 35 mm.* To insure maximum photographic quality, many nontheatrical films are shot in 35 mm and then released in 16 mm reduction prints. Another reason for releasing in 16 mm is the advantage of greater mobility, the convenience of the small and easily operated 16 mm projector. In this reduction process the 1000-foot reel of 35 mm is reduced to a 400-foot reel of 16 mm, with the running time remaining identical, as given in the preceding ratios. However, the average reel of 35 mm does not run the full 1000 feet, but instead runs 900 to 960 feet per reel. There are about 360 feet in a 16 mm reel.

---

* 16 mm film is coming into increased usage in some areas of production, particularly the peripheral. However, most film editors prefer to work with 35 mm because of its greater ease in physical handling and its larger viewing proportions, as well as for the greater durability of the film itself in the work print stage; it also simplifies lab processing problems and has a wider range for optical effects.

 **3** **The Qualities of Narration**

The narrator's voice should be pleasing to the ear and stimulating to the mind. But the narrator is only a voice. It is *what* he says and *how* he says it that is important. The narration should flow smoothly. Clichés, awkward words, stilted phrases, and pedantic language must be avoided.

Good narration has a quality of human conversational warmth which encourages rapport with the viewer-listener. Give the narrator words and phrases which he can read easily and which can be understood as easily by the listener. The possible exception to this is the technical film limited to a high-level audience of advanced technicians or professional men capable of understanding and digesting extremely technical terms and phraseology. Even then, well-written narration can give greater flexibility or more natural flow than the static style of a textbook on the same subject.

Integrating the Narrative and the Visual

Narration must be closely integrated with the visual and closely synchronized in time and mood. It must be written with economy of expression and yet with emphasis on those points which the writer wants to make.

If you have to make a point which is mostly abstract, and thus predominantly dependent on the narration for explanation, do not write visual support which requires concentration on that visual. Instead, write visual support which does not tax the visual concentration of your audience — so that the message carried by the audio may be more easily absorbed and understood.

The "Live" Narrator

The usual all-narration film is narrated by a "disembodied voice" whose owner never appears on the screen. But the writer should also consider the use of a live narrator for more effective presentation: for example, the narrator is introduced visually in the opening of the film,

17

while his voice continues over scenes which do not include his image. After introducing the subject in the beginning of the film, a live narrator may appear again at the end to sum it up. Frequently a live narrator may appear several times on the screen to speak directly to the audience between segments of the film.

More Than One Narrator

The writer may also consider indicating the use of more than one narrator, depending on the subject matter or the greater effectiveness which might be obtained with the use of more than one voice. In certain types of film a single voice throughout can become monotonous as it drones on and on, while the change to another voice may freshen up the presentation and recapture greater audience interest. Effective use can be made of one narrator to open and close the film, with a second narrator to voice the main body of your picture.* Sometimes it is desirable for one of the actors to serve as the narrator to introduce the subject, after which his voice comes over scenes in which he may or may not appear. The choice of one of these several ways of handling narration lies with the writer, in his conception of the most effective manner of presentation.

Avoiding the Static

In using a live narrator, the writer should avoid keeping him on camera for too long a time. Otherwise you have a lecturer being photographed, and that is not a *motion* picture. When it is absolutely necessary to have a live narrator on camera for lengthy periods, you must overcome a static situation either by moving the narrator about the set or by using the dolly shot to move the camera in and out on him to change the angle and give a sense of movement. Camera movement can be used to emphasize a segment of narration, the camera moving in to a closer angle to underscore what is being said. You can also break up what would otherwise be one long, monotonous scene into several scenes — separate camera setups from different angles for direct cuts.

Your job as the writer, whichever narration technique you use, is to avoid any static element, to make the narration flow along naturally with the visual, to be sure that you have synchronized the audio with the visual.

* See example scripts in Part V for complete examples of how an on-camera host narrator can be used to introduce the subject and to editorialize, while a voice-over narrator is used for straight reportorial comment over the main body of the film.

Part II: The Two Kinds of Script Format

Format "A" — The Hollywood or One-Column Format

Unless he is the author of an original idea or story on which a film will be based, the writer of nontheatrical films seldom works on a subject of his own choice. He may be assigned to write a script on a totally unfamiliar subject or on one involving a basic idea in which he has no personal interest. It may even be a subject distasteful to him. But since it is his profession, he goes to work, whether or not he likes the subject or is familiar with it.

What every reader would like to see, I am sure, would be an example production script presenting a familiar subject. He could then follow the mechanics of the script's development with clarity and understanding. But the wide variety of subject matter, manners of treatment, and presentation techniques appropriate to the demands of particular subjects make it impossible to write a "pilot model" motion picture script.

For the purpose of practical illustration a script has been chosen which may serve as a general model, since it contains elements of the public relations or promotional film, as well as of the technical and documentary types of presentation. But let us consider writing the "Treatment" on which the production script was based and from which it was developed to its final form.

The Treatment

The writer is given an assignment to write a three-reel script (about 28 minutes of running time) on the purebred dog and what it takes to make a purebred dog champion of his breed. The sponsor is a manufacturer of dog-food products who is producing the film as a public service to stimulate interest in the breeding and buying of the purebred. At the same time the manufacturer wishes to promote the sale of his dog-food products.

The film must emphasize the advantages of owning and breeding the purebred dog. It must show just how a breed is kept standardized in physical type and characteristics. The film must have strong human interest.

It has been decided that the popular dachshund will represent the purebred dog in the film. The first thing the writer must do is to familiarize himself with the dachshund, the background and history of the breed, the purpose for which it has been bred, the reasons for the characteristics and capabilities sought after in the development of the breed.

The best source of rudimentary information for research is a local breeder of pedigreed dachshunds. Through the breeder, the writer picks up some essential facts. He learns something about the characteristics of the breed: that a purebred dog has a documented pedigree and is registered with the American Kennel Club. He also learns about the authorized published standard that sets forth in detail the physical characteristics and qualities necessary to establish an ideal for the breed. The standard also defines serious, secondary, and minor faults.

The writer learns that there is a local or regional Dachshund Club of owners, breeders, and exhibitors. He interviews several members of this group, and, from this experience, if he is a good reporter, he can evaluate their opinions. He will attend one of the regional American Kennel Club dog shows held throughout the year. There he will observe and study dog-show procedures. He will talk to an American Kennel Club judge, from whom he will gather information on the techniques of judging a dog, the application of the breed standard, and how those factors apply to the dachshund.

After he has completed his initial research, he will write his treatment, remembering the sponsor's requirements as well as the technical aspects involved in interpretation and in application of the dachshund standard. The writer will create and develop his story line and general manner of presentation as given in the following example:

THE MAKING OF A CHAMPION

Treatment

Our film opens with the Sponsor's presentation title:

A—TO—Z DOG FOOD PRODUCTS, LTD.

Presents

THE MAKING OF A CHAMPION

To Encourage a Greater Interest in
and Appreciation of the Purebred Dog

Following the Main Title is a Foreword:
    Just as Nature has evolved characteristics designed
    for utility and survival of her creatures, Man has

```
followed the same pattern in his breeding of the dog
for specific purposes—a hunter, a worker, a guardian
of life and property, a loyal and lovable companion.
Each purebred dog is bred to a standard so that he
will faithfully reproduce his type, characteristics,
and capabilities.
```
Foreword is superimposed on a series of shots of different
breeds of dogs.

[COMMENT: The first rough, overwritten, and unedited draft of the
foreword is given below to show what can be done in necessary
cutting and rewriting to eliminate the superfluous:

```
    Somewhere back in the misty reaches of Time, primi-
tive man and wild dog first came together in the hunt
and formed a cautious alliance by which both obtained
food.  Through the ages a growing mutual trust and
affection forged a mystic bond between the lowly quad-
ruped and the sovereign biped.
    Just as Nature has evolved characteristics designed
for utility and survival in its many creatures, Man
has followed the same pattern in his breeding of the
dog for specific purposes—a hunter, a worker, a
guardian of life and property, a loyal and lovable com-
panion.
    Each purebred dog is bred to a standard so that he
will faithfully reproduce his type, characteristics,
and capabilities.  The integrity of the breed is pre-
served so that the buyer of a purebred young puppy may
be assured that the puppy he has bought will develop
into the type of dog he wants.
```

This was written for a roll-up title. It contains 148 words which, at
the rate of 1 word to 1 foot of 35 mm film, would take up to 148 feet,
or a running time of over 1½ minutes. It is too lengthy for what it has
to say. Further, a long roll-up title is difficult for many viewers to
follow, since some read more slowly than others.

The finished foreword contains 63 words, requiring about 64 feet
of film with a running time of about 43 seconds. It is *lean* writing, a
clear and pertinent introduction to the theme of the picture.

This does not mean that a writer should not overwrite in his first
rough draft — many do to "get into the story." It is better to let first
thoughts flow fully and freely, to have too much rather than too little
to work with. Craftsmanship manifests itself in the rewriting and final
editing. There is an old adage in the theater: "Plays are not written —
they are *rewritten*." The same holds true for motion picture scripts.]

Following the foreword we introduce the film's four-
legged leading character, Van the dachshund. We show him
in a Limbo Shot on a dog-show bench, surrounded by the
ribbons and trophies he has won. The Narrator introduces
him with a "Meet the Champ!" Larry, Van's owner, is introduced as he enters the scene, accompanied by a fellow
dog fancier, to admire and pet Van, who greets them enthusiastically.

To tell the story of all that went into making Van a
champion, we go into retrospect. It all began a little
more than two years ago in Larry's kennel house. On a
table in the background are cartons of canned dog food and
kibble which are plainly labeled "A-TO-Z DOG FOOD PRODUCTS."
Feeding pans have "A-TO-Z" printed on the side. Next we
meet Van's mother, Hexie, just before Van was born.

It is obvious that Hexie is heavy with puppies, and due
to whelp very soon. Larry is especially attentive to the
expectant mother dog as he feeds her a pan of A-TO-Z. The
Narrator remarks that from the beginning of her pregnancy
Hexie has been fed the best of food, scientifically prepared, rich in protein, vitamins, bone-building calcium,
and other essential minerals. She doesn't know it, but she
is building a future champion.

With Hexie so near her whelping time, Larry takes her
into a small adjoining room that the narrator calls "the
maternity ward." In the room is a whelping box with a
hinged top and a wide, low-cut opening at the front. Larry
caresses Hexie reassuringly as he talks to her, coaxing her
to enter the whelping box. His manner is very gentle and
the little mother dog expresses her devotion to her master
by licking his hand. Larry leaves when he sees that Hexie
is settling herself contentedly in the whelping box.

The next morning Larry returns to the whelping room to
find that Hexie has given birth to four or five puppies
without his help. He looks over the litter and selects one
little male which he picks up and examines closely. It
may be wishful thinking, but he has a hunch that this
sturdy little fellow has the makings of a champion.

We then see Hexie's litter eight or nine weeks later.
The pups are weaned and occupy a pen to themselves. Van,
the puppy Larry selected as best in the litter, is still
his favorite; now he starts to train the pup, teaching him
to respond to his commands. One of his first lessons is to
hold a pose, essential to show-ring discipline. Young Van
is very responsive to posing and to gaiting properly on a
light lead. Throughout these early training periods we

become acquainted with the technique of training a show
dog and the patience that it takes.

We next see Van at the age of five months. Now the dog
is beginning to show the results of Larry's expert handling
and care, as Larry continues to give him workouts on a
light show lead.

Next we see an almost fully matured Van at the age of
eleven months in a dog-show ring. It is the Nine to Twelve
Months Puppy Class and Van, handled by Larry, is in competition with nine or ten other entries. The background
atmosphere of the dog show is now established. An American
Kennel Club Judge is in the dachshund ring, judging the
class. Thanks to Larry's expert training, Van behaves like
a veteran.

The Judge watches the young dogs parading around the ring
in a counter-clockwise circle for his initial appraisal.
The Judge stops the parade and selects Van as the first dog
to examine. An examination table is made available to the
Judge so that he may go over each dog comfortably and effi-
ciently.

Larry poses Van on the examination table for the Judge's
scrutiny. Over these scenes the Narrator remarks that many
people think a dog show is a beauty contest in which the
most beautiful and personable dog is chosen winner. But,
in judging dogs, this is true only to the extent that a dog
meets the requirements of a set standard of perfection.

The Narrator goes on to say that a dog may appear to be a
beautiful specimen of his breed, yet a close examination by
an expert can reveal structural faults. Each breed of
purebred dog is judged according to a rigid breed standard
defined in detail, describing serious, secondary, and minor
faults. The standard also defines the characteristics of
perfection. Good and bad features of a dog's conformation
and body structure are what a judge looks for.

Van is posed on the examination table. It is a close,
broadside shot, with his image filling the screen. Freeze
Frame is used to hold the image of Van immobile long enough
for the Narrator to say that the official dachshund standard states that in general appearance the dachshund should
be low to the ground, short-legged, long-bodied, but with
compact figure and robust muscular development, as is seen
in Van's image.

We see the Judge examine a particular feature of Van's
anatomy, which is almost perfect, and then we show a still
photo of a dachshund with a bad example of that particular
feature. Arrows Pop On to indicate the features which the

narrator is identifying and discussing. Since the picture
will be filmed in color, the still photos of the bad examples should be in black and white to give greater contrast between the good and the bad. (Drawings could be
used instead of still photos.)

The first bad specimen we see in a still picture is
short-chested, low behind the shoulders, and high in the
rear, presenting a very bad top-line. The second bad
specimen has a roached or carp back, with flanks drawn up
like those of a greyhound. In contrast we cut back to Van,
showing his well-developed trunk, long and fully muscled,
with good top-line. We see the back, with sloping
shoulders, and short, rigid pelvis lying in a straight
line between the withers and the slightly arched loins.
Arrows Pop On to identify the individual features.

During the Judge's examination of Van's head the Narrator comments that, viewed from the side or from above,
the head should taper uniformly to the tip of the nose and
should be clean cut. Van's head fits the description. By
contrast we show a still photo or drawing of a dachshund
with a very skully, coarse head with a pronounced "stop."
Then back to Van showing his head with little or no stop,
the slightly arched muzzle, resembling the curve of a
ram's nose, with bridge bones strongly prominent over the
eyes.

The Judge examines Van's teeth, or "bite." The teeth
should fit close together, the outer side of the lower
incisors tightly touching the inner side of the upper--the
"scissors bite."

Next our attention is called to Van's eyes, which are
oval and of medium size. In contrast, a still photo of a
bad example is shown--a dachshund with goggle eyes.

The Judge finds that Van's ears are set perfectly. The
Narrator explains that the ears should be near the top of
the head and not too far forward. In contrast, a bad
specimen is shown with low-set, folded ears--a sad sack.
The carriage of the ears should be animated, and the forward edge should touch the cheek.

Van's neckline is judged next. The Narrator tells us
that the standard says the neck should be long, muscular,
without dewlaps on the throat, clean cut, like Van's. In
contrast we show a still photo of a dachsie with dewlaps
hanging like double chins about his throat--"Double Chin
Charlie," as the Narrator calls him. We cut back to Van
as the Judge runs his hand lightly and approvingly over
Van's neck, which is slightly arched in the nape, extend-

ing in a graceful line into the shoulders, carried proudly,
but not stiffly.

The next feature is Van's front quarters. The Narrator
explains that the dachshund has been bred as a hunting dog
for beating the bush, trailing, and going underground to
fight and kill a badger, or drive him from his burrow.
For the dog to endure the arduous exertion underground,
his front must be muscular, deep, long, and broad. Van's
front quarters are a good example of the standard. In
contrast we show a still photo of a thin, scrawny, poorly
developed dachsie front, the result of poor breeding or
nutritional deficiency or a combination of both.

The placement of the shoulder blade and the upper arm is
important. The Narrator, quoting the standard, states
that the shoulder blade should be long, broad, obliquely
and firmly placed on the fully developed thorax, furnished
with hard and plastic muscles. The upper arm should be
the same length as the shoulder blade and at right angles
to it, strong of bone and hard of muscle, lying close to
the ribs, capable of free movement.

In a close shot, the Judge shows how, by using his experienced fingers, he can measure and calibrate the components of the skeletal structure not clearly visible to
the eye. He probes gently with his fingers to determine
the length of the shoulder blade, the length of the upper
arm, and their angulation, which should be, according to
the standard, at right angles. A drawing illustrates the
point.

By contrast, we show a drawing of a poor specimen which
graphically illustrates a noticeably short forechest.

The Narrator comments on the visual, saying, "Here's
what happens when the upper arm is shorter than the
shoulder blade. It drops to a more vertical position.
This lack of proper development results in shortening the
forechest, lessening lung and heart room required for endurance in underground work. It is more like a terrier
front." We cut back to Van's forechest—a good and very
typical example.

The Judge moves to examine Van's chest. To the camera
it is a frontal view. The Narrator comments on the visual
by remarking that the breast bone should be strong, and so
prominent in front that on either side a depression appears like a dimple. In a very close shot of Van's front,
the Judge's hand appears and his forefinger traces the
oval appearance of the thorax and the extension of the
bottom of the chest downward to the mid-forearm. The Nar-

rator makes comments appropriate to the visual. In contrast is shown a still photo of a dachsie with a narrow
and relatively high front chest--the leggy type.

The Judge next appraises Van's rib cage, which should
appear full and oval from above or from the side, to allow
ample capacity for development of heart and lungs.

Van's feet are examined next. They meet the perfection
of the standard, the paws being full, broad in front, and
a trifle inclined outward. They are compact, with well-
arched toes close together and with tough pads. In contrast, we show a still photo of a pair of weak and badly
splayed forepaws.

The Judge examines Van's hindquarters, which should be
sturdy and of equal width with the hind legs, robust and
well muscled, with well-rounded buttocks, well spaced and
aligned like the example we are showing in Van's image.
By contrast, we see a still photo of a bad example of hind
legs, showing a dachsie rear with legs that are cow-
hocked, a sign of weakness. They are not like Van's hind
legs--strong and capable of powerful thrust for good movement.

The rear angulation, important to strength and movement
capability, is then examined. The Judge examines Van's
calf bone which should be short and perpendicular to the
thigh bone. The Judge's finger indicates the calf bone,
the thigh bone, and their respective angulation.

Although they may vary according to the different specifications of the individual breed standards, all these
factors determine the makings of a champion.

After his table examination of Van, the Judge asks Larry
to trot Van from one end of the ring to the other, so that
he can study Van's ability to move. Good movement is required of any breed. Van's legs are straight and strong--
no cow hocks--and his movement is excellent; the Narrator
comments to that effect.

The Judge returns Larry and Van to their place in the
lineup of dogs and handlers and calls for the next dog to
come to the examination table.

A Dissolve covers a time lapse to the final judging of
the entire senior puppy class. Each dog has been examined
on the table. The handlers and their dogs are lined up
along one side of the ring, the dogs placed at short in-
tervals--head to tail. Larry and Van are at the head of
the line. The Judge is about to select his first, second,
third, and fourth choices.

We watch the Judge deliberate as he looks over the
lineup of dogs posed before him, and we cut back and forth

between the poker-faced Judge and the anxious handlers and
their dogs. After a moment's final consideration, the
Judge makes his decision. He waves Larry and Van to a
place in front of the No. 1 marker at the head of the ring.
The spectators applaud approvingly. The Judge motions his
second, third, and fourth choices to their numbers.

It is Van's first blue ribbon win and he won it in stiff
competition. But it is only a "class" win, which carries
no championship points. The really tough competition will
come later in the show when Van will have to meet the
winners of the other classes. But the class win is the
first step upward and Larry is elated.

Later in the day the big moment arrives when Van is
again in the ring, with the other class winners. Winner's
Dog is about to be selected, and that win carries the
coveted points toward championship. Suspense is developed
as we cut in reaction shots of the intensely interested
spectators and anxious competing handlers.

The Judge very carefully looks over the lineup. All are
unusually fine dogs. It isn't going to be an easy decision
to make. Larry is sweating it out. This time he and Van
are at the end of the line. The Judge starts his appraisal, coming first to Larry and Van. But, after a
moment, he moves on up the line. Larry shows his disappointment, feeling that the Judge did not give Van much
attention.

The Judge deliberately appraises each dog in the lineup,
giving two dogs in particular a little more attention.
The suspense builds. Finally he makes his decision and
calls to the ring steward to bring the Winner's ribbon and
the trophy. They meet in the center of the ring, and the
Judge takes the ribbon and trophy and exits back toward
the lineup. We do not have any immediate indication of
his selection, but the spectators burst into enthusiastic
applause when they see the Judge heading for a particular
dog.

Larry is astonished when the Judge comes to him with the
ribbon and the trophy. He can hardly believe it. It's a
big win in top-flight competition. It carries Van's first
points toward his championship.

The Narrator tells us that, in other shows which followed, Van topped this win by going Best of Winners and
Best of Variety of Breed. It didn't take long for this
outstanding specimen to become a champion.

We Dissolve back to the present with Van on the show
bench as we first saw him in the beginning of the picture.

We Dissolve to Larry (a Limbo shot) who is holding a

very young (6 to 7 weeks old) mongrel puppy in his hands.
He turns and speaks to the audience:
  "Now you've some idea of what it takes to make a champion. I've always loved dogs ever since I was a kid. But
look at this little fellow. Will he grow up to be like
this . . ." (Close Shot of a drab mongrel with no personality) ". . . or like this?" (Close Shot of another
unattractive mongrel) ". . . or what you want him to look
like and be like when he grows up. That's where you can
depend on the purebred dog, whether you want . . ." (A
series of Limbo shots of individual specimens of different
breeds as Larry's voice comes over the scene to identify
each one) ". . . a dachsie . . . a cocker . . . a collie
. . . a beagle . . . or his cousin, the basset . . . a
bird dog, the English setter . . . a pointer . . . a
poodle . . . a Great Dane . . . or a very doggy little
dog--the Miniature Pinscher."
  Back to the Limbo shot of Larry as he resumes speaking
directly to the audience, briefly commenting on the advantages of choosing a purebred puppy, ending with the
friendly admonition: "Remember, your dog, whether he's a
purebred, or a lovable mutt, looks to you for two things--
love, and plenty of it--and good food, and plenty of that,
too!"
  THE END is superimposed over a rear view of Van as he
looks back over his shoulder at the Camera.

Upon completion of his treatment, the writer should have it checked
for accuracy by one or more of his technical advisors. In this case a
technical advisor would be an authority on dachshund breeding, as
well as the American Kennel Club judge from whom he obtained his
show-ring information. With the treatment approved for technical
accuracy, the writer will then submit at least three neatly bound
copies to the sponsor or producer.

If he has reason to believe his treatment is what it should be, the
writer usually will not wait for formal approval from the sponsor or
producer. He will proceed with the writing of his first-draft shooting
script. Even if a treatment is well written, the producer may suggest
changes. They usually are such that a first-draft shooting script can
easily be adjusted to accommodate them. However, if the producer
does not approve of the writer's approach as given in the treatment,
then the writer will have to come up with a different concept, unless
the producer furnishes a new one for him to develop.

An Inadequate Treatment

For the purposes of our example, the producer has approved the treatment as submitted by the writer. But, before we go on to see how the treatment was developed into a shooting script, let us consider an inadequate treatment of the same subject and then compare the two:

THE MAKING OF A CHAMPION
Treatment

This is a story of a man, Larry, and his dog, Van, and how a purebred dog becomes a champion. Larry's hobby is the breeding of prize—winning dachshunds. He keeps his pets in a small kennel house with outdoor runs. His favorite is Van, a beautiful specimen of his breed, every inch a prize winner, a friendly dog with an attractive personality.

To show how Van became a champion we go back in time about two years, just before Van was born. His mother, Hexie, is heavy with puppies. Larry feeds her a diet of the best food he can obtain so her pups will not suffer from prenatal malnutrition.

Soon after Hexie gives birth to her pups, Larry picks one as the outstanding specimen in the litter. His choice, of course, is Van as a puppy. When Van is old enough, Larry starts training him for the dog—show ring. Young Van responds to the training until by the time he is about eleven months old he is a very obedient dog.

Larry is delighted with Van and enters him in a dog show. He is in competition with many other fine speci-mens of his breed. The American Kennel Club Judge judges the dogs according to the specifications of the standard for the breed. The standard gives the good points of the breed and also the bad points which can disqualify a dog in competition with others of his breed. As the Judge examines Van, the Narrator tells us about the details of the standard as applied by the Judge.

In the show ring Van behaves like a well—trained vet-eran, but Larry has a hard time suppressing his feeling of excitement and his eagerness for Van to win. Here sus-pense is developed until finally the Judge selects Van for first place.

It is a good win, but only what is known as a "class win." Van receives a blue ribbon and a trophy, but the class win carries no championship points. Larry and Van

must stand by until the Judge has gone over the dogs in
all the other classes.
  Later, Larry and Van come into the ring again to com-
pete with the winners of the other classes. Winner's dog
is about to be chosen by the judge. The winner will
receive points toward his championship. Suspense is
developed as the Judge carefully studies the competing
dogs. Larry becomes discouraged. He believes the Judge
has his eye on another dog.
  Finally, in a surprise finish, Van is chosen Winner's
Dog and gains the first points toward his championship.
Larry is elated.
  Our story returns to the present, showing Van as having
won his championship. Larry ends the picture by appearing
in a live scene to address the audience and tell them
about the advantages of breeding and owning the purebred
dog.

While this brief second version tells a story, it leaves many things
to be desired. It is not really a treatment. It is no more than a sketch
or outline. It is not "pictorial writing." It fails to give the reader a
clear idea of what the writer has in mind. The detailed development
in the first version is a professional presentation that leaves no doubt
in the reader's mind just what the writer is going to put in his shooting
script and just how he is going to develop it for pictorial presentation.

Faults and Consequences of an Inadequate Treatment

The very first paragraph of the second version is an uninspiring
statement written in pedestrian language, as is the rest of the treatment. It fails to establish any idea of the scope which the shooting
script and the completed film must have.

The second version fails almost entirely to present the possibilities
for developing human interest. The flat statement is made that Van's
mother, Hexie, is heavy with puppies, that Larry feeds her a diet of
"the best food" he can obtain so her pups will not suffer from malnutrition. Such a cold, uninspiring statement leaves the reader with
a "So what?" attitude. Such writing does not cause the reader to
visualize the mood, action, and atmosphere of the sequence. The
same scenes of Hexie and Larry, as delineated in the first version,
enable the reader to visualize and appreciate the warmth of the relationship between Larry and the little mother dog.

In the second version the writer tells the reader that Larry starts
training Van for the show ring. He does not give the reader any indication of what this training is. The reader is told that the judge

judges dogs according to the standard for the breed, but gives the reader no idea of what that standard is, what it specifies, or how those specifications will be presented visually. The writer tells the reader that "here suspense is developed" without giving the reader some way to visualize just how that suspense will be developed.

In the last paragraph of the treatment, the reader is given no indication of what Larry is going to tell the audience about the advantages of owning and breeding the purebred dog, or what visual support will be given what he says. Again the reader has been given little to visualize. And the writer has made the serious mistake of not giving a clear idea of how he is going to weave the "sponsor's message" into the script. He has neglected the sponsor's primary concern — that of promoting the sale of his products.

From reading such a treatment, the producer or sponsor has every reason to question the writer's competence. In such a case, the writer has reduced his value to the men who pay him, and who consequently may not give him future assignments.

Each writer has his own way of working. Many write a rough outline for their own guidance in the preparation of a well-developed presentation. No one else sees this rough outline. The professional has learned through experience the error of submitting a hastily devised treatment or script which does not give the critical reader a clear and interesting picture of *what* will appear on the screen and *how* it will be presented. It must be a *pictorial* or *visual* style of writing.

The Shooting or Production Script

While the treatment is a fairly detailed narrative account of events in the order of their occurrence, the shooting or production script is the final blueprint in which the greatest emphasis is given to development of detail and clarity of description. It is the master guide for the director and cameraman to follow in translating story to film. Finally, it will be a master guide for the film editor when he cuts and assembles the footage.

The importance of proper script format and setup cannot be overstressed. It is important, not only for the guidance of the director and film editor, but for the benefit of those who break down the script for cost and budget planning. Those who must analyze the script for the various phases of actual production also need a detailed format, for determining shooting schedule, studio set construction and dressing, requirements for exterior shooting on location, casting and scheduling of actors, assembly of props and wardrobe equipment, crew requirements, transportation, and the many other details which make up the production of a motion picture.

The production script must incorporate these requirements. If proper individual scene headings and camera setups are lacking, if alphabetical abbreviations of designations are run together carelessly, the script is neither usable nor professional.

The example shooting script which follows happens to have been written in the "Hollywood" type of format, which we will designate as Format "A." It could just as well have been written in the form which carries the visual on the left side of the page and the narration on the right, as given in Chapter 6. It is a fully written script, leaving little room for doubt in the reader's mind as to *what* will be seen on the screen and *how* it will be seen. It presents detailed instructions to the director, the cameraman, and others of the production staff.

For live shooting using actors, a "Cast Sheet" should accompany the script, describing the approximate age, type, and characteristics of each character. In addition, it is always advisable to have a page or two of "Production Notes," as cover pages to the shooting script. These notes are written after the shooting script has been completed, but inserted as an introduction to the script in the bound copies submitted to the producer.

Example Script: Format "A"

THE MAKING OF A CHAMPION

PRODUCTION SCRIPT

PRODUCTION NOTES

Professional actors should not be cast in the roles of the characters in this film unless, by chance, they are expert dog handlers experienced in training and show-ring procedures. The leading character, Larry, hopefully should be a photogenic professional dog handler (there are several attractive women who are professional handlers). The person chosen should have a good speaking voice, to carry the narration and on-camera speeches. A professional narrator can be used to carry the main body of the narration unless it is decided to use Larry's voice throughout.

The character of the Judge should be played by an American Kennel Club judge who is photogenic, or a photogenic professional handler who is experienced in judging procedures.

The casting of the leading dog character, Van, can be arranged with any one of several important dachshund breeders and exhibitors. Van should be an alert, friendly dog who will enhance the human-interest element.

Since the film is to be shot in color, Van should be a red dachshund. Black does not photograph well.

There are three interior sets involved: The interior of a kennel house, an adjoining whelping room, and a stage for scenes shot in Limbo.

The exteriors are: The yard outside the kennel house, and a judging ring at a dog show.

However, there would be advantages in filming the judging sequence in the studio. Shooting on the stage would do away with the necessity of fighting time and the uncertainties of weather and light, since the picture is to be shot in color. If an interior set is used, the background atmosphere of a dog show can be established by taking random shots, but pertinent to the story, at any dog show held indoors. The impression could be given that the dachshund ring is more or less isolated.

[COMMENT: The writer's suggestion concerning the advantages of shooting the judging sequence in the studio, instead of as an exterior, is a practical one. Shooting in the studio can save time and money, since greater control can be exercised in the shooting. These are examples of the many factors which the writer must think about in order to be a responsible member of the production team.]

Special Effects: Freeze Frame and the simple Popping On
of arrows to indicate the specific body features of a
dachshund as shown in the judging sequence, where Freeze
Frame, drawings, or photos are used.   A pointer can be
used in still photos and drawings to show "good" and "bad"
examples.

Thought and consideration have been given to the production problems involved in photographing the dogs indicated
in this script.   No action has been written in that cannot
be practicably photographed, if care is exercised in
selecting the right dogs and handlers to appear in the
film.   The use of Freeze Frame will simplify holding dogs
in any pose desired for the duration of necessary narration.

Any further information and needed cooperation may be
obtained from the Executive Secretary of the American
Kennel Club, 221 Fourth Avenue, New York City, telephone
ALgonquin 4-2540.   Arrangements for exterior or interior
shooting at a dog show, and for necessary props, can be
made through the Foley Dog Show Organization, Inc., 2009
Ranstead Street, Philadelphia 3, Pa., telephone LOcust
4-6133.   The Foley organization has charge of putting on
almost all the East Coast dog shows.

As a result of the writer's research, he suggests the
dachshund as probably the best choice of breed to be used
in this film.   According to American Kennel Club figures,
the dachshund has occupied fourth place in popularity in
recent years.   He is a small dog and easily handled; more
important, the smooth-haired dachshund is photographically
ideal for showing a dog's conformation, body structure,
and features.   If a long-haired dog were used, it would be
difficult for the camera to show those structural features.

[COMMENT: The writer's comment on the selection of the dachshund
as the best choice of breed to be used in the film is a helpful observation to the producer concerning the photographic practicality of showing the dog's conformation and structural features. The writer remembered the sponsor's remark that, although the part of Van was to
be written for a dachshund, he might have to use a different breed
as a matter of policy or because of pressure from fanciers of other
breed groups. By presenting practical reasons for choice of the
dachshund, the script writer has given the sponsor a strong supporting
argument of this choice.

In his "Production Notes" the writer of this script presents the
problems of casting, and then recommends the most practical solu-

tion, for the information and guidance of the producer. Even though the script has been written for a male lead (Larry), the writer is still aware of an alternative. In the first paragraph of his production notes he remarks that there are several attractive women dog handlers. It is a suggestion which shows the writer's interest and concern in aiming for the best possible presentation. An attractive woman might add glamor and sex appeal. On the other hand, she might be a distraction from Van, the dachshund. However, that is something for the producer and sponsor to decide. If a Mary is used instead of a Larry, the rewrite of the script is simple.]

CAST OF CHARACTERS

Larry	A dog breeder and handler, a pleasant man in his thirties.
Judge	A mature man in his forties or early fifties, dignified in appearance and manner, typical of a veteran American Kennel Club judge.
Handlers (in first ring) and their dogs	Nine or ten men and women of varying ages with their dogs.
Handlers and their dogs in second ring for Winner's dog	Six handlers and their dogs including Larry and Van. Larry is the only handler from among those who appear in the first ring.
Ring Steward	Either man or woman of neat appearance and efficient manner. From 30 to 40.
Larry's friend	A man about 30 who appears in the very opening scenes and who can also be used as one of the ringside spectators.
Ringside spectators	A dozen or so men and women of varying ages. Some are casually dressed, others are in street attire.
Van	A mature male dachshund.
Hexie	Van's dam.

Van........................... Nine weeks old.

Van........................... About five months old.

First puppies................. Four or five about two
                               days old.

Second puppies................ Representing the same litter
                               about nine weeks old.

Other dachshunds.............. Four or five in background
                               in Larry's kennel.

FADE IN:

PRESENTED

BY

A–TO–Z DOG FOOD PRODUCTS, LTD.

To Encourage a Greater Interest
in and Appreciation of the
Purebred Dog

   (The Titles and Foreword are superimposed Over a
Cutting Montage, a fast-moving series of very brief
scenes, or "quick cuts," of several of the more popular
breeds of dog as they appear on dog-show benches and
parading around the show ring.)

DISSOLVE

FOREWORD

Why the Purebred Dog?

   Just as Nature has evolved characteristics designed for
utility and survival of her many creatures, Man has
followed the same pattern in his breeding of the dog
for specific purposes—a hunter—a worker—a guardian
of life and property—a lovable and loyal companion.

   Each purebred dog is bred to a standard so that he will
faithfully reproduce his type, characteristics,
and capabilities.

DISSOLVE

[COMMENT:

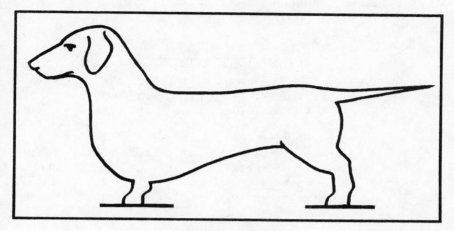

CLOSE SHOT
Broadside View

This is an illustration of a representative CLOSE SHOT as it would appear framed by the screen.

Van's "screen direction" is from right to left, that is, he is facing the left side of the screen as the viewer sees it. This screen direction, from right to left, should remain consistent throughout. It establishes and maintains a consistent image of Van, less confusing to the viewer than if he saw the dog facing screen left in one scene and screen right in the next, with such reverses being repeated, particularly in the major sequence in the dog show ring when Van is examined by an American Kennel Club judge.

Anyone who is interested in learning about film production is probably familiar with CAMERA ANGLES, having seen many entertainment films in the theater and on television.

The CLOSE SHOT, CLOSE UP, EXTREME CLOSE UP, MEDIUM CLOSE, MEDIUM SHOT, and LONG SHOT should by now be easily recognized.

However, the beginner should study very closely the use of CAMERA ANGLES throughout this script, visualizing the action as the writer describes each scene. He should study each scene in its relationship to the one preceding it and the one that follows. He will see how the writer "moves" the camera, keeping it focused on the CENTER OF INTEREST, with the exception of necessary brief cutaways and reaction shots.

Scene 2-A was added in writing the final draft. While any profes-

sional director would probably shoot such a CLOSE ANGLE, it was
thought best to include one specifically in the script.]

MAIN TITLE--

THE MAKING OF A CHAMPION

> (The last scene in the montage of live shots that
> background the Titles shows a fine specimen of a
> smooth-haired male dachshund (Van) with his owner
> (Larry). The dog is on a show lead and trots from
> the background toward the camera until his image
> fills most of the screen in a large head CLOSE UP)
> (The choice of whether Van will be a black and tan
> or a red dachsie depends upon color of dog avail-
> able and suitable for the part at time of casting)

DISSOLVE

1. INT DOG-SHOW BENCH--LIMBO
   CLOSE SHOT--VAN

This is shot in LIMBO (a Limbo scene is one shot against a
neutral or blacked-out background to the exclusion of all
else except the principal object or objects to be
photographed, together with any necessary furnishings and
props). It is a VERY CLOSE ANGLE on Van, the male dachshund we saw in the last title background montage. Van is
standing broadside to the camera, on a conventional dog-
show bench. While Van holds the pose, he faces Screen
Left. This same Screen Direction, from right to left,
should be consistent throughout, particularly through the
judging sequence beginning with Scene 49. For photographic
purposes the dog-show stall should be wide enough to
accommodate three dogs, although we are showing only one.
Van wears the usual benching collar and chain. His stance
at the opening of the scene is one learned in the
discipline of the show ring, and he appears every inch a
champion, well groomed, in superb condition. The Background Music Fades Under And Out as the Narrator starts
speaking:

NARRATOR

> Meet the Champ!

The CAMERA DOLLIES BACK TO WIDER ANGLE to show an
impressive display of ribbons tacked to the upper rear
wall of the stall and several imposing trophy cups on each

side that stand taller than the dog. Van breaks his pose,
relaxing on the bench.

> NARRATOR
>
> He could be introduced by his high-sounding
> registered pedigree name, but it's as long as he
> is. His owner calls him Van.

2. MED SHOT

Van's owner, Larry, a man in his early thirties, enters,
accompanied by a dog-fancier friend. Van greets Larry
enthusiastically as he sits down on the edge of the bench
to fondle the dog. His friend sits down on the opposite
end of the bench to admire the champion. They discuss the
dog's fine points, the beautiful head, fine feet, and good
top-line.

> NARRATOR
>
> Despite his prestige, Van's the informal type. He
> may not be able to talk, but his demonstration of
> love for Larry, his owner, is eloquent apprecia-
> tion of all the kindness, good care, and handling
> that Larry has given him.

2-A. CLOSE SHOT--FEATURING VAN

Van continues to respond to his owner's attentions.

> NARRATOR
>
> Good care and wise handling made Van a champion.
> It started a little more than two years ago,
> before Van was whelped . . .

FADE OUT.
FADE IN:

3. INT. KENNEL HOUSE--DAY
   FULL SHOT

This is the spotlessly clean interior of a representative
type of kennel used by small breeders. In one corner is a
set of laundry trays and a grooming bench. On a table
against the wall are cartons of canned dog food and
containers of kibble stamped with the label, "A-TO-Z DOG
FOOD PRODUCTS." There are several pens, divided by solid
wooden panels, with heavy wire gates in front through
which we can see half a dozen or so dachshunds. A sleep-

ing box is in one corner of each pen. Openings in the
rear lead to individual outdoor runs. Benching chains and
show leads hang from pegs outside each pen. It is feeding
time and Larry has placed pans filled with food in all the
pens but one. He goes to a table, picks up the remaining
food pan and crosses to a pen in the foreground where
Hexie, a bitch heavy with pups, is hungrily awaiting her
meal. (Note: In the vernacular, a female dog is usually
referred to as a "bitch.")

                              NARRATOR
          Here is where it really began.

4. MED SHOT--LARRY & HEXIE

Larry enters, places the pan of food on the floor just
outside the pen and opens the gate. The heavily burdened
bitch comes out to the pan and starts devouring the food
as Larry squats down beside her to run his hand gently
along her back.

                              NARRATOR
              This is Van's mother, Hexie. Ordinarily she's a
              fine, trim specimen of her breed, but approaching
              motherhood has done things to her waistline.

5. CLOSE SHOT--HEXIE

Low Camera Setup.
This is shot at such an angle so as to accentuate her
distended sides and low-hanging belly as she eats. On the
side of the food pan we can plainly see the letters
"A-TO-Z." Larry's hand is in the scene, stroking Hexie's
back.

                              NARRATOR
              As the French would so delicately put it, Hexie is
              a trifle enceinte. But she's in fine shape--for
              the shape she's in.

6. CLOSE UP--HEXIE

Low Camera Setup.
This is a head-on angle as Hexie eats her food with relish.

                              NARRATOR
              From the beginning of her pregnancy, Hexie has
              been fed the best of food, scientifically pre-

pared, rich in protein and vitamins, bonebuilding
calcium and other essential minerals.

7. CLOSE UP--LARRY

Low Camera Setup.
As he watches Hexie eat. (This is a "CUT-AWAY" SHOT to
save time and footage while the dog is eating all her food
--a time bridge or contraction.)

8. MED CLOSE--HEXIE & LARRY

Low Camera Setup.
Hexie cleans up the last of her food and licks the dish
clean while her owner, still squatting down by her side,
pets her approvingly.

> NARRATOR
>
> In their prenatal development <u>her</u> unborn pups are
> not suffering from the deficiencies that result
> from a poorly balanced, unscientifically prepared
> diet.

[COMMENT: Beginning with Scene 5 there are several CLOSE SHOTS
of Hexie. The writer also specified LOW CAMERA SETUP. He could
have gotten by with merely indicating a CLOSE SHOT, but, by specify-
ing a LOW CAMERA SETUP, he has given the critical reader a more
exact visualization of just how that CLOSE SHOT will look on the
screen—a view of Hexie from more of a ground-level angle. He has
also made the director and cameraman aware of the need for a very
low angle to more plainly show the little mother dog's distended
sides and low-hanging belly.]

9. CLOSE UP--HEXIE

Low Camera Setup.
She licks the crumbs of food from her muzzle and looks up
and off at Larry. (The bitch can easily be induced to
lick her lips by rubbing a small amount of cod-liver oil
or sweet syrup about the outside of her muzzle.)

> NARRATOR
>
> She doesn't know it, but she's building a sturdy
> future champion--with the help of her knowing
> owner.

[COMMENT: In his parenthetical note in Scene 9, the writer has anticipated a problem in having Hexie lick her chops as a human might lick his lips after a good meal.

Writing in such action is not difficult, particularly where animals are involved. It is more difficult and sometimes impossible to obtain such effects during the actual shooting. The writer should always think through the possibilities of such problems arising during the shooting. By anticipating them, he can alert the director or cameraman, and can offer ways and means of overcoming such problems.

Time is money on the set or on location. The delays, with an expensive crew standing by, caused while the director or cameraman is struggling with an unforeseen problem, can amount to hundreds and even thousands of dollars. That is why the writer should not thoughtlessly write in "business" and actions which are not photographically practical, or may be so difficult to obtain that they are just too expensive to shoot.

To make his job easier, it is very convenient for the writer to do a slick piece of writing. He may say to himself: "I'll let the director or cameraman worry about that." Such an attitude is unprofessional and irresponsible. A writer of integrity, who has a sense of responsibility and professional pride, will reduce such production problems to a minimum. The essence of his job is to turn in a script that is shootable.]

10. MED SHOT—HEXIE & LARRY

As Larry gives Hexie a final pat on the head, he gets to
his feet and calls for her to follow him. He leads the
way to a doorway in the b.g.

                         NARRATOR

          With Hexie due to whelp any day now, Larry has
          made all preparations for the event . . .

11. INT. WHELPING ROOM—DAY
    FULL SHOT

This is a very small room. In one corner is a standard
whelping box with hinged top and a low-cut opening to
allow the low-built, heavily laden bitch to come and go
without having to jump over a high sill. Larry enters,
followed by Hexie. He coaxes her toward the whelping box.

                         NARRATOR

          . . . in what he refers to as "the maternity ward."

12. MED SHOT—LARRY & HEXIE

Larry coaxes Hexie to enter the whelping box which she
does. She disappears for a moment and then peers out
through the opening at Larry, who stoops down to talk
reassuringly to her.

> NARRATOR
>
> Here he has placed a whelping box with a hinged
> top and an opening wide enough and low enough to
> allow easy passage for the low-slung expectant
> mother.

13. CLOSE SHOT—LARRY & HEXIE

Low Camera Setup.
The man is talking reassuringly to Hexie as her head and
shoulders are extended through the opening in the whelping
box. She licks his hand in appreciation of his attention.
(Use cod-liver oil or sweet syrup if she will not vol-
untarily lick hand.)

> NARRATOR
>
> It will be Hexie's first whelping, and Larry knows
> that she needs all the loving attention she can
> get to relieve much of the restlessness and
> nervousness which affect many bitches at their
> first whelping.

DISSOLVE

14. INT. WHELPING ROOM—DAY
    MED SHOT—LARRY

Larry enters to pause before the whelping box. He calls
Hexie and snaps his fingers to coax her out of the box.
She does not show herself. Larry carefully raises the
hinged top of the whelping box and peers down into the interior.

> NARRATOR
>
> The very next day Larry discovered that Hexie had
> taken care of things quite nicely during his ab-
> sence, without his help as midwife.

15. MED CLOSE—HEXIE & NEWBORN PUPS

This is shot over Larry's shoulder as he bends over the
open box. Hexie is lying on her side and four or five
newborn puppies are nursing.

NARRATOR

It was a fine litter. One sturdy little male
caught Larry's eye.

16. MED CLOSE--LARRY

He reaches down into the whelping box and gently takes out
one of the puppies. He holds it up and smiles, especially
well pleased with such a fine little specimen. (Note:
Many bitches are cross immediately after a whelping and
will growl or snap even at their owner. To avoid disturb-
ing the bitch, she should be removed from the area while
Larry reaches down into the box, picks up and handles the
pup. Also, the pups can be two to three days old instead
of just recently born.)

[COMMENT: The parenthetical note in Scene 16 is another illustration
of factors which can affect shooting and which might not be anticipated by the director or cameraman. In this instance, there is the possibility of someone being bitten by the protective mother dog. The
writer has anticipated the problem and has offered a simple solution.
This is the result of the writer's thorough research.

While the problem given here has to do with photographing a dog
and her pups, other difficulties may be encountered in photographing
actions and objects of a mechanical nature. The writer should find solutions to such problems before shooting; where hazards exist, he
should document them and recommend safety measures which can be
taken. It might be necessary to shoot scenes in an area where there
are inflammable or explosive fumes and gases or other dangerous
materials. There might be danger from overhead timbers or falling
rocks.]

17. CLOSE UP--PUPPY IN LARRY'S HANDS

Featuring the pup's wrinkled little face.

18. MED CLOSE--LARRY

Larry continues to examine and admire the pup, carefully
turning it about in his hands, appraising its conformation.

NARRATOR

Perhaps it was wishful thinking at the time, but
Larry thought he might have a future champion in

his selection of the best in the litter. Time
would tell.

Larry gently returns the puppy to the whelping box. Other
pups and Hexie are not seen in this shot.

19. CLOSE SHOT--HEXIE & PUPS

The returned pup starts nursing again.

DISSOLVE

20. INT. KENNEL HOUSE--DAY
    MED CLOSE--8-9 WEEKS OLD PUPS

The four or five pups of Hexie's litter are now weaned.
They are clamoring at the wire gate of their pen to greet
Larry as he is approaching off scene. (This is the same
pen occupied by Hexie when we first saw her.) Hexie is
now in an adjoining pen.

21. MED SHOT

Larry enters to the pen to lean over the gate and play-
fully fondle the lively pups. They are in fine condition.
Larry picks up one (Van as a small puppy) and exits toward
the grooming table.

                    NARRATOR

        Van began his education at the early age of eight
        or nine weeks.

22. MED CLOSE--LARRY & PUP

Larry enters to the grooming table and, standing behind
it, facing the camera, he gently but firmly "sets up" the
pup on the table in an initial training session to teach
him to strike a good show-ring pose and to hold it upon
command. Lifting the pup off his feet by a firm hold on
the muzzle with one hand and the fingers of the other hand
thrust between the pup's hind legs, Larry gently lowers
the pup to its feet. Throughout, Larry talks quietly but
firmly to the young trainee, repeating the word "hold!"

                    NARRATOR

        The first thing that little Van had to learn was
        to respond to his owner's wishes and commands.

Van's puppy exuberance at first makes it difficult for
Larry to get him to hold a pose.

NARRATOR

Like all young ones, Van didn't want to hold still
for very long at a time.

(Run long enough for sufficient footage for intercutting
with Close Shots to follow.)

[COMMENT: In Scene 22, a MEDIUM CLOSE SHOT of Larry and the pup,
the writer notes that enough footage should be shot of the action at
this angle to allow for intercutting with CLOSE SHOTS to follow
Scene 23, CLOSE UP of the pup, and Scene 24, CLOSE UP of Larry,
which also carry notes to shoot enough footage for added intercuts.

These added notes not only show the writer's awareness that there
may be difficulties in getting a recalcitrant puppy to respond to discipline, even though he might have had a few previous lessons, but
the writer capitalizes on those anticipated difficulties in his recogni-
tion of the almost certain human interest and amusement in the situation showing a man trying to make a puppy behave. In any event,
added footage gives the film editor greater choice in his cutting. It is
good insurance. In one sense, these could be called "protection
shots."

The term FREEZE FRAME should be self-explanatory. The animate
image, or action, as it appears at a particular second in a single frame
of film, is "frozen" and the image, or action, is held immobile in that
one position for whatever length of running time is necessary. This
effect is accomplished by optically printing a single frame over and
over to desired Freeze Frame length of footage required.]

23. CLOSE UP—-PUP

Van's hands are in 'the shot as the pup squirms, resisting
the efforts to make him pose.   (Run long enough for footage for two or three scenes for intercutting.)

24. CLOSE UP—-LARRY

He shows patience and determination as he works with the
pup. (Run long enough for footage for added scenes for
intercuts.)

NARRATOR

But Larry was a firm and patient trainer.

25. MED CLOSE--LARRY & PUP

The pup starts to respond to Larry's will and holds reasonably still as Larry, talking to him reassuringly, sets
each of the pup's feet in the correct position with one
hand while with the other he holds the pup gently but
firmly by the muzzle. (Note: The pup will have had several training lessons before being brought before the camera.) Larry shifts his hand from the muzzle to hold the
pup only by the tip of one finger placed in the hollow under the jaw to raise the pup's head to the desired angle.

26. CLOSE UP--PUP

The pup is holding a reasonably steady pose, almost broadside to the camera. (FREEZE FRAME can be used here to
hold pup in pose.)

                         NARRATOR
          This lesson in ring manners was repeated several
          times each day.

27. CLOSE UP--LARRY

He shows he is well pleased with the progress he is making
with the pup.

28. MED CLOSE--LARRY & PUP

Same angle as Scene 25. Larry picks up the pup in his
arms, fondling him and praising him for his response.

                         NARRATOR
          Like any smart handler, Larry kept the training
          sessions brief so as not to tire or aggravate his
          pupil. And he never failed to reward a good per-
          formance with praise.

DISSOLVE

[EXPLANATORY NOTE: Once a set or location and time of day are established in a scene heading, such designation of place and time need
not be repeated at the heading of the scenes to follow immediately,
as long as the action taking place occurs on the same set or location.
When the camera is moved to a new set or location, then the new set
or location and time of day (whether day or night) are again established at the head of the script scene.

An example is found after a time lapse has occurred between Scene 28 and Scene 29. In the heading of Scene 29 the set and time of day are designated. Such heading is not used again until the camera is moved to the exterior of the yard in Scene 31 when that location and time of day are given. There is no further designation until Scene 36, when the exterior of the dog-show ring and daytime are established.]

```
29. INT. KENNEL HOUSE--DAY
    MED. SHOT
```

Larry enters to the puppy pen with a large pan of puppy
food. On the side of the pan can be seen the letters
"A-TO-Z." Larry leans over the gate to set the food pan
on the floor of the pen.   ,

```
30. MED CLOSE--PUPS
```

Low Camera Setup.
The pup and his brothers and sisters crowd the dish, eating ravenously.

                          NARRATOR
          The same nourishing food that was a part of their
          dam's prenatal care continued to build bone and
          muscle and good coats in her growing offspring.

DISSOLVE

```
31. EXT. YARD--DAY
    FULL SHOT
```

In the background are the outdoor runs and the kennel
house. In the foreground Larry has Van (still about nine
weeks old) on a lead and is walking him back and forth.
The pup may make a break or two, but responds pretty well
to the lead since he has had a few previous training ses-
sions on it.

                          NARRATOR
          Good food and regular exercise, walking on a light
          lead, is all part of a dog's life--that is, in the
          life of a dog being trained for the discipline of
          the show ring. And a wise handler starts training
          at a very early age.

```
32.⎤ To cover Added Scenes with Closer Angles on Larry and
33.⎦ the pup for intercutting into previous scene.
```

34. CLOSE PAN SHOT—PUP

This is a broadside view of the nine-weeks-old pup as the
CAMERA PANS with him as he trots along at the end of the
lead. Larry's feet and legs are in the scene. Moving
from right to left.

MATCHED DISSOLVE

35. CLOSE PAN SHOT—VAN, AGE 5 MONTHS

Same location as preceding scene. Same broadside view of
Van, only now he has grown larger. He is now about five
months old. CAMERA PANS with him as he trots along at
lead's-end with a rhythmic gait without a break. Larry's
feet and legs are in the shot, moving in the same direction as in preceding scene—from right to left.

MATCHED DISSOLVE

36. EXT. DOG—SHOW RING—DAY
    CLOSE PAN SHOT—VAN, AGE 11 MONTHS

We now see a more mature Van as he moves in the show ring,
CAMERA PANNING with him from right to left to match the
two preceding scenes. Larry's feet and legs are in the
scene as he moves along with the dog. He is wearing
dressier shoes and slacks.

[EXPLANATORY NOTE on MATCHED DISSOLVE — Scenes 34 to 36: Used
for a smooth transition of progression in time or mood from one action
to an identical or closely related action in the next scene immediately
following.

In this instance (Scene 34), we DISSOLVE from the CLOSE PAN SHOT
of Van as a nine-weeks-old pup as he trots along from right to left. As
we DISSOLVE into Scene 35, we pick up Van at the age of five months
at the same distance from the camera as he continues to move from
right to left, the camera panning with him. DISSOLVING from Scene 35
to 36, we pick up Van as a mature dog. He is the same distance from
the camera, still moving from right to left, the camera continuing to
pan with him. By using the MATCHED DISSOLVE we have covered
some nine months of time and Van's growth and progressive training
in three scenes, taking him from the untrained puppy to the disciplined mature show dog.

To maintain the same smoothness of transition from one time and
place to another we continue to pan from right to left with the camera
in Scene 37, a WIDER ANGLE, which is an ESTABLISHING SHOT to es-

tablish the location and atmosphere of the dog-show ring, to orient
the audience to a new setting. By suggesting the Judge in the shot,
we have also established him and his position in the center of the ring.
When we cut to the Judge in Scene 38, a CLOSE SHOT, there is the
same sense of movement as he slowly turns his head, his gaze following the dogs parading around the ring off scene. Next we cut to a
FULL SHOT, Scene 39, to more completely orient the audience before
we move the camera in to a CLOSE ANGLE on THE CENTER OF INTER-
EST — Van and Larry.]

37. WIDER ANGLE PAN SHOT--VAN & LARRY

(An Establishing Shot--Establishing location and atmosphere to orient audience.)
PANNING from right to left, this is shot from the Judge's
Angle--from where he stands in the center of the ring--
suggesting the Judge in the shot, back to Camera, as he
watches the dogs parading around the ring from right to
left. Spectators and ringside atmosphere in the background. Other dachsies parading in line.

                    NARRATOR

          Then came the big day when Van made his debut as a
          show dog . . .

38. CLOSE SHOT--JUDGE

This is close enough on the Judge for us to plainly see
the official judge's badge on the lapel of his coat. The
man turns his head, following the progress of the line of
dogs circling about the ring.

                    NARRATOR

          . . . under the critical eye of an American Kennel
          Club judge.

39. FULL SHOT--SHOW RING

This is a WIDE ANGLE on the show ring in which the dachshunds are being judged. It is the 9 to 12 Months Puppy
Class. The Judge stands in the center of the ring while
ten or twelve young dogs are being paraded around the ring
in a circle by their handlers so the Judge may make his
initial appraisal of the individual entries. They are
moving counter-clockwise. Larry is in the line with Van.
In the background are other rings where other breeds are

being judged. Spectators are seated and standing outside
the rings. In one corner of the dachshund ring is the
trophy table where a ring steward is arranging the ribbons. Nearby is an examination table.

> NARRATOR
>
> It was all very new and exciting to Van, with all
> the strange dogs and strange people . . .

40. MED PAN SHOT—FEATURING LARRY & VAN

The CAMERA PANS with Larry and Van as the man leads the
dog at a brisk trot around the ring with the other entries.

> NARRATOR
>
> . . . but at a little over eleven months, Van be-
> haved like a veteran in the Nine to Twelve Months
> Puppy Class.

41.⎤ To cover SHOTS OF SPECTATORS from the angle of the
42.⎦ ring, as they watch the proceedings and make comments
on this or that dog.

43. CLOSE SHOT—JUDGE

The Judge is standing in the center of the ring, watching
the young dogs being paraded before him. His expert eye
is appraising each dog as it passes in review. He turns
his head as his gaze follows a particular individual that
has caught his fancy.

> NARRATOR
>
> The Judge saw he had a good entry of fine young
> dogs. It wasn't going to be an easy choice.

44. MED PAN SHOT—FEATURING LARRY & VAN

This is from the Judge's angle as the man and the dog continue their brisk gait counter-clockwise around the ring,
CAMERA PANNING with them.

> NARRATOR
>
> Many people think a dog show is something like a
> beauty contest in which the most beautiful dog is
> chosen winner. Such a choice is subject to vary-
> ing and conflicting human opinion . . .

45. FULL SHOT--SHOW RING

The Judge leaves the center of the ring and crosses to the
line of handlers and their dogs and stops the parade with
Larry and Van at the head of the line, nearest the Judge,
and near the examination table.

                    NARRATOR

        . . . but in judging dogs it is true only to the
        extent that a set standard of perfection and what
        goes to make that standard of perfection is
        beautiful.

46. MED SHOT--LARRY & VAN

Larry has stopped with Van at the Judge's signal. The
Judge enters to pause for a moment a pace or so away from
Van to look him over as the young dog takes a good stance
at the end of his lead.

                    NARRATOR

        Superficially, a dog may appear to be a beautiful
        specimen of his breed, yet a close examination by
        an expert can reveal structural faults.

47. MED CLOSE--VAN

This is shooting down at Van from the Judge's angle. The
dog stands steady enough at the end of his lead. He is
in superb condition. His coat is sleek. He is a fine
specimen of his breed.

                    NARRATOR

        Each breed of purebred dog is judged according to
        a rigid breed standard that is defined in detail,
        describing serious, secondary, and minor faults.

48. MED SHOT--LARRY, VAN, & JUDGE

After studying Van for a moment or two, the Judge speaks
to Larry and waves his hand, indicating the nearby examination table that has been set up so that the Judge may
more conveniently and thoroughly go over a small dog such
as the dachshund. Larry picks up Van in his arms and
exits with the Judge toward the examination table.

NARRATOR

The Standard also spells out the characteristics
of perfection. Good and bad features of a dog's
conformation and body structure are what the Judge
is looking for.

49. MED CLOSE--LARRY, VAN, & JUDGE

They enter to the examination table where the Judge gives
Larry a moment to deftly set up Van in a pose to show him
to best advantage, arranging his feet and adjusting his
legs to the proper angles with one hand while with the
other he holds Van's head up on a close lead.

NARRATOR

In judging small breeds, an examination table is
usually provided for the convenience of the Judge
so he will not have to squat, stoop, or kneel in
going over each dog, especially when there is a
large entry.

Larry moves back a step to give the Judge an unobstructed
view of the dog, as he has Van set up in a perfect pose.
The Judge stands back a pace to give Van an overall appraisal. In this and all other judging scenes, the Judge
works behind or to one side of the dog so that the audience will have an unobstructed view of the dog.

50. CLOSE UP--JUDGE

He looks off at Van appraisingly.

51. CLOSE UP--VAN

This is a BROADSIDE VIEW of Van on the examination table.
He is beautifully posed, his image filling the screen. It
is from the Judge's angle. It is what he sees.

FREEZE FRAME to hold the image of Van immobile for the
length of the narration.

NARRATOR

The official dachshund standard states that in
general appearance the dachshund should be low to
the ground, short-legged, long-bodied, but with
compact figure and robust muscular development
like this . . .

52. CLOSE UP--FIRST POOR SPECIMEN

This is a Still Photo of a dachshund in the same pose as
that of Van in previous scene--a broadside view--only this
dog is short-chested, long-legged, low behind the shoulders
and high in the rear, altogether a very sorry specimen.

> NARRATOR
>
> . . . not like this sorry specimen, short-chested,
> low behind the shoulders, high in the rear. A
> very bad top-line.

(Note: Since this film should be shot in color, it is
recommended that this and other Still Photos of poor
specimens be in black and white to give even greater contrast between the good specimen and the bad. Also,
drawings can be used instead of photos.)

53. CLOSE UP--SECOND POOR SPECIMEN

A Still Photo. A broadside view of another bad example of
a dachshund with roach or carp back, excessively drawn up
flanks like those of a greyhound.

> NARRATOR
>
> . . . nor like this equally bad top-line. Roached
> back and excessively drawn up flanks. Altogether
> a weak figure.

54. CLOSE UP--VAN

Same FREEZE FRAME as Scene 51.

> NARRATOR
>
> . . . in contrast Van has a well-developed trunk
> like this, long and fully muscled, with good top-
> line. The back, with sloping shoulders, and
> short, rigid pelvis should lie in the straightest
> possible line between the withers and the very
> slightly arched loins.

As the Narrator calls attention to each body feature, an
ARROW POPS ON to identify that particular feature--the
trunk--the top-line--the sloping shoulders--the pelvis--
the withers--the arched loins.

UNFREEZE FRAME--As Van moves his head to reestablish live
action, CUT TO--

55. MED CLOSE—VAN & JUDGE

Larry may be suggested in the shot as the Judge runs his
hand lightly and appreciatively along Van's good top-line,
and then moves to get a frontal view of the dog, particularly the head. He appraises Van's head from the side
and from above, as the Narrator synchronizes his commentary with what the Judge is doing.

> NARRATOR
>
> Viewed from the side or from above, the head
> should taper uniformly to the tip of the nose and
> should be clean cut.

[COMMENT: In Scene 54 the Judge is concentrating on Van's top-line.
When we cut to Scene 55, we pick up a continuation of the action in
the preceding scene as the Judge finishes his contemplation of Van's
top-line and then moves to appraise the dog's head. This overlapping
of the action from one scene to the next scene makes for smooth
visual transition, without the effect of jumping too abruptly from one
thing to the next.]

56. CLOSE UP—VAN'S HEAD

This is a Very Close Side View of Van's head.

FREEZE FRAME

> NARRATOR
>
> The skull is only slightly arched, and should
> slope gradually without stop, the less stop, the
> more typical—like this . . .

An ARROW POPS ON to identify the location of the faint
"stop."

57. CLOSE UP—BAD-HEADED DACHSHUND

A Still Photo of a very skully, coarse head with a pronounced stop and lack of arched muzzle.

> NARRATOR
>
> . . . not like this skully, coarse head with its
> pronounced stop . . .

As the Narrator mentions "stop," an ARROW POPS ON to
indicate the very pronounced stop.

58. CLOSE UP--VAN'S HEAD

Side View.   Same as Scene 56 with FREEZE FRAME.

> NARRATOR
>
> . . . but like this, with little or no stop,
> slightly arched muzzle, resembling the curve of a
> ram's nose. The bridge bones over the eyes should
> be strongly prominent.

UNFREEZE FRAME

59. MED CLOSE--VAN & JUDGE

Larry may be suggested.   The Judge opens Van's mouth to
examine his teeth.

> NARRATOR
>
> Powerful canine teeth should fit closely to-
> gether . . .

59-A. EXTREME CLOSE UP--VAN'S FRONT TEETH

This is extremely close on Van's front teeth as the
Judge's fingers hold back the dog's lips to expose the
teeth to view.

FREEZE FRAME

> NARRATOR
>
> . . . the outer side of the lower incisors tightly
> touching the inner side of the upper--the scis-
> sor's bite.

59-B. MED CLOSE--VAN & JUDGE

The Judge gives his attention to Van's eyes.

> NARRATOR
>
> The eyes should be of medium size and oval . . .

60. CLOSE UP--GOGGLE-EYED DACHSHUND

Still Photo of dachshund with round, protruding eyes.

> NARRATOR
>
> . . . not goggle eyes, like these.

61. MED CLOSE--VAN & JUDGE

The Judge examines Van's ears for proper set, length, and shape.

> NARRATOR
>
> Ears should be set near the top of the head, and not too far forward--like this . . .

62. CLOSE UP--BAD-EARED DACHSHUND

Still Photo of a specimen with very low set, too long, and folded ears. This should show an almost exaggerated example to make clear the comparison.

> NARRATOR
>
> . . . not like the low-set, folded ears of this doleful but lovable sad sack.

63. MED CLOSE--VAN & JUDGE

Same Angle as Scene 61, as the Judge finishes examining Van's ears, according to the standard.

> NARRATOR
>
> Their carriage should be animated, and the forward edge should touch the cheek.

The Judge shifts his position slightly to examine Van's neckline.

64.
65. } To cover very brief REACTION SHOTS of spectators at ringside as they follow the judging. Taken from the
66. angle of the examination table. To be cut in, if needed, to break the monotony of staying too long with Close Angles on the judging alone during this sequence.

67.
68. } To cover very brief CLOSE REACTION SHOTS of Larry as he follows the judging with intense interest.
69.

70. } To cover very brief REACTION SHOTS of the other
71. Handlers in the ring as they await their turn and watch the Judge working with Van at the examination table. Taken from the angle of the examination table.

(Note: These added scenes are cutaways which can be cut in by the editor anywhere appropriate—when and if he should need one or more of such scenes.)

72. MED CLOSE—VAN & JUDGE

This is a change of angle, a little toward a three-quarters side view of Van, with the dog directly in front of CAMERA, and the Judge working on the other side of the dog, examining his neckline.

> NARRATOR
>
> The neck should be long, muscular, without dewlaps on the throat—clean-cut, like this . . .

The Judge runs his hand along Van's clean under neckline.

73. CLOSE SHOT—BAD EXAMPLE NECK

Still Photo of a dachsie with pronounced dewlaps hanging about his throat like double chins. A pointer or arrow comes into the scene to indicate the heavy dewlaps.

> NARRATOR
>
> . . . not like Double Chin Charlie here.

74. MED CLOSE—VAN & JUDGE

Same angle as Sc. 72. The Judge runs his hand lightly along the back of Van's neck as he takes in the slightly arched nape.

> NARRATOR
>
> The neck should be slightly arched in the nape, extending in a graceful line into the shoulders, carried proudly, but not stiffly.

75. CLOSE UP—JUDGE

As he appraises Van's front quarters.

76. MED CLOSE—VAN & JUDGE

The Judge examines Van's front quarters, which are featured in the shot.

> NARRATOR
>
> The dachshund has been bred as a hunting dog for beating the bush, trailing, and going underground

```
            to fight and kill a badger, or drive it from its
            burrow.

77. CLOSE UP--VAN

This is a Close Broadside view of Van's front quarters.
They are all that the Narrator describes.

FREEZE FRAME

                          NARRATOR
            For the dog to endure the arduous exertion under-
            ground, his front must be muscular, deep, long and
            broad.
```

[COMMENT: As an example of redundant, digressive narration, let us assume that the narration in Scene 76 had been written in this fashion:

```
The dachshund originated in Germany and firsし gained popu-
larity outside of that country when Queen Victoria of
England imported a pair of the little dogs.  Courtiers and
others throughout Britain soon became fanciers of the
breed.  Most pet owners do not know that the dachshund was
first bred as a hunting dog, to trail small game and to go
underground and hunt out the badger, a fierce fighter
when cornered in his burrow.
```

The immediate concern is the judging of the dachshund's body structure, not the history of the breed, nor its popularity, nor the fierceness of the badger which it is called upon to fight.

There are 73 words in the wordy discourse above, which would require about 32 seconds of running time, or about 49 feet of 35 mm film, at the rate of 1½ words per foot. The visual action at this point in the film could not be dragged out to support narration irrelevant to what we are seeing on the screen.

In contrast, the narration in Scene 76 is composed of 30 words requiring 20 feet of film, or about 13 seconds of running time. It is *lean audiovisual* writing that is entirely pertinent support for the visual, briefly explaining what the visual cannot entirely explain, that is, the need for development and strength in a dachshund's front quarters.

This illustration of how *not* to write narration in support of the visual might be considered an exaggerated example. It is not as exaggerated as many may think. The tendency toward digressive writing

is prevalent among beginners and those who lack sufficient professional experience in the field.]

78. CLOSE UP--BAD EXAMPLE FRONT

Still Photo of a thin, scrawny, poorly developed dachsie
front.

                    NARRATOR

        Not like this sorry specimen--the result of
        either poor breeding or nutritional deficiency
        going back to his dam's prenatal care, or a com-
        bination of both.

79. CLOSE UP--VAN

Same angle as Scene 77 in FREEZE FRAME. An ARROW POPS ON
to indicate the shoulder blade.

                    NARRATOR

        The shoulder blade should be long, broad, ob-
        liquely and firmly placed upon the fully developed
        thorax, furnished with hard and plastic muscles.

An ARROW POPS ON to indicate the upper arm.

                    NARRATOR

        The upper arm should be the same length as the
        shoulder blade, and at right angles to it, strong
        of bone and hard of muscle, lying close to the
        ribs, capable of free movement.

UNFREEZE FRAME. As Van "comes alive" CUT TO:

80. MED CLOSE--VAN & JUDGE

The Judge is using his experienced fingers to examine the
length and angulation of the dog's shoulder blade and
upper arm.

[COMMENT: In this sequence on the judging of a dog according to a
very comprehensive, detailed, and exacting breed standard, the same
basic photographic principles and techniques are employed as are
used in the presentation of a mechanical device in the example script
formats used in Part IV.

There is a definite relationship between the functional mechanical
components of a complex piece of machinery and the functional
components of a living mechanism. A machine is built to certain

specifications to perform certain functions. A living creature is built with certain component parts and with capabilities to perform certain functions. The problem of breaking down the component parts in either category for photographic purposes is identical. The automobile has a motor and wheels. The dog has a heart and legs. An auto's wheels must be well constructed, durable, and well balanced. A dog's legs must be well constructed, strong, and capable of movement.

The only difference between shooting scripts on these two subjects would be in the subject matter. The identical fundamental principles of script writing apply to each. *What* do we want to show? *Why?* Exactly *what* is it? *How* does it work? *What* results from *what* it does? *How* best to present it on film so that the *what*, the *why*, and the *how* can be understood clearly by the intended audience?]

NARRATOR

The Judge knows the anatomy of a dog and he uses his experienced fingers to measure and calibrate the skeletal structure not visible to the eye.

81. CLOSE UP—NO. 1 DRAWING OF A DACHSHUND

See Figure 1. It shows the broadside outline of a good specimen of a dachshund. It shows the shoulder blade and upper arm in proper length and in proper juxtaposition, or angulation.

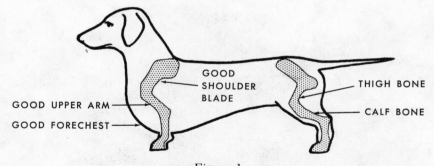

Figure 1

NARRATOR

Only by probing gently with his fingers can the Judge determine the length of the shoulder blade, the length of the upper arm, and their respective angulation, which should be at right angles.

82. CLOSE UP--NO. 2 DRAWING OF A DACHSHUND

See Figure 2. It shows the broadside outline of a poor
specimen of a dachshund with a noticeably short forechest.
It is the same type of outlined and shaded drawing as in
Figure 1 with the exception that the shaded area showing
the shoulder blade and upper arm differs in that the upper
arm is only about two-thirds as long as it should be--one-
third less than the length of the shoulder blade--and it,
the upper arm, has lost angulation, dropping to a nearer
vertical angle in its relationship to the angulation of
the shoulder blade. A pointer, or arrow, comes in to
(first) point out the shortness of the upper arm, (second)
its drop in angulation, and (third) the short forechest.

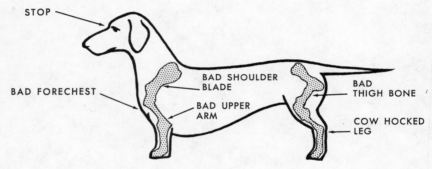

Figure 2

NARRATOR

Here's what happens when the upper arm is shorter
in length than the shoulder blade--it drops into a
more vertical position. This lack of proper development results in a short forechest like this,
lessening lung and heart room which is a vital
requirement for endurance in underground work.
More like a terrier front.

83. CLOSE UP--NO. 1 DRAWING

A pointer or arrow enters to indicate the typical, well-
developed dachshund forechest.

NARRATOR

. . . than that of a typical dachsie forechest
like this . . .

84. CLOSE UP--VAN

Featuring his excellently developed forechest.   Side view.

NARRATOR

. . . and this.

[COMMENT: In Scenes 81, 82, and 83, drawings are used to illustrate certain features of the dog's anatomical structure which are specifically identified through the use of POP ON ARROWS (to be accomplished by Special Effects process). These drawings serve as an X-ray effect to give the viewer a clear understanding of what the narrator is saying about the anatomical features which are not apparent on the surface.

The same graphic method of presentation can be applied when machinery and mechanical devices are involved, where the internal working parts and functions cannot be seen from outside. Such clear and precise illustration is essential to the audiovisual medium. Degree of audience interest and understanding depends entirely upon the degree of clarity in the presentation.

Lack of essential detail, whether it is the absence of necessary drawings or in inadequate, skimpy writing, does not carry the message. That is why it is so necessary to develop the visual fully and not depend upon the narration to get across the more technical points. (This is *what* it *looks* like. This is what is *said* about it.) Be explicit in your writing.

It is best to develop the visual first, to have a very clear picture of what you are going to talk about in the narration before you write it. Again—*give primacy to the visual* in every way.]

85. WIDER ANGLE--VAN, JUDGE, & LARRY

This is tight on the three as the Judge finishes examining Van's shoulder and upper arm placement.   He smiles and remarks to Larry that the dog has excellent length and angulation of shoulder and upper arm.   Then he moves to examine the front of Van's chest.

86. MED CLOSE--VAN & JUDGE

This is a frontal view of Van's chest.   The Judge stands a little to one side, leaning into the shot so he will not block the Camera's view of the front chest.

NARRATOR

The breast bone should be strong, and so prominent in front that on either side a depression appears —-like a dimple.

87. EXTREME CLOSE UP--VAN'S CHEST--FRONT VIEW

NARRATOR

When viewed from the front, the thorax should appear oval, and should extend downward to the midpoint of the forearm.

The Judge's hand enters the scene and his forefinger indicates the oval appearance of the thorax and the extension of the bottom of the chest downward to the midforearm.

88. EXTREME CLOSE UP--BAD EXAMPLE FRONT OF CHEST

Still Photo of a dachsie with a front chest that is narrow, and relatively high off the ground--the leggy type.

NARRATOR

Not narrow and high like this weak structure.

89. EXTREME CLOSE UP--VAN'S CHEST--FRONT VIEW

The Judge's hand pats Van's chest approvingly.

90. WIDER ANGLE--VAN & JUDGE

The Judge moves around to get a top and then a side view of Van's rib cage. Van is broadside to the Camera, the Judge on the opposite side of Van, or to one side, so as not to obscure what we want to show and talk about.

NARRATOR

The enclosing structure of ribs should appear full and oval when viewed from above or from the side, full-volumed to allow ample capacity for complete development of heart and lungs.

The Judge turns to look at Van's feet.

NARRATOR

Good feet are another one of the many points a judge likes to see.

91. CLOSE UP—VAN'S PERFECT FEET

NARRATOR

The paws should be full, broad in front and a
trifle inclined outward. Compact with well-arched
toes close together and with tough pads like
these . . .

The Judge's hand comes into the scene to raise a paw and
show the good pad.

92. CLOSE UP—SPLAYED FOREFEET

Still Photo of weak and badly splayed forepaws, turned
outward like a turtle's feet.

NARRATOR

. . . not like these weak, badly splayed, and
turned-out turtle feet.

93. CLOSE UP—VAN'S PERFECT FOREFEET

Same angle as Sc. 91.

NARRATOR

Van's feet are excellent.

94. MED CLOSE—VAN & JUDGE

The Judge finishes examining Van's feet. The Camera Pans
with the Judge as he moves toward Van's rear.

95. MED SHOT—VAN, JUDGE, & LARRY

The Judge appraises Van's hindquarters.

NARRATOR

Hindquarters should be sturdy and of equal width.
The hind legs robust and well muscled, with well-
rounded buttocks . . .

95-A. CLOSE UP—VAN'S HIND LEGS

This is shot from the rear, showing Van's well-aligned
hind legs.

NARRATOR

. . . well spaced and aligned like this . . .

95-B. CLOSE UP--BAD EXAMPLE HIND LEGS

Still Photo, shot from rear, showing a dachsie's rear with
legs that are very cow hocked.

> NARRATOR
>
>   . . . not cow hocked as these weakly formed hind
>   legs . . .

95-C. CLOSE UP--VAN'S HIND LEGS

Same angle as Sc. 95-A.

> NARRATOR
>
>   . . . but strong and capable of powerful thrust
>   for good movement, like Van's.

96. CLOSE SHOT--VAN & JUDGE

The Judge now examines the position of the calf bone for
proper length and angulation. This shows a side view of
Van's hindquarters.

> NARRATOR
>
>   Proper rear angulation is also a mark of strength
>   and movement capability.

97. EXTREME CLOSE UP--VAN'S CALF--SIDE VIEW

> NARRATOR
>
>   In comparison with other breeds, the calf bone of
>   a dachshund is short and should be perpendicular
>   to the thigh bone . . .

The Judge's finger comes into the shot indicating the calf
bone and the thigh bone.

98. CLOSE UP--NO. 3 DRAWING OF A DACHSHUND

See Figure 3. The calf bone is shown along with the
pelvic bone, thigh bone, hock joint, the hock, and foot.
An ARROW POPS ON to identify the calf bone and its relationship to the rest of the rear structure.

> NARRATOR
>
>   . . . like this, for excellent rear angulation.

99. EXTREME CLOSE UP--VAN'S CALF

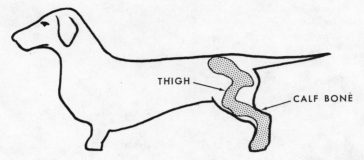

Figure 3: Good Specimen

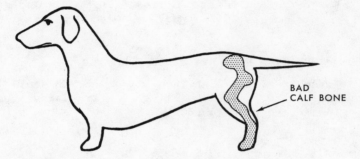

Figure 4: Bad Specimen

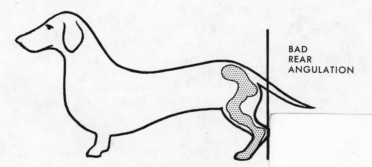

Figure 5: Bad Specimen

NARRATOR

Although they may vary according to the different
breed standards, all these factors and many others
decide whether or not a dog has the makings of a
champion.

100. MED SHOT--VAN, JUDGE, & LARRY

The Judge has now finished his table examination and
motions for Larry to walk his dog, saying, "Let's see how
he moves." Larry picks Van up from the table and places
him on the ground. The Judge motions for him to walk Van
the length of the ring away from him and then toward him.

NARRATOR

There is one more important thing. The Judge
wants to see how Van moves. Good movement is required in any breed of dog.

101. MED SHOT--VAN & LARRY--JUDGE SUGGESTED

This is from the Judge's angle. Larry and Van are in the
foreground. Larry leads Van at a brisk trot away from the
Camera toward the background.

102. CLOSE SHOT--JUDGE

LOW CAMERA SETUP. The Judge squats on his heels to watch
off after Larry and Van who are moving directly away from
him.

103. MED LONG--VAN & LARRY

LOW CAMERA SETUP. This is from the squatting Judge's low,
eye-level view as the dog and man move away from the
Camera.

NARRATOR

No cowhocks here--Van's legs are straight and
strong.

104. CLOSE SHOT--JUDGE

Low Camera Setup.
He squats on his heels, intently appraising Van's move-
ent as the dog trots away from him.

105. MED LONG—VAN & LARRY

Low Camera Setup.
Man and dog reach the far end of the ring and turn to trot
back toward the Judge at a brisk pace.

106. MED—VAN & LARRY

LOW CAMERA SETUP. Man and dog move from the background
toward the Camera at a brisk pace. From Judge's angle.

> NARRATOR
>
> Van can sure move!

107. CLOSE SHOT—JUDGE

Low Camera Setup.
He squats on his heels, watching Van's movement as the dog
trots toward him.

108. MED SHOT—VAN, LARRY, & JUDGE

Larry and Van enter to the Judge, who gets up from his
squatting position and motions Larry back to his place in
the line of handlers and dogs. Larry exits with Van as
the Judge motions for the next handler in line to bring
his dog to the examination table.

109. FULL SHOT—SHOW RING

Larry takes his former place in line with Van as the next
handler takes his dog toward the Judge and the examination
table.

> NARRATOR
>
> The showing of purebred dogs in competition can be
> just about as exciting as horse racing. It's a
> great sport.

110. MED CLOSE—LARRY & VAN

Low Camera Setup.
They are back in line and Larry is kneeling beside the
dog, petting him and praising him for his well-disciplined
performance. Larry shows the tension of the last few
minutes at the examination table. He quickly wipes his
brow.

> NARRATOR
>
> And there's an even greater emotional tie here--
> the love of a man for his dog and the love of a
> dog for his master.

DISSOLVE

111. FULL SHOT--SHOW RING

All the handlers and their dogs are lined up along one
side of the ring, the dogs placed at short intervals, head
to tail. Larry and Van are still at the head of the line.
Each handler behind one side of his dog, presenting the
other side, a broadside view, to the Judge for his final
appraisal and selection. Each handler is deftly "setting
up" his dog so that he will appear to his best advantage.
The Judge is near the center of the ring, scanning the
line of dogs.

> NARRATOR
>
> All the dogs in the class have been examined. Now
> comes one of the handler's or exhibitor's tense
> moments--the Judge is about to select his first,
> second, third, and fourth choice.

112. CLOSE UP--JUDGE

As he looks over the line of dogs posed before him. He is
thoughtful and deliberate in his appraisal.

113. MED LONG PAN SHOT--HANDLERS & DOGS

This is from the Judge's angle as he appraises the line-up
of dogs. The CAMERA PANS from the tail end of the line-up
to Larry and Van at the head of the line.

114. MED CLOSE--JUDGE

The Judge's gaze fastens on the head of the line-up. He
has made up his mind. He points off to Larry, indicating
his number one choice. He waves his hand for Larry to
take his place before the first-place marker at the head
of the ring.

115. CLOSE--LARRY & VAN

Larry is quietly jubilant. He exits with Van toward the
first-place marker at the head of the ring.

116. MED—SPECTATORS

They applaud enthusiastically.

117. MED—LARRY & VAN

As Larry enters with Van to place-marker No. 1. In the
background we see 2, 3, and 4. Larry proudly sets Van up
in a pose in front of the marker.

[COMMENT: Scene 116 of the Spectators is more than a necessary
REACTION SHOT; it also serves the purpose of covering the time it
takes for Larry and Van to walk from where they made their exit in
Scene 115 to where they make their entrance to the No. 1 Marker in
Scene 117.

The CUTAWAY is used not only to cover a reaction, but as a time
lapse device, such as would apply to photographing a service station
attendant filling a gasoline tank. We show him removing the cap and
inserting the hose. To cover the time it takes to fill the tank, we can
cut to a CLOSE UP of his face, or to the car's driver inspecting his
tires, or to another man wiping the windshield, or to the driver taking
out his wallet to get money to pay for the gasoline. After one or two
quick cuts, we can go back to the station attendant as he finishes filling
the tank and removes the hose.]

118. FULL SHOT—SHOW RING

The Judge quickly motions his choices for 2nd, 3rd, and
4th to their positions at the markers. The three cross to
the markers at the head of the ring as the ring steward
crosses to the Judge, carrying the ribbons and trophies.

119. MED—LARRY, VAN, JUDGE, & RING STEWARD

The Judge and ring steward enter to Van and Larry. The
Judge hands Larry a blue ribbon and a small trophy. Larry
is delighted. The Judge moves on to give out the other
awards.

                    NARRATOR

     It was Van's first blue ribbon won in stiff com-
     petition, but it was only a class win. The really
     tough competition would come later on in the show
     when he would meet the winners of the other
     classes.

120. CLOSE SHOT--LARRY & VAN

As Larry grabs Van up in his arms, hugging him, jubilant
over his win.

> NARRATOR
>
> But the class win was the first step upward and
> Larry was elated.

DISSOLVE

121. FULL SHOT--SHOW RING

It is later in the day and the Judge is making a final
appraisal of the class winners for his selection of
Winner's Dog. The class winners are lined up in the ring.
The Judge is in the center of the ring looking them over.
This time Larry and Van are at the tail-end of the line-
up.

> NARRATOR
>
> Then came the big moment when he was in the ring
> again with Van to compete with the winners of the
> other classes. Winner's Dog was about to be
> selected and that win carried the coveted points
> toward championship.

122. MED CLOSE--LARRY & VAN

Low Camera Setup.
Broadside view of Van. Larry is kneeling behind Van,
setting up the dog to show him to the best advantage.
Larry is sweating out this important moment. He gives a
quick glance off toward the judge and then off toward the
line ahead of him. He's not too optimistic.

123. MED CLOSE--JUDGE

He is looking them over.

124. MED LONG PAN SHOT--LINE-UP OF CLASS WINNERS

From the Judge's angle. It is what he sees. CAMERA PANS
SLOWLY from the head of the line to the tail-end of the
line where Larry and Van are placed. All handlers have
their dogs well posed, broadside to the Camera. (Background MUSIC builds for suspense through Scene 143.)

NARRATOR

It was a line-up of unusually fine dogs--the outstanding male dachshunds from all the classes.
The selection of the winner wasn't going to be
easy.

[COMMENT: Following the narration in Scene 124, the background
music builds up and there is no narration over Scenes 125 through
143. The element of suspense in the visual, augmented by background music, tells the story. Narration over such scenes can break
the mood of suspense and become a distraction.

125. MED CLOSE--JUDGE

He is looking them over carefully.   He exits in the direction of Larry and Van.

126. MED SHOT--LARRY, VAN, & JUDGE

The Judge enters and looks down at Van.

127. CLOSE SHOT--LARRY & VAN

Larry is sweating it out under the Judge's close scrutiny
of Van.   He quickly adjusts one of Van's feet to more
proper position and then looks off up at the Judge hopefully.

128. MED SHOT--LARRY, VAN, & JUDGE

The Judge studies Van for a moment more, poker-faced.
Then he glances off toward the middle of the line-up and
exits toward another dog.

129. CLOSE UP--LARRY

He shows disappointment at seeing the Judge move on.

130. MED SHOT--HANDLER NUMBER 1 & DOG--JUDGE

Handler Number 1 is conscious of the Judge's approach and
quickly adjusts his dog's pose.   The Judge enters, pauses
to study the dog, a fine specimen.

131. CLOSE UP--HANDLER NUMBER 1

He looks up off at the Judge hopefully.   It is a moment of
suspense for all concerned.

132. MED SHOT--HANDLER NUMBER 1, DOG, & JUDGE

The handler shows disappointment as the Judge exits on up
the line.

133. MED SHOT--HANDLER NUMBER 2, DOG, & JUDGE

The handler is aware of the Judge's approach and quickly
checks his dog's stance. The Judge enters and looks down
at the dog, another very fine specimen that seems to
impress the Judge who bends over and touches the dog's
hindquarters. Then he straightens up and takes one more
look up and down the line.

134. CLOSE UP--JUDGE

As he takes one more look up and down the line-up.

135. CLOSE SHOT--LARRY & VAN

Larry appears discouraged as he watches off toward the
Judge who seems to be well impressed by another dog.

136. MED SHOT--HANDLER NUMBER 2, DOG, & JUDGE

The Judge studies the dog for a moment more before he
turns and gestures off to the ring steward waiting at the
trophy table. He has made up his mind.

137. MED SHOT--RING STEWARD

The ring steward responds to the Judge's call and exits
toward him with Winner's Dog ribbon and a handsome trophy.

138. MED SHOT--JUDGE & RING STEWARD

The Judge and the ring steward enter from opposite directions, meeting near the center of the ring. The steward
hands the Judge the ribbon and trophy.

139. MED LONG SHOT--LINE-UP FOR WINNER'S DOG

Shooting at an angle from near the head of the line-up.
Larry and Van are at the far end.

140. MED SHOT--JUDGE & RING STEWARD

The Judge exits back toward the line-up, carrying ribbon
and trophy.

141. MED SHOT—SPECTATORS

The ringside spectators see which of the dogs the Judge is
heading for and burst into enthusiastic applause.

142. MED SHOT—JUDGE

He enters smiling, carrying ribbon and trophy.   To hold
suspense, there is no indication in shot as to which dog
he has chosen Winners.

143. MED CLOSE—LARRY & VAN

Larry looks up, and slowly registers astonishment when he
sees the Judge is approaching him.

144. MED—LARRY, VAN, & JUDGE

Larry gets up from his squatting position beside Van
as the Judge enters and smilingly presents him with ribbon
and trophy.   Larry can scarcely believe his good fortune.
He grins and thanks the Judge heartily.

                    NARRATOR
          A great win for so young a dog in the face of top-
          flight competition.   Winner's Dog and the first
          points toward Van's championship.

145. WIDER ANGLE

As Larry picks up Van to hug him close.   Competing handlers enter to congratulate Larry on his win and to admire
Van.   A show of good sportsmanship.

                    NARRATOR
          In other shows that followed, Van topped this
          first win by going Best of Winners and Best of
          Variety of Breed . . .

146. CLOSE SHOT—VAN & LARRY

This features Van as he is held in Larry's arms.

                    NARRATOR
          . . . and it didn't take long for this outstanding
          specimen to complete that championship.

DISSOLVE

147. INT. DOG SHOW BENCH--LIMBO
      CLOSE SHOT--VAN

Same as Scene 1--LIMBO--with Van on the bench, back-
grounded by his array of ribbons and with impressive
trophies set up on either side of him.

DISSOLVE

148. LIMBO
      CLOSE SHOT--LARRY

He is holding a very young (6 or 7 weeks) nondescript
puppy in his hands. He is cuddling it. He turns and
speaks into the Camera.

                    LARRY
          Now you've got some idea of what it takes to make
          a champion--it's interesting and exciting.
          (Pauses as he glances back at puppy.) Like you,
          I've always loved dogs--all kinds of dogs--ever
          since I was a kid. But look at this little fel-
          low. Will he grow up to be like this . . .

149. LIMBO
      MED CLOSE--First ugly mongrel. Not very attractive.

150. LIMBO
      MED CLOSE--Second mongrel. Drab. No personality.

                    LARRY
                  (Off Scene)
          . . . or like this?

151. LIMBO
      CLOSE--LARRY

He smiles into the Camera, still holding the mongrel
puppy.
                    LARRY
          . . . or what you want him to look like and to be
          like when he grows up. That's where you can de-
          pend upon the purebred dog, whether you want
          . . .

152. LIMBO
      CLOSE SHOT--DACHSHUND (VAN)

He is posed.

> LARRY'S VOICE
>
> A dachsie . . .

153. LIMBO
     CLOSE SHOT—COCKER SPANIEL

He is posed.

> LARRY'S VOICE
>
> A cocker . . .

154. LIMBO
     CLOSE SHOT—COLLIE

He is posed.

> LARRY'S VOICE
>
> A collie . . .

155. LIMBO
     CLOSE SHOT—BEAGLE

He is posed.

> LARRY'S VOICE
>
> A beagle . . .

156. LIMBO
     CLOSE SHOT—BASSET

He is posed.

> LARRY'S VOICE
>
> . . . or his more droll cousin, the basset . . .

157. LIMBO
     CLOSE SHOT—ENGLISH SETTER

He is posed.

> LARRY'S VOICE
>
> . . . a bird dog—the English Setter . . .

158. LIMBO
     CLOSE SHOT—POINTER

He is posed.

> LARRY'S VOICE
>
> . . . a pointer . . .

159. LIMBO
     CLOSE SHOT--MINIATURE POODLE

A white poodle in contrast to the LIMBO background.

                    LARRY'S VOICE

         . . . a poodle . . .

160. LIMBO
     CLOSE SHOT--GREAT DANE

He is posed.

                    LARRY'S VOICE

         . . . or a nice little lap dog like this Great
         Dane . . .

161. LIMBO
     CLOSE SHOT--MINIATURE PINSCHER

A sleek-coated red posed beside a dummy fire hydrant to
give contrast to the Miniature's size.

                    LARRY'S VOICE

         . . . or one of the doggiest of the little dogs--
         the Miniature Pinscher.

162. LIMBO
     CLOSE SHOT--LARRY

He is holding the mongrel puppy as he speaks to the Camera.

                         LARRY

         . . . that's the advantage of choosing a purebred
         puppy. He will look exactly like his purebred
         parents--just what you ordered--you'll know what
         you're getting and you'll be proud of him--for
         he's a purebred dog! (Brief pause to smile at
         puppy he is holding.) Remember, your dog, whether
         he's a purebred, or a lovable mutt, looks to you
         for two things--love, and plenty of it--and good
         food, and plenty of that, too!

DISSOLVE

163. LIMBO
     CLOSE SHOT--VAN

This is a view of Van's rear end as he looks back over his

shoulder toward the Camera.   FREEZE FRAME.   The title——
THE END——is superimposed over this shot.

FADE OUT.

(Note: The series of LIMBO shots of the several dogs can
be beautiful, individual cameos that should be very impressive.   However, if the Sponsor should desire to show
other and additional breeds, as a matter of public relations, or if it is necessary to sacrifice such cameo—like
shots for a simpler form of production, the different
breeds can be paraded by their owners or handlers before
the Camera against a LIMBO background.)

5

Analysis of
The Making of a Champion

The Making of a Champion includes the elements of more than one type of film—the public-relations or promotional, the documentary, the informational, and the technical. In Scene 47, the writer tells us that there is a breed standard by which a purebred dog is judged. In scene 51, he gives us a more intimate picture of the "component parts" of a dog—the "technical" aspect.

The purpose of the film is to promote the sale of dog-food products, and it gets across the sponsor's message with a punch. Thus it is a promotional or sales type of film. It serves as an information film for those with no knowledge of the purebred dog. For the amateur breeder it has orientational and instructional value. It could serve as an audiovisual aid in training dog-show judges.

It is also a documentary film in that it records the life of a dachshund from birth, through his early training, and on to his championship. It shows how a breeder of purebred dogs raises them, how he trains them for show, and how he handles them in the ring. And it shows a day in the life of an American Kennel Club judge.

From Treatment to Script

After having read the two contrasting treatments and the shooting script, it should be apparent that the writer of a well-detailed treatment has a great advantage when it comes to the development of his shooting script. He has given his producer or sponsor a clear idea of *what* will be shown and *how* it will be shown, thereby winning their confidence. He has simplified the writing of the shooting script for himself. He has followed the orderly procedure of taking first things first.

With a well-developed story line in proper continuity, the writer can concentrate on the development of scene content and progression, the action, camera angles, production problems, and the narration and/or dialogue. There is enough to think about in laying out a production script without having to "fight" major story problems, although there are adjustments to be made as the final form takes shape.

Some sponsors and associated personnel do not always know how to "read" a production script with the same practical understanding as those familiar with the form and technical breakdown of a shooting script. They can more easily follow and envision the cinematic development and progression of the story line in the treatment's narrative form — another reason why a detailed and well-polished treatment is important.

Script Scenes

The shooting script of *The Making of a Champion* is meticulously developed in scene description and in its complete breakdown into camera angles. It can be referred to as a "cutting script" — that is, a script in which the breakdown into detailed camera angles closely approximates the way it actually will be shot, scene by scene, and (when assembled by the film editor) how it will appear on the screen. That is one reason why it was chosen as an example script, as a clear and detailed illustration for the student or the beginner, to make him aware of the techniques of camera angles and camera movement as indicated in a shooting script.

Breaking down a script into a great number of individual scenes should not be accepted as absolute doctrine in writing all types of films. Cutting from one camera angle to another capriciously is amateurish and affected.

The number of script scenes or individual camera angles is meaningless unless the visual action from scene to scene, from camera angle to camera angle, constitutes a smooth movement forward in the natural visual unfolding of the story line. An action or "piece of business" that can be played through with its purpose plainly understood by the audience should not be interrupted by cuts to different angles. Too much intercutting can destroy a scene's effectiveness. The movement of the actors, or the use of the Dolly Shot, Crane Shot, the Pan, or Tilt, avoids monotony.

When a more effective manner of presentation can be achieved, the director frequently combines two or more script scenes in a single scene covered by a single camera setup during the actual shooting. Cutting from one scene to another is used to maintain continuity and to re-establish or to emphasize action, reaction, or mood.

Lean Writing

In Chapter 1 we stressed the importance of the visual. The audio must give the visual the greatest possible support with clarity, eloquence, and emphasis — complementing the visual. Therefore good narration must be *lean writing*. Lean writing is positive, not passive. It is colorful but not flamboyant. It has understanding and sincerity, and must be convincing. It establishes and maintains empathy with the audience. An ostentatious style puzzles and frustrates the audience.

Analysis

Two examples of redundancy have already been given. Now let us study the difference between wordiness and lean writing. We will use examples based on narration in the dog script, since they will now be familiar:

Not like this:

```
This is dachshund Champion
Schuyler van Rensselaer with
all the important ribbons and
trophies he's won in many dog
shows throughout the country.
Schuyler van Rensselaer is
the name that appears on his
pedigree, but his owner calls
him Van and that's the only
one Van responds to.  Most
purebred dogs have short ken-
nel names.  It would be a
little ridiculous to have to
call out to your dog: "Come
here, Schuyler van Rens-
selaer!"
```

Like this:

```
Meet the Champ! . . . He
could be introduced by his
high-sounding registered
pedigree name, but it's as
long as he is.  His owner
calls him Van.
```

There are 26 words in the short narration, requiring 17 feet of film for support—a little over 11 seconds of running time. The narration on the left contains 75 words requiring about 56 feet of film or 37 seconds of running time. That's over half a minute required for visual support. We must remember that this is a three-reel film with fixed running time of a little less than 30 minutes. Under such restrictions, 37 seconds is a span of time which does not permit redundancy. It must tell a small part of our story economically.

Consider again the lengthy version above. Is it necessary to identify Van as a dachshund? The breed is a very popular one and almost everyone recognizes specimens of the breed as dachsies. Why identify the ribbons and trophies? The presence of such props is self-explanatory and impressive enough. Why explain that Van won the ribbons and trophies in dog shows throughout the country? The fact that he has won them is obvious. The statement that most purebred dogs have short kennel names is gratuitous.

Suppose that in the cutting room you found that only 12 feet of film were available to cover this one scene. That would mean you would have to shorten the narration to 18 words or less:

> Meet the Champ . . . his pedigree name is as long as he is, so his owner calls him Van.

or use FREEZE FRAME to obtain sufficient footage to cover narration.

Underwriting is as ineffectual as overwriting. In scenes 2 and 2-A it is essential that the narration complement the human-interest element in the visual. Also, it must lead into the sponsor's message.

Not like this:	Like this:
Like all dogs, Van loves his owner.	Despite his prestige, Van's the informal type. He may not be able to talk, but his demonstration of love for Larry, his owner, is eloquent appreciation of all the kindness, good care, and handling that Larry has given him. [This narration explains why Van loves his master, one of the reasons being the good care (good food) that Larry gives him.]
It was Larry's smart handling that made Van a champion. But let us go back in time to Larry's kennels just before Van was born.	Good care and wise handling made Van a champion. It started a little more than two years ago, before Van was whelped. . . . [In this narration "good care" is repeated, but this time it has a different connotation—for it now relates to the vital part that "good care" (good food) plays in the making of a champion.]

In Scene 4 the narration establishes the identity of Van's mother. The remark that "approaching motherhood has done things to her waistline" establishes the fact that Hexie is pregnant and not just a fat, overfed little dog. It also carries a note of quiet humor.

Not like this:	Like this:
This is Van's mother, Hexie, a day or two before Van was born. [This is pedestrian writing.]	This is Van's mother, Hexie. Ordinarily she's a fine, trim specimen of her breed, but approaching motherhood has done things to her waistline.
(Scene 5) Like all pregnant bitches she eats a lot. . . . [This is flat, pedestrian writing.]	As the French would so delicately put it, Hexie is a trifle enceinte. But she's in fine shape——for the shape she's in. [This narration lightens up the scene with another touch of humor.]
(Scene 6) . . . but Larry sees to it that it is the best food obtainable. [The visual has identified the food as being "A-TO-Z," but the above narration fails to explain why it is "the best food obtainable."]	From the beginning of her pregnancy, Hexie has been fed the best of food, scientifically prepared, rich in protein and vitamins, bonebuilding calcium, and other essential minerals. [This narration by contrast lets the viewer-listener know why "A-TO-Z" is such good dog food. It explains what the visual cannot explain.]
(Scene 8) With Hexie eating such good food her puppies will be strong and healthy. [A very flat, unimaginative, and uninformative statement which isn't much of a contribution to the sponsor's message.]	In their prenatal development her unborn pups are not suffering from the deficiencies that result from a poorly balanced, unscientifically prepared diet. [This narration builds up the value of "A-TO-Z," emphasizing that poorly bal-

anced and unscientifically prepared food results in weak, undernourished puppies.]

(Scene 9)
Good food builds champions. [A very positive statement which could fit in very well elsewhere, but here it is too cold and succinct a statement to cover the content of the visual in which there is human interest appeal which should be exploited.]

She doesn't know it, but she's building a sturdy future champion—with the help of her knowing owner. [This narration complements the human-interest appeal inspired by the little mother dog. It also states that Larry's knowing selection of a dog food is responsible for the development of a future sturdy champion.]

Although the visual in these scenes carries a plug for the sponsor's product, the audio has not once mentioned "A-TO-Z." The visual is sufficient to identify the product, but the support of the narration is necessary to explain the particular value of the product which we cannot see: that it is scientifically prepared and rich in the elements which guarantee a balanced, nourishing diet.

As another example of lean writing, let us return to the narration in scenes 39 and 40:

Not like this:

The atmosphere of the dog show with hundreds of other strange dogs of many different breeds, their owners and handlers, and the hundreds of spectators who had come to watch the judging, was all very new and exciting to Van as he and others of his breed paraded around the ring while the Judge looked them over . . . [This narration contains 57 words—38 feet of film—about 25 seconds of running time. It represents a "literary" type of writing

Like this:

It was all very new and exciting to Van, with all the strange dogs and strange people. . . . [This narration contains 17 words—11 feet of film—about 8 seconds of running time. It tells all it needs to tell in support of the visual, and it brings Van (the Center of Interest) into sharper focus.]

--not audiovisual writing.
In the background of the visual, the viewer can plainly
see the atmosphere of the dog
show--the other rings where
different breeds are being
judged, the groups of people.
It is all so obvious in the
visual that the narration
need not explain it. We know
that almost all the people
present came to watch the
judging, so there is no need
to mention that. In the visual we can plainly see that
Van and the other dachshunds
are parading around the ring,
so it is superfluous to tell
the viewer-listener what he
is seeing and can understand
so clearly. We can see the
Judge looking over the parading dogs. The Judge and his
mission were already established in Scene 38.]

(Scene 40)
. . . but even though Van was
only a little over eleven
months old, and it was his
first appearance in a dog-
show ring, as a result of the
excellent training he had received, Van behaved as if he
had had many years experience
as a show dog. [This narration contains 47 words--about
31 feet of film--about 21
seconds of running time.]

. . . But at a little over
eleven months, Van behaved
like a veteran in the Nine
to Twelve Months Puppy
Class. [This narration contains 20 words--15 feet of
film--10 seconds of running
time.]

So that there will be no misunderstanding on the reader's part, the
number of words, number of feet of film (35 mm), and number of
seconds of running time given in the comparative examples above
apply to running time of the narration only. It does not mean that a
block of narration of 20 words requiring 15 feet of film for visual sup-

port running 10 seconds necessarily indicates the actual length of the visual alone. The visual might run 20 to 30 or more feet.

It is not necessary to crowd every scene with the maximum number of words its length can support. Some scenes are entirely without narration when the visual is completely self-explanatory. However, there are scenes which may run many feet in length but require only a very few words of narration. *Narration should be used only to explain, or to complement in mood, what the visual cannot completely explain.*

A minimum of at least a couple of seconds of running time should be allowed at the beginning of a scene before the narration starts, and an equivalent time at the end of a scene. The exception occurs when there is an overlapping of continuous action from one scene to the next requiring continuous explanation by the audio.

Dangers of Under-Writing

Lean audiovisual writing is neither too succinct nor verbose. It can be carried to such an extreme that it ceases to communicate. This applies to writing the visual—scene description—as well as to the narration. Scenes 54 and 55 of the dog script can be used as an illustration:

54. CLOSE UP—VAN [As it appears in script]
Same FREEZE FRAME as Scene 51.

NARRATOR

. . . in contrast, Van has a well-developed trunk like this, long and fully muscled, with good top-line. The back, with sloping shoulders, and short, rigid pelvis, should lie in the straightest possible line between the withers and the very slightly arched loins.

As the Narrator calls attention to each body feature, an ARROW POPS ON to identify that particular feature—the trunk—the top-line—the sloping shoulders—the pelvis—the withers—the arched loins.

UNFREEZE FRAME. As Van moves his head to reestablish live action, CUT TO—

As an example of too succinct and quite inadequate writing, it would be written as follows:

54. CLOSE UP--VAN

Same FREEZE FRAME as Scene 51.

                    NARRATOR
     . . . but like Van's perfect top-line.

UNFREEZE FRAME

55. MED CLOSE--VAN & JUDGE [As it appears in script]

Larry may be suggested in the shot as the Judge runs his
hand lightly and appreciatively along Van's good top-line,
and then moves to get a frontal view of the dog, particularly the head. He appraises Van's head from the side
and from above, as the narrator synchronizes his commentary with what the Judge is doing.

                    NARRATOR
     Viewed from the side or from above, the head
     should taper uniformly to the tip of the nose and
     should be clean cut.

55. MED CLOSE--VAN & JUDGE [Example of inadequate writing].

In this scene the Judge examines Van's head.

                    NARRATOR
     The Judge finds that Van's beautiful head meets
     requirements of the standard.

   Such meager writing gives the critical reader little to visualize and
it presents the director and cameraman with nothing concrete to work
with. If an entire script were written in such staccato fashion, it
would be no more than a hastily prepared shooting outline.

Special Effects

   In Scene 54, as it appears in the script, the writer specifies the use
of Special Effects—arrows popping on the screen to identify each
anatomical feature that goes to make up Van's perfect top-line. Such a
device is used in the visual to identify what the Narrator is talking
about, to make certain that the viewer-listener understands.
   The use of such Special Effects is important in the instructional or
orientational film. Pop-on arrows are used to identify specific areas
and locations on maps, diagrams and photographs, parts of machinery
and equipment, or on drawings to show the direction being taken

(and progress made) along a road or trail by a body of men or a group of vehicles.

Summary

Illustrations of verbosity and extreme brevity have been given. Somewhere between the two is the effective area of mass and individual communication. The writer must express himself in such a way that what he says is clearly understood by his audience.

6 Format "B" — The Two-Column Format

The format that writers of most all-narration films find more convenient and practical to use is the form we shall identify as Format "B." It is used for the average industrial film, training film, or filmed progress report. It carries the visual, or scene description, in a column on the left side of the page and the audio, or narration, in a column on the right side. It is also used for certain kinds of documentary film (see Part V). It is employed whether the film is made up of stock footage or new footage.

This form is more convenient for writer and film editor in timing the length of narration against the visual's length in footage and running time. It is perhaps easier to follow in synchronizing the audio content with the visual content—what is being said in the narration with what is being shown in the visual.

Example Script: Format "B"

SMITH LABORATORIES——X DEVICE

PRODUCTION SCRIPT

FADE IN:
                        MAIN TITLE

DISSOLVE TO:
                        CREDIT TITLES
                        (or Foreword)

FADE OUT.
FADE IN:

1. EXT SMITH LAB——DAY

    FULL SHOT featuring Main   NARRATOR
    Entrance. (This is an
    ESTABLISHING SHOT. If the   (Introductory narration,
                      identifying Smith Labora-

94

film is not being made
from stock footage, de-
scribe the action and
visual fully—such as peo-
ple coming and going—a
car driving up and dis-
charging a passenger
carrying a briefcase who
walks toward the en-
trance, etc.)

(If this were being writ-
ten for stock footage, in
this and succeeding
scenes, the writer would
briefly describe the con-
tent of the selected
scenes and indicate the
source of such stock footage. He also might in-
dicate the length of the
scene, or available usable
footage, and its capacity
to support a certain num-
ber of words of narration
which would affect his
writing of the narration.
He would not write a block
of narration containing 30
words for a scene where
the visual could carry
only 20 words.)

tories and their function.
Double space for greater
convenience to the narrator
in reading his lines.)

2. CLOSER ANGLE—ENTRANCE

Featuring identifying sign
which is plainly read-
able—

                    NARRATOR
(Continues the introduction,
explaining the Lab's function.)

SMITH RESEARCH AND
DEVELOPMENT LABORATORIES.

DISSOLVE:

3. INT. SPECIAL DEVICES
   ROOM—DAY

   FULL SHOT—X DEVICE &
   TECHNICIANS

(This, too, is an ESTAB-
LISHING SHOT. Describe
the visual--the setting,
the action, and the people
involved, so that the
reader of the script can
visualize how the scene
will look on the screen,
how it will play. "Four
technicians are gathered
about X Device which
stands on a large work
bench. Dr. Rawlins, the
group leader, is pointing
out certain features of X
Device to his colleagues."
Identify in this scene
description those par-
ticular features which Dr.
Rawlins must indicate in
the action.)

NARRATOR

(The narration is closely
synchronized with the
visual, identifying the
group and its leader, Dr.
Rawlins, and X Device, and
identifying the particular
features of X Device which
Dr. Rawlins is pointing out
to his colleagues in the
visual--the narration ex-
plaining that which the
visual alone cannot com-
pletely explain.)

4. MED SHOT--GROUP

Featuring Dr. Rawlins as
he continues to point out
particular features of X
Device; however, he holds
his remarks to the mini-
mum, instead using his
forefinger to identify the
features which the nar-
rator will identify and
explain. Dr. Rawlins may
pause to answer a question
or two put to him by his
colleagues, but he relies
more on a nod or a shake
of the head to signify his
agreement or disagreement.

(When silent characters
carry on unheard conversation in a scene covered by
narration, or without
narration, the unheard ex-
change of comment should
be held to a minimum.

(The narrator continues,
closely synchronizing the
narration in time and subject matter with the action
as it appears on the screen
--talking only about what is
actually being seen or is
very closely related to what
is appearing in the visual.)

Actually we are seeing
pantomime. Use gestures
to indicate questions,
nods of approval or agreement, negative shakes of
the head to show disagreement or puzzlement. In
this scene Dr. Rawlins is
pointing out the specific
features of X Device with
his forefinger. The
narration replaces the
live sound. Too much
silent lip movement is
distracting to the audi-
ence. Some viewers will
try to read lip movement
and will not get the mes-
sage that the voice of the
narrator conveys. A
pantomime scene should
never run too long.)

5. MED CLOSE SHOT—X DEVICE

Dr. Rawlins is suggested   NARRATOR
in the shot as he con-   (The narration continues to
tinues to indicate   support the visual, iden-
specific features of X   tifying and explaining what
Device with his finger. Dr. Rawlins is pointing out
                         on the screen.)

6. CLOSE UP—ACTIVATING
   MECHANISM OF X DEVICE

(The visual is described   (The narration continues to
in detail so that the   support the visual—explain-
critical reader and the   ing that which is happening
director or cameraman will on the screen—explaining
clearly understand exactly the function of the activat-
what is to be photo-   ing mechanism as Dr. Rawlins
graphed—what will be   would tell it.)
taking place on the
screen. Dr. Rawlins' hand
comes in to the scene and
his forefinger points out
the activating mechanism
which the Narrator will

simultaneously identify
and explain in the absence
of Dr. Rawlins' voice.
The activating mechanism
has now become the center
of interest, hence the use
of the close angle to
exclude everything but
Dr. Rawlins' forefinger,
necessary for exact visual
identification.)

7. EXTREME CLOSE UP--
    ACTIVATING MECHANISM

    (Since the activating   NARRATOR
    mechanism is now the cen-
    ter of interest, we have   (The narration continues,
    moved in to an Extreme   closely synchronized with
    Close Up. Here again,   the visual.)
    describe the visual, the
    specific feature that the
    narrator will be talking
    about.)

8. MED CLOSE--GROUP

    Featuring Dr. Rawlins and   (The narration covers the
    Technician No. 1 as the   substance of the question
    latter asks a brief ques-   asked by Technician No. 1
    tion concerning a certain   and the substance of Dr.
    component of the activat-   Rawlins' reply, continuing
    ing mechanism. Dr.   over Technician No. 2's com-
    Rawlins makes a brief   ments, etc.)
    reply.

    CAMERA DOLLIES BACK TO
    WIDER ANGLE to include
    Technician No. 2 as he
    makes a comment to which
    Dr. Rawlins briefly
    replies. Explain the
    substance of this ex-
    change, what they are
    talking about.

```
(If the camera could not
be moved, due to lack of
facilities for a Dolly
Shot during the actual
shooting, this wider angle
would then be shot as a
separate scene, i.e. by
cutting at the time the
camera would start to move
back to a Wider Angle;
instead, a different
camera setup would be
used, resulting in a
direct cut from the
Closer Angle to the Wider
Angle.)
```

In a comment on the dog script, mention is made of the similarity between photographic coverage of the functional components of man-made machinery and the functional components of living organisms. While there are other examples, let us compare Scenes 86 and 87 of the dog script with Scenes 5, 6, and 7 of the example script above, as an illustration of this similarity—the employment of basic techniques. In the former, the dog-show judge appraises the chest of a dachshund, his forefinger (in Scene 87) tracing the oval appearance of the thorax and the extension of the bottom of the chest downward, while the narrator explains this particular "component" of a dog's anatomy. Scene 86 is a Medium Close Shot of the dog with the judge suggested in the shot. The next scene is an Extreme Close Up of the dog's front chest—the absolute center of interest.

In scenes 5, 6, and 7 of the Format "B" script, we have the identical coverage in photographing X Device and its features or components— going from a Medium Close Shot of the device's activating mechanism to an Extreme Close Up of the activating mechanism, focusing close on *the center of interest*, while the narrator identifies and explains what appears on the screen.

Comment is also made in the dog script on the use of drawings to show the internal anatomical structure of a dog, a technique which could also be used to show the internal working parts of a machine— parts which cannot be seen from the outside. Undoubtedly, drawings or a cutaway model would be used to show the internal working parts of X Device in a complete development of the Format "B" script.

If Format "A" were used for the script on X Device, employing a mixture of live dialogue and narration, it would be written as follows:

1. EXT SMITH LAB--DAY

   FULL SHOT--MAIN ENTRANCE

   (This is your Establishing Shot. Describe setting, action, or visual fully, as indicated in the illustration of Format "B", using width of the page, margin to margin.)

                         NARRATOR

           (Introduction as in Format "B." Double
           space narration and live dialogue.)

2. CLOSER ANGLE--MAIN ENTRANCE

   Featuring identifying sign which is plainly readable: SMITH RESEARCH AND DEVELOPMENT LABORATORIES.

                         NARRATOR

           (Continue introduction and identify the
           Lab's mission.)

   DISSOLVE:

3. INT. SPECIAL DEVICES ROOM--DAY

   FULL SHOT--X DEVICE & TECHNICIANS

   (This is another Establishing Shot. Describe the setting, people and action, same as set forth in the description of the visual as written on the left side of the page for Scene 3 in previous example of Format "B.")

                         NARRATOR

            (If a narrator is used to introduce the group,
            otherwise it will be live sound with the murmur
            of natural background noises and voices--a
            "presence track.")

4. MED SHOT--GROUP

   Featuring Group Leader, Dr. Rawlins, a studious man of about 45 or 50. He is discussing certain features of X Device.

DR. RAWLINS

(He is on live sound and is talking about
certain features of X Device.)

FIRST TECHNICIAN

But, Dr. Rawlins, it is my understanding
that X Device...

DR. RAWLINS

(Replies to the other's comment)

5. CLOSER SHOT—GROUP

Featuring Dr. Rawlins and the First Technician as the
latter asks another question.

FIRST TECHNICIAN

(Asks the question)

DR. RAWLINS

(Replies)

6. CLOSE UP—DR. RAWLINS

(We go to a Close Up of Dr. Rawlins because what he
now has to say is of prime importance and therefore
becomes the CENTER OF INTEREST.)

DR. RAWLINS
(Becoming more thoughtful)

(Continues speaking. He starts talking about
the Activating mechanism of X Device.)

7. CLOSE UP—ACTIVATING MECHANISM

Featuring trigger mechanism. (It is what Dr. Rawlins
is talking about—the CENTER OF INTEREST.) Dr.
Rawlins' voice comes in over the scene.

DR. RAWLINS' VOICE

(Rawlins' voice comes in over the scene to explain
trigger mechanism of the activating unit.)

8. CLOSE UP—DR. RAWLINS

He continues talking about the activating mechanism.

DR. RAWLINS

(Continues speaking)

9. MED CLOSE SHOT--OTHER TECHNICIANS

This is a reaction shot from Dr. Rawlins' angle on the
other technicians as they listen intently to Dr.
Rawlins and show reactions to what he is saying. The
doctor may be suggested in the scene, the camera
shooting over his shoulder.

DR. RAWLINS' VOICE

(He continues his discourse)

10. CLOSE UP--DR. RAWLINS

DR. RAWLINS

(Continues to speak on one of the more vital
aspects of his subject.)

11. MED SHOT--GROUP

DR. RAWLINS

(Finishes speaking)

SECOND TECHNICIAN

(Makes a comment)

DR. RAWLINS

(Replies)

(The scene would be further developed with each of the
technicians speaking in turn to make it a group discussion. Other scenes would follow showing close
angles on X Device and its components as such shots
would become pertinent to the discussion.)

By now you should have a fairly clear working idea of the general
guidelines to follow in setting up your script. Format "B" is more
widely used in writing for silent footage which requires all narration.

Part III: The Script Writer and His Craft

7 Camera Angles, Optical Effects, and Background Atmosphere

CAMERA ANGLES

Intelligent and dramatic use of camera angles, suggested by the writer in his script, comes with experience. The choice of camera angles is in part determined by the type of film, the subject matter, and probable shooting conditions. However, the inexperienced writer may safely plan the progression of his film by selecting the camera angle which emphasizes the importance of each scene's content.

First, use an ESTABLISHING SHOT, usually a FULL SHOT, LONG SHOT, or MEDIUM LONG SHOT. Second, move the camera by indicating camera angles in your script, in a progression of Closer Angles, MEDIUM, MEDIUM CLOSE, CLOSE, CLOSE UP, EXTREME CLOSE UP, whichever may be necessary to get to the *center of interest*. Third, keep the camera focused on the center of interest, and whatever is closely related to that interest, as *close in* as possible.

Variations

These are the basic rules of procedure, but, of course, there are always variations that can be introduced. Sometimes the establishing shot might open with a very close angle on a person or an object — depending on the mood or dramatic impact the writer or the director might want to establish — and then pull back to a wider angle.

For instance, we might Fade In on a Close Shot of a dying or dead man lying in the mud. It is night and a light rain is falling. The Camera Dollies Back to a Wider Angle to include the back of a man standing with a gun in his hand, staring down at his victim. As the Camera Dollies Back to a still Wider Angle, the gunman runs away from the Camera toward a car in the middle background. In the Wider Angle we see that the scene is a lonely country road.

Progression of camera angles from MEDIUM CLOSE SHOT to EXTREME CLOSE UP.
U.S. Army Photo.

Common Faults

One of the common faults in the use of camera angles is found in extreme FULL SHOTS, LONG SHOTS, ESTABLISHING, or RE-ESTABLISHING SHOTS, especially in the filming of exteriors. This is usually the director's or cameraman's fault, and essentially is their responsibility.

The writer can influence proper coverage by indicating in his script that "tight" shooting is desirable. Even though the writer can rarely control such things in shooting, he should know that such problems exist. The LONG SHOT should include only what is necessary for an ESTABLISHING SHOT, or for coverage of an action that obviously requires a very wide angle and a scene in depth.

Another related problem, again primarily the director's responsibility, comes when a picture shot in 35 mm is then reduced to 16 mm prints for release. When shooting in 35 mm, the subject may be shot at a close enough angle so that details are clearly visible — in 35 mm. But in the 16 mm reduction print the same object often appears too far away because it was not shot close enough in 35 mm. Hence much or all of its value is lost to the viewer. Many directors and cameramen in the nontheatrical field do not use close enough angles where they are required. Even though such strictly photographic problems are the director's or cameraman's responsibility, the writer can recommend more effective coverage by stressing in his script the necessity for close camera angles when it is important to see an object or an action in detail.

Unfortunately, many writers do not have the opportunity to take part in the actual production of a film. And, unfortunately, too, it is in the shooting phase that problems arise which require on-the-spot solutions involving changes in the script. A practical knowledge of production and its problems learned through close observation on the set or on location is a valuable asset to a script writer. There, he has the opportunity to learn what the camera can and cannot do.

Working with the Film Editor

Inevitably, many problems arise in the actual shooting of a picture, but a good shootable script by a writer experienced in production can keep those problems to a minimum. The best training for a new writer is the opportunity to work closely with a film editor in the cutting room. It is in the cutting room that a writer sees the result of his work, and the director's work, and how it is put together. It is here that he will face the problems of script writing, of direction, and of techniques necessary to good audiovisual production. A film writer's education is rounded out by spending some time with a film editor.

Film Editor working at his Moviola in the cutting room. U.S. Army Photo.

The Stock Footage Film

When a picture is being put together of previously shot film using Format "B," a detailed description of the visual in the script is not necessary. When stock footage is used predominantly, this form is frequently called "Scene Continuity and Narration Script" (see Part IV for examples). The content of an individual scene may be indicated. Based on the length of available footage, the approximate length of the scene may also be indicated when necessary, to let you know the limitations in your use of narration—the number of words the visual can support.

When you are putting together an all- or part-narration stock footage picture, where you are using more than one source of stock shots, you should indicate in each scene the exact source of that particular stock; this should include the film library can number.

In the stock footage film, the approximate ratio of scenes and pages of script per reel of film which applies to a script for production shooting may be reduced or exceeded—obviously so, since there are no "added scenes" to be shot by the director. Again, this depends on the subject matter and the length of individual scenes.

In this type of film it is necessary for the writer to work closely with the film editor. They must preserve proper continuity (making necessary adjustments in the editing, which will require rewriting), and must match the length of narration to footage, and the length of footage to narration. It is in this phase of editorial coordination that problems arise requiring ingenuity on the part of writer and editor — for example, the problems of sufficient or suitable footage to cover necessary narration. Here the opportunity to exercise imagination and inventiveness presents itself.

OPTICAL EFFECTS

Having read the example shooting script in Part II, you should recognize the close relationship between the theatrical and non-theatrical film. The basic principles and techniques of script writing are the same. Whatever the nature of your story, it can only appear on the motion picture or television screen as originally seen by the camera. The smooth unfolding and progression of your story — the continuity of events and actions — depends on the camera placement and camera movement from one angle to the next closest related angle, in that progression.

The Matched Dissolves between Scenes 34, 35, and 36 of *The Making of a Champion* are used to cover a period of time. This is a transitional device designed to preserve the even flow of the story. The Matched Dissolve is an optical effect that should be used only infrequently. It is the means of achieving an uninterrupted flow of visual action. Each scene must blend into the next until a succession of visual impressions forms the closely related and well-integrated whole. It is the art of pictorial relationships. Optical effects — dissolves, wipes, fades — should be used sparingly and judiciously. If employed excessively, they can be distracting. Visual or spoken transitions are far more effective.

BACKGROUND ATMOSPHERE

Essential background atmosphere is a part of those pictorial relationships. It provides a setting and a mood which lend realism, color, and depth to a situation and story, especially in the human-interest film.

Imagine a long shot of Diamond Head in the far background, with the beach stretching into the middle distance and a palm tree in the foreground. There follow shots of surfboard riders. Other shots, taken along Kapiolani or Kalakaua Boulevards, of Hawaiian women in their native dress weaving leis, establish the atmosphere of Honolulu's colorful Waikiki district. Such background shots establish one of the most peaceful and romantic settings in the world.

In sharp contrast, only a few miles away, is Honolulu's commercial, gaudy Hotel Street district. It is filled with crowded bars, restaurants, hotels, shops, small businesses, and cheap tourist attractions. It is the other face of Honolulu, the melting pot of races. In the daytime the district is alive with commerce. At night, a honky-tonk atmosphere pervades the district.

If you were writing a script with this background, you would try to capture its rich and wonderful color by writing in a montage of scenes showing the cheap bars, shops, and eating places. You would include CLOSE SHOTS and CLOSE UPS of various racial types among the shopkeepers, their customers, the drinkers at the bars, sailors and soldiers with their girl friends, and a Chinese-Hawaiian cop directing traffic. If you were writing for live sound, the Waikiki sequence would include Hawaiian background music. In the Hotel Street sequence you would capture the sound of auto horns, the piercing whistle of the traffic cop, and the chatter in the crowded smoke-filled bars. The viewer-listener must be made to feel that he is *there*—in Honolulu.

However, once having established the background atmosphere, you must not let it overpower the story and its principal characters. Do not permit background objects, people, or activities to distract from your script's center of interest. A writer must be aware of and sensitive to the background of the locale he is going to write about. He must be aware of its people, their mores, and their physical surroundings, as well as the influence of geographic, economic, political, or religious factors. When he writes about people whom the critical script reader and the viewer of the film have never seen, the writer must give his reader and viewer-listener a clear picture of those people—how they live, and why they live as they do.

In preparing for this kind of film, the writer must submit a detailed treatment and shooting script, conveying all his observations and impressions, which are indispensable to the director or cameraman-director. For this type of film, the writer should also indicate in detail in his production notes the local conditions which might present production problems. Local government officials and business-firm personnel who can be helpful in the shooting of a film on location should be listed in the production notes.

8 Pace, Memory Retention, and Persuasion

PACE

A good way to learn script-writing is to see several consecutive screenings of a well-produced entertainment film. A first viewing can distract attention from the study of technique. Entertainment films are recommended because they generally represent a high level of competent film-making.

Study such films scene by scene. Try to envision how they were photographed, the position of the camera, and how they were edited. Study the emphasis achieved by the use of effective camera angles and camera movement. Train yourself to think in terms of visual action — of unity and form.

Varieties of Pacing

Tempo, or pacing, is one of the most important elements in making a film. The subject matter, the type of story, mood, and situation dictate the pacing.

A western picture, or melodrama, must be packed with action. A murder mystery may move more slowly, but building suspense replaces the need for continuous physical action. The love story usually is told in a slower, quieter tempo. Comedy must be fast paced.

The pace of an instructional film is necessarily slow in order to clarify and emphasize each teaching point, to give the student audience time to understand each point before moving on. In the straight didactic film dealing with highly technical and complex subject matter, images will be held on the screen for a long time, even though the camera angle may be changed. The narration must be slow and deliberate, closely synchronized with the visual. The writer can avoid monotony through an imaginative approach in writing both the visual and the narration. The narration can be fresh without being "cute." Avoid the deadliness of stilted and pedantic language.

The instructional film has certain requirements of presentation

111

peculiar to its purpose. It must be written with clarity and with emphasis on the teaching points. The instructional film has three parts: an introduction to the subject, the teaching of the subject, and a recapitulation of the major points. First, briefly tell your viewers what you are going to teach them; second, teach them; third, tell them again what you have taught them.

The introduction should define the subject, so that your audience will be prepared for what they are going to see. The main body of your film is a thorough presentation of your subject. Each teaching point is shown to its best visual advantage and explained in the audio by clear and simple narration.

Pacing with Camera Shots

The use of the RE-ESTABLISHING SHOT is more important in the instructional film than in any other type of audiovisual presentation. Let us say the subject is a large telephone switchboard, ten feet long and six feet high. If you were writing a script about such a complicated panel, first you would establish the entire board in a FULL SHOT, then you would move the camera in close to the area on the board to be discussed.

If you kept moving around such a board, confining yourself to a series of CLOSE ANGLES only, your audience would lose touch with that part of the panel you were discussing. To avoid this, you would DOLLY BACK, or cut, from the area being shown to a RE-ESTABLISHING SHOT—a FULL SHOT of the entire board—to reorient your audience. Then you would move in again from the re-establishing shot to the next area. Always let your audience know where they are in following movements of the camera.

Teaching with Films

In this form of didactic presentation little should be left to the imagination. The teaching film is an instructional film. If your film is to train mechanics in the repair and maintenance of bulldozers, you should ascertain the educational level, the knowledge, and the experience of your audience. How much experience has your audience had in bulldozer repair and maintenance, or are they completely inexperienced? This will obviously influence your manner of presentation. If your audience is ignorant of the subject, your script will be a simple presentation. If the audience has had a course in the subject, your script will be written on a more advanced plane. Confine yourself to the repair and maintenance of a bulldozer; do not introduce material on the operation of a bulldozer unless the film is to include this subject. They are two different subjects, and should be made as separate films.

If you were given an assignment to write a film on the atom, you would follow the same preparatory procedures: What is the audience's educational level? What is its knowledge or experience? You would familiarize yourself with the subject before beginning to write, whether it is about a bulldozer or the atom. On either subject you would find a great deal of material. You cannot write authoritatively on a subject you do not understand.

All educational or instructional films do not deal with specifics. Some are concerned entirely or in part with theories that are still in the drawing-board stage. Such instructional films rely on the use of technical symbols, drawings, diagrams, and animation. If you are writing for a producer who plans to use animation, confer with his animation department, or with the artist doing the animation for the picture.

In preparing the script for an instructional film, the writer must know at what point in the teaching course the film will be used as an audiovisual aid. For this type of film the writer should also prepare a few introductory remarks for the instructor's use before the screening. He should, in addition, prepare a list of "true or false" questions for a quiz after the showing.

MEMORY RETENTION

The content of your film must remain in the memory of the viewer-listener long after he has seen it, if it is to accomplish its purpose. If an instructional or orientation film deals with physical danger, such as the handling of lethal devices, the viewer-trainee must remember what the film teaches him. If circumstances should bring him into actual contact with or use of such deadly devices, he must remember exactly what to do to avoid injury or death. He must *retain* everything the training film taught him. The film can help him recall what he must do to stay alive through your skillful use of memory retention devices in the film script.

An Unforgettable Example

An outstanding example of effective use of a memory retention device occurred in a British training film used at the beginning of World War II, and subsequently shown to American troops after we entered the war. It was a four-reel film which presented the lethal hazards of hidden mines and booby traps. Trip wires and other triggering mechanisms were identified, as well as danger signs of their presence: in short, a thorough instruction in precautionary measures.

To get across the teaching points, a realistic situation was presented in the form of a story—that of a small advance party of mine and booby-trap experts whose mission was to clear the way for the main force to follow. Their objective was the enemy's recently abandoned headquarters in what had been a private home. Along the way, they discovered and rendered harmless a series of mines and booby traps. At last they reached the abandoned headquarters.

Employing every precaution, they examined the interior for booby traps. There were the usual "props"—the "forgotten" pistol lying on the floor, the cigarette box on the table, a picture askew on the wall— all of which looked harmless. But the pistol, if picked up, might set off a lethal charge; a man "dying for a smoke" might just do that, if he lifted the lid of the cigarette box on the table; if someone tried to straighten the picture, he might trigger an explosion.

Each suspected device was carefully identified and then as carefully made harmless. The booby-trap experts successfully finished clearing out all the planted hazards. The building could now be safely occupied as a temporary headquarters by their own command. Since the job was done, the experts could relax for a moment.

Heeding the call of nature, a soldier went into the toilet. The door was left ajar and he stood at the urinal, back to camera. When he was through, he reached up and pulled the chain of the old-fashioned flushbox. Instantly there was an explosion that sent plaster and timbers flying. The last shot in the film was a close angle on the expert who had pulled the chain. He was alive, but dazed and badly shaken. The Fade Out on the close shot of the besmudged face of the expert was a "Laurel and Hardy" ending and invariably brought roars of laughter from the audience.

It was a surprise serio-comic ending to a deadly serious training film, and it served as an exceptionally effective memory retention device. Those who saw the film never forgot that last scene. And, in the association of ideas, they remembered most of the major teaching points of the film as well. After many years, I spoke with veterans who had seen it. Almost all remembered its lesson vividly, although they couldn't recall much from other training films. Human-interest appeal, especially used with a sense of humor, makes a dry subject palatable, entertaining, and hence memorable.

Much can be done by imaginative men with talent in the audiovisual field to raise the instructional film to a sophisticated and effective level. The audiovisual training aid is a useful teaching device but its potential has by no means been realized.

Reaching Your Audience

If a film is to reach its audience, it must speak the language of that audience. In writing a script dealing with teenagers and their problems, you wouldn't write it from the point of view of a middle-aged man, who obviously would have no rapport with the teenage world. You would write it from the viewpoint of the teenager, speaking *his* language, so that he could identify himself with the problem. Hopefully, he would be stimulated into thinking for himself, although the film may have adroitly guided him into such thinking.

PERSUASION

The orientation film requires a less didactic presentation than the training or educational film, since it is not a teaching film. It may be used as an introduction to a study course, or it may help people adapt themselves to unfamiliar circumstances, activities, or environments. The orientation film lends itself to imaginative treatment. Generally, it is faster paced than the instructional film, since it does not have to explain technical points. A film which deals with human relationships is intended to change or reaffirm existing attitudes. It is usually dramatic, and offers the writer an opportunity to be creative.

The film intended to influence attitudes and opinions can be either a "soft sell" or a "hard sell." In preparing the script for such a film, the writer must perform extensive research to become acquainted with the audience he hopes to influence.

Let us assume that you have an assignment to write a civil defense film with an emphasis on survival measures. If the producer of the film has no fixed ideas, you will have to determine the style of the film. Which will be the most effective style? A moderate appeal to reason in describing the measures to be taken when an atomic attack is imminent, while it is occurring, and after the attack? Can you assume that your audience is already sufficiently terrified by the threat of blast and radiation? Or will you employ shock technique by showing the devastation of Hiroshima and Nagasaki? Would you show the dead, the maimed, and those sick with radiation? Would you end with a final grim warning?

Your choice of the "soft sell" or the "hard sell," the shocker, in this case, would depend on the degree of complacency of your audience. The effectiveness of the shocker depends on psychological factors. It might result in panic among your viewers. Others might rationalize that it could happen, but probably won't. Still others may have a peculiar resistance to the shocker, manifesting itself in resentment and withdrawal. Whatever the audience attitude, you must analyze the core of the problem.

Changing Mass Attitudes

An amusing illustration of how simple ideas can change mass attitude is found in a classic anecdote. An unemployed advertising man with great imagination was having a hard time selling his talents. He finally found himself in the Pacific Northwest. He approached the manager of a fish-canning company. He was received pleasantly enough, but there was the same discouraging answer: "No opening at present."

He was about to leave when the manager suddenly thought of something. He took the advertising man to a warehouse stacked high with cases of canned salmon. The manager pointed to one huge stack of cases covered with dust and said: "You see that pile over there? That's pink salmon. It's a very slow mover, hard to sell. For some unknown reason most people think of red salmon as being superior, but the pink is just as good. If you can help us move it, we'll give you a job."

The advertising man took a day or two to mull over the problem. Finally he came up with an idea that was to change the fortunes of the fish-canning company as well as his own. He launched a highly successful sales campaign that soon had the warehouse emptied of canned pink salmon. The cans had been relabeled:

GENUINE SALMON
GUARANTEED NOT TO TURN RED IN THE CAN!

Slightly misleading, perhaps, yet it *was* genuine salmon and it most certainly would not turn red in the can. There was nothing untrue about the statement but it did imply that a certain variety of salmon turned red after it was canned. And it did change a biased mass attitude. Such ingenious "gimmicks" are priceless in audiovisual presentations designed to influence people.

Types of Persuasion Films

The motivational film is closely related to the attitude-forming film, since it is designed to persuade the viewer-listener to a course of action which will improve his lot. The motivational factor is present in many types of nontheatrical films. Hopefully, it will increase efficiency in the performance of some task or operation.

A good instructional or training film should express the motivational element by showing the benefits of doing something the *right* way. The writer must do a convincing selling job in persuading his viewer-listener to be motivated in accordance with the central idea of the script.

The documentary film is usually a factual record, or dramatized account of some event, happening, or activity. The success of the documentary depends on its timeliness, and on the extent of its human-interest appeal. It can, of course, be made from stock footage or from footage shot from a prepared script or shooting outline.

The writer of the documentary reaches a broad audience. In some instances, the audience may be as large as that drawn by a popular entertainment film. CBS' *Twentieth Century* series of award-winning documentaries is an example. *Victory at Sea* had millions of TV viewers. Among others are Walt Disney's semi-documentaries, *The Saga of Western Man;* David L. Wolper's series, *The Valiant Years;* and the more recent TV documentary series, *Army in Action.* Four production scripts from *Army in Action* are reproduced in Part V of this book.

Whatever the story, a subjugated people, a chapter in the life of an Eskimo, or the story of migrating salmon, the writer has high standards to meet which require all of his talent, imagination, and craftsmanship.

 **9** **Dialogue**

Dialogue Versus Narration

Dialogue is essential in certain types of nontheatrical films, but a dialogue situation usually takes up much more footage than the same subject covered by narration. Also, the necessary sound crews and equipment make the use of dialogue expensive and even prohibitive with low budgets. The average instructional or documentary film employs narration, which is both economical and effective.

What Is Good Dialogue?

However, when dialogue is used in audiovisual presentations, it should be lean writing for a medium in which the element of time is important. When the lines are spoken by actors they must sound like actual speech. As with narration, it is not how dialogue reads, but how it sounds. Good dialogue incorporates economy of expression by saying what it has to say and no more.

The writing of good dialogue is too broad and complex a subject to be included in a book confined to the fundamentals of audiovisual script writing. There are a number of other books concerned with the writing of dialogue to which the reader may refer.

No form of writing requires greater craftsmanship than good dialogue; as the musician must have a good ear for music, the writer must have a good ear for natural speech.

Good dialogue is the result of writing and rewriting. The experienced professional writer writes, rewrites, and polishes. The big-name writer has not achieved his high standing overnight. Talent, craftsmanship, and hard work are his stock in trade. The nonprofessional writer who walks into his producer's office with a "polished" draft and states positively, "This is it!" is usually in for a shock, when he discovers how wrong he is.

Characterization Through Dialogue

There are, however, a few comments which can be made here. When you are building a story, your objective is to create a group of characters your audience will understand and believe in. Even if they involve fantasy, all stories, situations, and characterizations should be convincing.

No two characters talk alike. A character should speak from his own point of view. Similarity of dialogue among different characters is a flaw which the beginner guards against. Dialogue is a vital part of convincing characterization. People express themselves in ways peculiarly their own if they are to be believable. The speech of a salesman is friendly. The speech of a bill collector is not friendly. The salesman would not be harsh or demanding in speaking to a customer any more than the bill collector would be meek and mild. The efficient, ambitious secretary of a corporation executive would not be given the same speech as a high-school dropout working as a waitress. For consistency of characterization in dialogue, the writer must understand his character completely to give that character dimension. The beginning writer has to learn to bring his characters to life, to give them warmth, vitality, depth, and color, to make them human and believable.

In contrast to the stereotyped character is the exotic character. There are some stories which cannot be told without exotic characterizations. However, in an attempt to be original or different, beginners sometimes make their characters exotic when down-to-earth characterizations are needed. This does not mean that an offbeat character should not be used when an offbeat characterization is essential to the story.

Achieving Audience Interest and Empathy

The degree of audience interest aroused and sustained depends on the writer's talent in developing situation, characterization, and dialogue. The beginning writer must guard against overplaying or overdramatizing, especially in a highly dramatic situation. The best drama is underplayed and avoids overemotional and flamboyant dialogue. Good dialogue must have a warm, human quality, and flow smoothly from one speech to another. Keep the dialogue human, and keep it believable. Then your audience will understand it, and, through it, empathize with your characters.

The best advice that could be given the beginning writer would be to revise, rewrite, and polish until you have achieved the best you are capable of producing. The statement that writers are born, not made, is substantially true. A writer needs natural aptitude to tell an interesting, colorful, and convincing story.

There are different kinds of natural writing talent. There are writers who excel in technical writing who cannot write informational, documentary, or dramatic films. Yet these men are qualified specialists who do well financially. Then there is the writer who has a flair for the public relations, documentary, or dramatic film, but who cannot write complex technical films. The beginning writer should try to find out what kind of film suits his talents, and then concentrate on becoming a specialist in that field. Perhaps, in time, he may develop versatility. The versatile professional capable of doing a good job on any type of film is a rare writer. There are writers with talent and versatility who prefer to specialize in the unglamorous technical film. They have become so proficient in that speciality that they are in constant demand.

The skillful writer has an advantage over professionals in many other fields. There is no retirement age in the writing profession. For the encouragement of writers of all ages, I know two "old pros" in their seventies who are still going strong.

The Creative Process

This book cannot go into the more creative aspects of writing. It is not within my province to analyze the origin of ideas in story writing. Many other books are available which deal with the creative process of writing. To reduce creative thought and original writing to mechanical formulas is like presenting the skeleton of a human being to an anatomist and telling him, "This is the structure, these are the bones. Clothe them with warm flesh, give them a heart, a brain, emotions, intellect, imagination, and the capacity to love and to hate."

The "bones" or structure of a story must be there, but formulas cannot give them life. To give life to a story requires understanding of human relationships which involve love and hate, conflict and compromise, triumph and defeat, depression and exaltation. A sense of values is the core of good writing. The creative mind is endowed with powers of observation, imagination, and inventiveness.

The Writing Process

Good original ideas are hard to come by. It takes a lot of hard thinking to get them. The commercial writer cannot wait for inspiration. So he sits down and goes to work. He knows what his subject will be. He has a basic idea, a premise for his story or story line. First, he must satisfy himself that the premise is a sound one. Second, he must understand what the story is to present and develop. Third, he must set his stage—time, place, condition, and background atmosphere. Fourth, he must conceive the characters through whom he will tell his story. Fifth, he must create situations which are germane to the development of the story line. Sixth, he must make certain that what he is building is assuming unity and form.

All these elements slowly take shape. An author's first conceptions of his characters will change as they develop. And their development is usually simultaneous with the development of theme, situation, and story progression. I pointed out before that all characters do not talk alike. This is so obvious that mention of it again may seem gratuitous, but similarity of speech by different characters is a pitfall by no means limited to the beginning writer. Each character is a distinct personality and must retain that individuality in his speeches. The writer who understands his characters will let them react and express themselves in a manner consistent with the personality he has given them. Establish and develop convincing characters and they will help you tell your story.

Part IV: The Training Film

Chapter 10: Requirements of the Training Film
Example Script: Ohm's Law

10 Requirements of the Training Film

A great many training, educational, and orientation films rely on voice-over narration or an on-camera narrator to carry the audio. It is the easiest, most convenient type of presentation to produce. Low-budget films rely on voice-over narration or on an on-camera narrator. There are some subjects which can be taught quite effectively by voice-over narration. There are others which can be given a livelier style of presentation by using dialogue for dramatization. This requires an imaginative approach. It also demands greater craftsmanship, since it involves acting talent, good dialogue, strong characterization, and professional use of the camera.

As an illustration of how a live dialogue situation can be used in a training or educational film, I have chosen the production script for a film designed to teach a technical subject. It also shows how audience empathy may be aroused to accelerate the learning process. Through dramatization, the stilted effect of straight narration is avoided, minimizing the possibility of boring a captive audience. When a writer works on this kind of assignment, his principal source of specific information is usually a technical advisor. A good technical advisor is an invaluable asset to you as a script writer, since he can furnish you with fact, background, and general information. However, *you* are assumed to be the expert in transferring the subject to film.

Immediately preceding the script of *Ohm's Law* is a Film Synopsis. This synopsis is *not* a treatment; it is a brief outline attached to the draft of the script as submitted by the writer. There is also a list of production requirements compiled by the script writer, together with several rough sketches for diagrams. The instructional purpose of the film is stated briefly. The script writer has also prepared introductory remarks to precede screening of the film, a suggested follow-up discussion, and a quiz. This preparatory work is the professional "packaging" of a production script required by most nontheatrical film producers.

The example script to follow concerns Ohm's Law and the basic

125

training of electronics technicians. It is a subject which might appall an inexperienced writer who does not have a scientific background. The scientist or the mathematician probably cannot write a motion picture script, but he can give you the facts and the material you need to organize the teaching points in motion picture form. As an illustration of this, I shall cite an experience of my own which might be reassuring.

I was called in from Hollywood to write the script for a Navy film on Underwater Sound or, as it is known today, Sonar. It had to do with the Doppler effect, a phenomenon of physics, which was being applied to the detection by surface ships of underwater objects, specifically, submarines. My knowledge of electronic equipment was exactly zero. I *did* know how to pick a technical advisor's brains and acquire the knowledge to organize the material in proper continuity for cinematic presentation. The job took a lot of digging, but it turned out to be relatively simple. Authorities on the subject approved the script with only minor changes, and an excellent training film was made from it. Ohm's Law is a less difficult subject for the script writer.

OHM'S LAW

FILM SYNOPSIS

The film takes place in an Army classroom. A group of enlisted men has just received its initial indoctrination, and is receiving manuals from S/Sgt. Higgins, the instructor. When the class is dismissed, one man, Pvt. Allen, stays in his seat. When approached by Sgt. Higgins, he states that he is worried about the course, and doesn't think he is capable of becoming an electronics technician. Higgins decides to prove to Allen that he is worrying needlessly.

The bulk of the film follows Allen through a brief, simplified study of basic electronics as offered by Sgt. Higgins. This impromptu course follows a pattern dictated by areas in which Allen feels he is weakest: Theories, Circuits, Formulas, and Mathematics. Higgins begins with the electron theory, using blackboard illustrations to introduce the atom and the electron. The movement of the free electron is demonstrated through animation. The topics covered are presented in a give-and-take fashion: Higgins offers points of information, and allows Allen to draw his conclusions or formulate his own theories.

After covering electron theory, Higgins moves on to a basic circuit, explaining that electron flow (or current flow) cannot be achieved without a complete circuit. When Allen has grasped the fundamentals, they move on to a demonstration panel which includes a simple circuit, resistors, ammeters, ohmmeters, batteries, etc. Higgins introduces volts, ohms, and amperes, and shows Allen how to prove their existence and measure their amounts with the various meters.

By varying the resistances and voltages, Allen learns that there is a definite relationship between volts, ohms, and amperes, and determines for himself what some of these relationships are. When Allen realizes that he has devised a formula of his own, Higgins introduces him to an even better formula: Ohm's Law. He demonstrates a practical method of applying Ohm's Law, and we then see Allen use Ohm's Law to predetermine the amount of current flow that various combinations of voltages and resistances will give.

We see Allen's self-confidence building up, until he spots a complicated piece of equipment on a display table. Higgins then introduces Allen to the schematic, explain-

ing how it will guide him through the most complicated
equipment with which he will have to work.

The final sequence in the film shows Higgins deliberately inserting a defective, or incorrectly labeled, resistor into the circuit, and we watch Allen locate the defective component by applying Ohm's Law, the meters, and
his own intelligence. The film closes as Allen is assur-
ing a new student that the course is really not difficult.

INSTRUCTIONAL USE OF THE FILM IN THE TRAINING PROGRAM:

The film will serve as initial indoctrination in the
subject of basic electronics. It is aimed directly at the
beginner, to instruct and reassure him about his own qual-
ifications. But, more important, it will provide him with
a working knowledge of the fundamentals of electronics.

SUGGESTED INTRODUCTORY REMARKS:

No doubt many of you have some questions: about the
subject we will cover in this course, and about your own
capabilities. One of the leading characters in the film
you are about to see is sitting just where you are sitting
right now, entertaining the same doubts. If you watch and
listen carefully, you will probably hear him ask some of
the questions you would like to ask.

SUGGESTED FOLLOW-UP DISCUSSION AND ACTIVITIES:

The point should be made that much of the information
covered in the film was deliberately simplified, and that
it will be expanded upon during the course of study.
After a question-and-answer session, it is recommended
that students be allowed to examine and test simple, basic
circuits such as those shown in the film, using ohmmeters,
ammeters, and voltmeters.

SUGGESTED QUIZ: (after screening)
   1. Which ring of electrons contributes to current flow?
   A. The outer ring.
   2. What are the electrons in this outer ring called?
   A. Free electrons.
   3. In what direction does electron current flow?
   A. From negative to positive.
   4. What instrument is used to measure voltages?
   A. A voltmeter.
   5. What instrument is used to measure current flow?
   A. An ammeter.
   6. What instrument is used to measure resistance?
   A. An ohmmeter.

7. What are the three symbols used for current, voltage, and resistance?

A. I for current; E for voltage; R for resistance.

8. What is the formula for determining the amount of current flow in a circuit?

A. I equals E over R; or, the current equals the voltage divided by the resistance.

9. If the voltage is doubled, but the resistance remains constant, what will happen to the current flow?

A. It will double.

10. If the resistance is doubled, but the voltage remains constant, what will happen to the current flow?

A. It will be reduced by one half.

PRODUCTION REQUIREMENTS

EQUIPMENT TO BE FURNISHED BY THE TECHNICAL ADVISOR as representative of the originating agency:

  20 MANUALS, TM 11-661
   1 TA 219/U Modem, from AN/TCC-3, and manual.
   5 CHARTS, fairly large size, for display on walls of set; typical of those found at Fort Gordon in a classroom.

AND THE FOLLOWING materials for construction of the DEMON-STRATION PANEL described in Scene:

  2 TRIPLETT AMMETERS, largest available face.
  1 Voltmeter, with equally large face.
  8 BA-23 Dry Cell batteries; 1½ volts per. (4 in panel; 4 spares)
  1 Small light bulb, with socket and wire leads terminating in alligator clips.
  4 Simple, single-pole single-throw switches.
  6 Large terminal lugs, of a type that will allow quick installation of resistor leads.
  1 ASSORTMENT of resistors. These will include one 2 ohm, one 4 ohm and one 6 ohm resistor. Of large wattage; or with artificial frames so that the bodies are approximately one inch in diameter. These bodies should be light gray, with the resistance value printed on them in large, black numerals.
  1 Resistor, doctored as above, labeled INCORRECTLY as 2 ohms. (The actual value should be as far below 2 ohms as we can get.)
  8 Alligator clips.
   and . . .

WIRE, for construction of circuit in panel.

NOTE: Since it is impractical to utilize an actual ohmmeter for the panel, one of the ammeters will
"double" as an ohmmeter face. The technical advisor will devise a small battery-powered circuit, which can be controlled from a position off
the set, that will make the ammeter face read the
correct numerals.

SETS: There is only one set--the interior of a classroom.
It is modeled roughly after those in existence at
Fort Gordon:

About twenty arm chairs fill the center area of the
room. The back wall has a double door, the entrance. The far wall will have various display
charts. The front wall has a centrally located
blackboard which should be at least six feet wide,
with chalk and eraser. To the left of the blackboard is CHART NO. 1, which has a circular representation of the Ohm's Law formula--as shown in Figure 1, Page 60 of TM 11-661. Beneath the circle
there is further wording. (See Figure 1 attached to
script.) There is a lectern. Prominently displayed to the right of the blackboard is a demonstration panel which will play a prominent part in
the action. (See Figure 2 attached to script.)
This panel will have four 1½ volt batteries; an ohmmeter face, ammeter face, and voltmeter face which
will be revamped with larger needles and enlarged
scales. A wire circuit is in the panel, with a
switch to open and close the circuit and bring the
ammeter into the circuit. Lugs will be on the panel
that will allow quick installation of resistors.
The connecting cables for attaching the ohmmeter and
voltmeter will terminate the alligator clips, allowing instant attachment. A shallow box is attached
to the bottom of the panel. This box has two com-
partments. One contains a variety of resistors,
the other has ONE resistor. These resistors will be
PRACTICAL, but they will be doctored so that their
bodies are large and clearly visible. They will be
labeled (their resistance) with LARGE BLACK FIGURES.
To the right of the demonstration panel there is a
small workbench or display table. On this table
will be the chassis of a piece of electronic equipment, with dust cover removed and most of its cir-

I=E/R, or current equals the voltage
    divided by the resistance.

R=E/I, or resistance equals the
    voltage divided by the current.

E=I/R, or the voltage is equal to the
    product of the current times
    the resistance.

"OHM'S LAW" 215 25061

NOTE: ACTUAL CHART SHOULD BE PROPORTIONED
SO THAT THE ⊕ AND THE WORDS "OHM'S
LAW" CAN FIT COMFORTABLY INTO SCREEN
PROPORTIONS

Figure 1

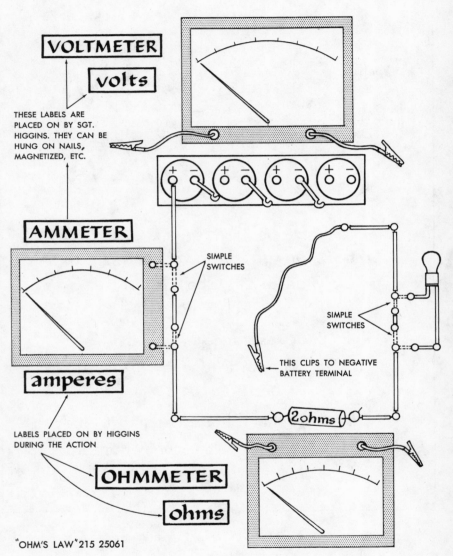

Figure 2

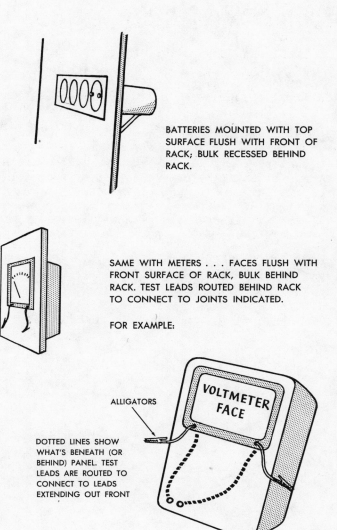

BATTERIES MOUNTED WITH TOP
SURFACE FLUSH WITH FRONT OF
RACK; BULK RECESSED BEHIND
RACK.

SAME WITH METERS . . . FACES FLUSH WITH
FRONT SURFACE OF RACK, BULK BEHIND
RACK. TEST LEADS ROUTED BEHIND RACK
TO CONNECT TO JOINTS INDICATED.

FOR EXAMPLE:

ALLIGATORS

VOLTMETER
FACE

DOTTED LINES SHOW
WHAT'S BENEATH (OR
BEHIND) PANEL. TEST
LEADS ARE ROUTED TO
CONNECT TO LEADS
EXTENDING OUT FRONT

"OHM'S LAW" 215 25061

Figure 2A

cuitry visible. Alongside the equipment is a manual, pertaining to it.

PROPS: (To be furnished by APC)
1. DEMONSTRATION PANEL, utilizing the materials described above.
2. Chalk and eraser for blackboard.
3. Blackboard, at least five feet wide.
4. OHM'S LAW chart.
5. Small Display Table, to accommodate the TA 219-U Modem.
6. Pencils and notebooks for twenty students.

ACTORS:

3 Professional Actors, to portray: S/SGT HIGGINS, in class A uniform, about 35, a competent, friendly individual. PVT ALLEN, in fatigues, about 20; serious and thoughtful; a worrier, but with a pleasant personality. PVT MATHEWS, in fatigues, about 20.

30 Non-Professional Actors, to portray students. EM, in fatigues. 20 in opening scenes; 10 for closing scenes. (Ad-lib lines.)

OHM'S LAW *

PRODUCTION SCRIPT **

*Written by Paul Caster as a free-lance writer on con-
tract for the United States Army Pictorial Center.

**This script is reproduced by permission of the United
States Army, Office of the Chief of Information.

FADE IN:

1. INT. CLASSROOM—DAY

   CLOSE SHOT—TOP OF OHM'S
   LAW CHART

   This is a Close Angle on
   the words "OHM'S LAW" at
   the top of the chart de-
   tailing Ohm's Law. Hold
   for reading, then

   DOLLY BACK TO FULL SHOT
   of classroom.

   About twenty enlisted
   men in fatigues are
   seated in the chairs.
   Each has a notebook and
   a copy of the informa-
   tion sheet entitled
   "Ohm's Law Circuits."

   S/SGT. HIGGINS, wearing
   a class A uniform,
   stands at the head of
   the class. He is holding a batch of manuals.

2. MED CLOSE SHOT—HIGGINS

   He hands the manuals in
   batches to the men in
   the front row.

                                    HIGGINS
                          Take one and pass the rest
                          back.

3. WIDER ANGLE—FEATURING
   STUDENTS

   The students pass the
   manuals back toward the
   rear of the room.

4. MED CLOSE SHOT—PRIVATE
   ALLEN

   Allen is seated in next
   to the last row. He
   takes a manual, passing

the remaining one to the
man behind him. Then he
looks at his copy of the
manual, his face skepti-
cal. He hefts it--as if
weighing the contents.

                                                HIGGINS

Allen looks up and off   All right--let me have your
toward Higgins.   attention, please.

5. MED CLOSE SHOT--HIGGINS   HIGGINS

He holds the manual   Everything that we'll be
aloft, waiting for the   studying in this class is
group's attention and   covered in the manuals you've
then speaks.   just been issued. Some of
                             you are probably already fa-
                             miliar with the basic funda-
                             mentals, but it won't do you
                             any harm to read through them
                             again. As for the students
                             who are starting from
                             scratch--

6. CLOSE SHOT--PVT ALLEN

We cut to this Close
Shot just as Higgins
mentions "starting from
scratch." Allen nods
imperceptibly, and we
realize that he is un-
happily in that cate-
gory--starting from   HIGGINS (OS)
scratch.
                             --I'd suggest you devote some
                             of your spare time to reading
                             it . . . particularly chapter
Allen opens the manual,   six, which explains Ohm's
flipping the pages.   Law.

7. MED SHOT--HIGGINS   HIGGINS

Some students in the FG,   SO much for introductions.
backs to Camera.   Tomorrow, we'll get to work.
                             And the day after that,
                             you'll be fixing radios.

(ALL: A GENERAL LAUGH AND A
CHORUS OF "OH, YEAH'S.")
That's all, men—-you're dis-
missed.

8. FULL SHOT—-CLASSROOM

The men get up and start
to exit.

9. CLOSE SHOT—-ALLEN

He is a depressed indi-
vidual. He flips pages
with his left hand and
seems more and more un-
happy with each page he
turns.

10. EXTREME CLOSE UP—-MANUAL
PAGES

Pages 60 and 61 of TM
11-661, from Allen's
point-of-view. His hand
is in frame, and it
flits across the circuit
illustrations. It then
makes a quick, tentative
turn of pages, glancing
ahead—-but lets the book
flop closed. His open
hand slaps down against
the cover, fingers out-
stretched, with an air
of finality and defeat.

11. CLOSE SHOT—-ALLEN

His left hand still on
the manual. He pushes
it a few inches away
from him, and now rests
his chin in both hands,
his expression gloomy,
as he looks down at the
floor.

                              HIGGINS (OS)

                    Would you believe I know
                    exactly how you feel?

ALLEN
(Looks up startled)

HUH?

WE DOLLY BACK QUICKLY TO
MEDIUM SHOT, Higgins has
moved in close to Allen.

HIGGINS

Sorry . . . I didn't mean to
creep up on you.

Allen holds up the man-
ual. Higgins takes it
and leafs through it.
Allen gets to his feet,
preparing to make his
exit.

ALLEN

That's OK, Sergeant. <u>You</u>
didn't scare me. But <u>this</u>
does.

HIGGINS

I felt the same way when I
was handed my first textbook
on the subject. A couple
hundred pages of completely
new material is enough to
frighten anybody.

12. CLOSE UP—HIGGINS

He smiles faintly.

HIGGINS

But there's another way to
approach it.

13. CLOSE UP—ALLEN

As he reacts and looks
off to Higgins skep-
tically.

ALLEN

There is?

14. CLOSE UP—HIGGINS
His smile broadens a
little.

HIGGINS

One page at a time.

15. MED CLOSE SHOT—ALLEN &
HIGGINS

Allen stares at Higgins
briefly and then shakes
his head dubiously as he
gathers up his notebook,
papers, and pencils and
prepares to exit.

ALLEN

Look, Sergeant—I'm not a
wise guy, and I mean no dis-

respect. But that sounds a
little bit like a pep talk—
and I'd need a lot more than
a pep talk to make it
through this course. I'm in
the wrong school. It's as
simple as that.

16. CLOSE UP—ALLEN

As he continues speak-
ing. He sincerely be-
lieves he's a very
square peg that can
never fit into this
round hole.

ALLEN

I'm just one of those guys
who can't even tune in a TV
set without dislocating a
knuckle. All this might as
well be Greek, for all I'll
get out of it. Theories—
circuits—formulas—mathe-
matics—everything I never
could understand.

17. MED CLOSE SHOT—ALLEN &
HIGGINS

Higgins listens pa-
tiently, poker-faced.
When he finishes speak-
ing, Allen exits,
Higgins staring after
him.

ALLEN

Let's face it: The Army
goofed. Trying to make me
an electronics technician
will be just a waste of time
and money.

Higgins suddenly real-
izes he is still holding
Allen's manual. He
holds it and calls off.

HIGGINS

Hey—you forgot something!

18. WIDER ANGLE—HIGGINS &
ALLEN

This is shot from Hig-
gins' angle, holding him
in the shot, back to
Camera. Allen pauses
and turns to glance back
to Higgins and then re-
traces his steps to get
the manual. He reaches

for the manual and
Higgins is about to give
it to him. He pulls it
back as he suddenly has
an idea. He turns to
face CAMERA as he
glances at his wrist-
watch. The two men are
in a MED CLOSE SHOT.

HIGGINS

No--wait a minute. I've got
some free time before chow.
You have too, right?

ALLEN

Yeah, but . . .

HIGGINS

I promise you no pep talks.
Just a little logic. We'll
both invest our free time on
a little research, and you
can decide later if it's
been wasted or not. Fair
enough?

ALLEN
(Reluctantly)

Higgins turns and exits
toward the blackboard,
slowly followed by
Allen.

I guess so.

19. MED SHOT--HIGGINS

As he enters to the
blackboard, picks up a
piece of chalk and turns
to face Allen off.

HIGGINS

Grab yourself a chair up
front.

DOLLY BACK TO WIDER
ANGLE featuring Higgins,
but including Allen as
the latter moves in to
seat himself in the
front row of otherwise
empty chairs.

HIGGINS
(Continuing)

Let's see now--you mentioned

Higgins starts to write
four words on the board,
one under the other.

four things. What were
they? Oh, yes--theories--
circuits--

20. CLOSE UP--ALLEN

He is looking off to-
ward the blackboard and
Higgins whose voice
comes in over the scene.
Allen's attitude is
still one of hopeless
frustration.

HIGGINS (OS)

. . . formulas--and mathe-
mathics.

21. MED CLOSE SHOT--HIGGINS

This is from Allen's
Angle. Higgins has fin-
ished writing the last
of the four words on the
blackboard.

HIGGINS

These four words have convinced you that you're in
the wrong school. But logic
convinces me that you're in
the right school. The Army
has evaluated your educa-
tional background, and
tested your abilities. You
wouldn't be here if they
didn't think you could
handle the material.

22. CLOSE SHOT--ALLEN

He is still very skep-
tical about his ability
to learn this particular
subject.

ALLEN

They could be wrong, too.

23. CLOSE SHOT--HIGGINS

He smiles and nods in
faint agreement.

HIGGINS

It's possible. But maybe
you're over-estimating the
subject and under-estimating
your own capabilities.

24. CLOSE SHOT--ALLEN

He makes a sour face,
and seems about to utter
a protest.

25. WIDER ANGLE--HIGGINS &
    ALLEN

This is from Allen's
angle, suggesting him in
the f.g., featuring
Higgins in the b.g. as
the latter raises his
hand to forestall the
protest.

HIGGINS

O.K., O.K.--no pep talks!
(Turns to blackboard and
draws a circle around the
word "THEORIES")
You're worried about the
fact that there may be a lot
of theory in this course.
Now what exactly is a
theory?

26. CLOSE SHOT--ALLEN

He searches for an an-
swer, and replies
slowly.

ALLEN

Well--it's something you
can't see, can't touch and
can't understand, unless
you're half a genius to begin with.

27. WIDER ANGLE--HIGGINS &
    ALLEN

Same as Sc. 25--Featur-
ing Higgins.

HIGGINS

You're half-right. In this
course there's really only
one theory you have to worry
about--the electron theory.
You can't see it, and you
can't touch it--but its results can be proven. And to
understand it, all you need
is a little imagination.

28. CLOSE SHOT--HIGGINS

He holds a piece of
chalk up between his
thumb and forefinger and
then lets it drop to
the floor.

He stamps on the piece
of chalk with his foot,
grinding it about.

HIGGINS

Take this piece of chalk,
for example. It has weight,
dimension--it's solid, just
like a piece of wood or
metal. Or so it seems. But
if I crush it . . .

29. CLOSE UP--HIGGINS' FOOT

As Higgins grinds the
chalk beneath his shoe.

30. WIDE ANGLE--FEATURING
HIGGINS

This is from Allen's
angle with him suggested
in the shot. Higgins
reaches down and picks
up some of the crushed
chalk and holds it in
the palm of his hand.

As Higgins finishes
speaking, Allen gets up
and crosses toward him.

HIGGINS

We find that it isn't as
solid as we thought it was.
Actually, it is a combination of many, many small
pieces.

31. CLOSER ANGLE--HIGGINS &
ALLEN

As Allen enters to
Higgins, the latter
calls attention to the
chalk fragments in his
hand.

Allen picks up a pinch
of crushed chalk between
his thumb and fore-
finger.

Higgins turns to the
blackboard, picks up a
fresh piece of chalk and
starts to make rough
sketch.

HIGGINS

Each of these small pieces
is composed of still smaller
pieces. (He pauses as Allen
contemplates the crushed
chalk)
The same is true of all
matter, regardless of how
solid it may appear to our
eyes, or how solid it may
feel to our touch. If you
could keep breaking any element down--subdividing it
into smaller and smaller
particles--eventually you
would come to the atom.

32. CLOSE UP--ALLEN

As he watches Higgins
sketching on blackboard.
Allen is beginning to
show aroused interest.

33. CLOSE SHOT——HIGGINS

As he is finishing
making a rough sketch of
an atom, with nucleus
and electrons.

HIGGINS

If you could see it, the
atom would look something
like this.

34. CLOSE SHOT——SKETCH

Higgins' hand is in the
shot, adding lines to
indicate the orbital
paths of the electrons.

(NOTE: This sketch
roughly matches the
CLOSE UP of the Atom as
shown in animation foot-
age from TF 11-1200)

HIGGINS (OS)

It has a nucleus and electrons which form rings
around the nucleus.

35. MED SHOT——HIGGINS &
ALLEN

We have a PROFILE of
each man, with the atom
sketch between them.

HIGGINS

Here's where you need your
imagination. These elec-
trons——(POINTS)——are not
just standing there, frozen
in position. On the con-
trary: they're in constant
movement.

36. CLOSE SHOT——ALLEN

His face is thoughtful
as he looks toward the
sketch of the atom.

HIGGINS (OS)

This movement is orbital.
Just as the planets orbit
about the sun . . .

37. CLOSE SHOT——BLACKBOARD
ATOM SKETCH

Higgins' hand indicates
the electrons' orbit.

HIGGINS (OS)

. . . electrons orbit about
the nucleus.

DISSOLVE TO:

38. STOCK--ANIMATION

From TF 11-1200. The
shot of the atom showing
the electrons orbiting
about the nucleus.

We watch this action
briefly, then--

DISSOLVE TO:

HIGGINS (OS)

This circling is constant.
Every electron is constantly
circling about its nucleus.

39. CLOSE SHOT--ATOM SKETCH

Hold briefly before
DOLLYING BACK TO WIDER
ANGLE to include Higgins
and Allen.

HIGGINS

Can you visualize that?

ALLEN
(Nodding affirmatively)

As you said, it's like the
planets and the sun.

HIGGINS

There are differences, but
we don't have to concern
ourselves with them.
(Pause) The nucleus of the
atom contains, among other
things, a number of protons,
or positive charges.

Higgins turns back to
the blackboard and be-
gins sketching a number
of small PLUS signs over
the nucleus.

40. CLOSE SHOT--ATOM SKETCH

Higgins' hand is in the
shot as he is finishing
sketching the small PLUS
signs over the nucleus.

41. MED CLOSE--HIGGINS &
    ALLEN

Higgins completes put-
ting the small PLUS

signs on the board and resumes speaking. Allen registers increasing interest.

HIGGINS

Electrons on the other hand are negative charges. That's why I've drawn them as short lines--the symbol we use for negative. (Slight pause) Every atom contains the same number of negative electrons as there are positive protons in the nucleus. (He pauses as he turns again to blackboard to draw rectangle about the atom sketch, then resumes speaking) A fundamental law states that like charges repel and unlike charges attract. Therefore, the positive charges in the nucleus . . . (He pauses expectantly for Allen to pick it up)

Higgins draws a rectangle about the atom sketch, then draws a large positive and a large negative sign below the rectangle. They are the same size.

ALLEN
(nodding)

Attract the negative electrons.

HIGGINS
(pleased)

Right. It binds them to the atom--holds them in orbit.

ALLEN

Well, however you put it, it means they can't get away because the nucleus has them locked in place.

HIGGINS

Hold on, let's not jump to conclusions. Look at the sketch . . .

He turns to the drawing on the blackboard.

42. CLOSE SHOT--ATOM SKETCH

Higgins' forefinger
points to various elec-
trons.

HIGGINS (OS)

These electrons in the inner
rings are locked tightly in
orbit, true. But what about
these--(POINTS TO OUTER RING
OF ELECTRONS)--the electrons
in the outer ring? They're
pretty far away from the
pull of the nucleus, and
they are describing much
wider orbits. They're not
as tightly bound to the
nucleus.

43. MED CLOSE SHOT--HIGGINS
    & ALLEN

Higgins turns away from
the board and back to
Allen.

Allen thinks a moment,
studying the sketch.
Stimulated by Higgins'
efforts, Allen's mind is
already starting to work.

HIGGINS

Bearing that fact in mind,
and remembering that electrons can move about, what
does this suggest to you?

ALLEN

I suppose it means that it's
possible to knock some of
the outer electrons out of
place.

HIGGINS

Out of orbit.

ALLEN

. . . out of orbit. If you
can find something to push
them with.

Higgins smiles in satis-
faction at the increas-
ingly positive response
of his pupil.

HIGGINS

Do you know what you just
did?

44. CLOSE UP--ALLEN

A very brief reaction
shot of Allen. He isn't

quite sure of what he's
done, but he's beginning
to realize he's starting
to make progress toward
understanding.

45. MED CLOSE--HIGGINS &
    ALLEN   HIGGINS

    Same angle as Sc 43.   You formulated a theory.
                                And apparently you're right,
                                for one of the things we
    Higgins turns back to   teach in this course is that
    the blackboard, Camera   these outer electrons are
    Pans with him as he   the ones that contribute to
    shifts to a clear spot   electrical current flow.
    on the board.

46. MED CLOSE SHOT--HIGGINS
                                            HIGGINS
    He starts to sketch
    another atom.   We're concerned only with
                                the outer ring of electrons,
                                so we'll only show that one
                                ring in this illustration.

47. CLOSE SHOT--NEW SKETCH

    Higgins' hand is in the   HIGGINS (VO)
    scene as he quickly
    draws the new sketch.   Here is that outer ring.
                                (His forefinger indicates
                                the outer circle) The prob-
                                lem is--what can be used to
                                force them out of orbit?

48. MED CLOSE SHOT--HIGGINS
    & ALLEN   HIGGINS

    HOLDING the new sketch   Any suggestions?
    on the blackboard be-
    tween them. Higgins   ALLEN
    turns away from the
    board to Allen.   No.

                                            HIGGINS

                                Well, since the positive
                                charge of the nucleus holds
                                these electrons in position,

we'll use a negative charge
to dislodge them.

He turns back to the
blackboard, raising his
chalk to the sketch.

49. CLOSE SHOT--NEW SKETCH

On the atom as Higgins
draws a large negative
symbol to the left of
it, and sketches an
arrow pointing from the
negative symbol toward
the atom.
THE CAMERA PULLS BACK A
LITTLE, PANNING TO THE
RIGHT. We now have a
frame that HOLDS the
sketched atom on the
left, EXCLUDING the
negative symbol and the
arrow, and has blank
blackboard space to the
right of the sketch--
enough space to accommo-
date two more atoms.
Higgins' hand reaches
in . . .

HIGGINS (OS)

We'll apply a negative force
in this direction--(SKETCHES
ARROW, POINTING LEFT TO
RIGHT). Now once again
we've got to use our imagin-
ations. And we've got to
remember that we're dealing
with more than one, single
atom . . .

HIGGINS (OS)

. . . There'd be another
atom here . . . another
there . . . and so on . . .

HIGGINS FOREFINGER
points to two imaginary
atoms alongside the
first atom . . . in
other words, he is
pointing to the spots
where they would be if
we could see them.

. . . Now try to visualize
these other atoms, and their
outer rings of electrons
. . .

DISSOLVE TO:

50. STOCK--ANIMATION

From TF 11-1200, picking
up the footage beginning

at 143 ft., showing
three atoms and rings of
electrons, side—by—side.
(THIS IS AS CLOSE TO A
MATCHED DISSOLVE AS WE
CAN GET.)

                           HIGGINS (OS)

We have a negative force
pushing from the left, which
means electrons will be
repelled toward the right.
The result is like a game of
musical chairs—with elec-
trons. An electron, re-
pelled by the negative
force, leaves its own orbit
and jumps into orbit around
the atom on the left . . .

We see an electron enter
the frame from the left,
pause, and then jump
into position in the
ring around the first
atom.

                           HIGGINS (OS)

. . . But the atom on the
left doesn't want an extra
electron—it would throw it
out of balance. So . . . it
throws one of its own electrons off. This electron,
also affected by the negative force, moves to the
right, joining the next atom
in the line . . .

We see the shifting of
electrons in the first
atom, and see an elec-
tron move out of posi-
tion, and then into
position in the second
atom. From this point
on, we let the inter-
changing run along at
its normal rate of
speed.

. . . This atom, too, accom-
modates the extra electron
by throwing off one of its
own. The result is a constant shifting of electrons,
all going in the same direction.

DISSOLVE TO:

51. MED CLOSE SHOT--HIGGINS
    & ALLEN

    Allen is staring
    thoughtfully at the
    board; Higgins is watch-
    ing him.

                                        HIGGINS

                            We call these electrons
                            Free Electrons--(HE WRITES
                            THE WORDS "FREE ELECTRONS"
                            ON THE BOARD NEAR THE
                            ELECTRONS). They're called
                            that because they are free
                            to move from atom to atom
                            under the influence of an
                            applied force. I've been
                            talking about a few atoms--
                            but actually there are
                            millions.

    DISSOLVE TO:

52. STOCK--ANIMATION

    From TF 11-1200, picking
    up the footage beginning
    at 162 ft. We see the
    three atoms previously
    established, then addi-
    tional atoms FADE ON,
    above and below the
    original three. We PULL
    BACK to show more and
    more atoms, and at 166
    ft. there is a DISSOLVE
    and we now see small
    circles surrounded by a
    sea of electrons. (THE   HIGGINS (OS)
    PULL-BACK CONTINUES.)
                            The amount of free electrons
                            varies with different ma-
                            terials. In copper, for
                            example, there are a vast
                            number of free electrons
                            . . .

The words: COPPER ATOMS
are SUPER'D, from 169 to
172 ft.

We see the small elec-
trons start to flow
(left to right, starting
at 174 ft.). We watch
this action briefly,
then:

DISSOLVE TO:

53. MED CLOSE SHOT--HIGGINS
& ALLEN

Allen still wearing the
thoughtful expression,
Higgins still observing
Allen as if to gauge how
much he is absorbing.

Higgins turns to the
board and starts to
erase the sketch of the
atom. Then he draws a
long, thin horizontal
line.

54. CLOSE UP--ALLEN

He shrugs.

. . . Therefore, when we
apply an electromotive force
to copper, there is a con-
siderable flow of electrons.

HIGGINS

Think you've got that?

ALLEN
(A little hesitantly)

I think so. I hope so.

HIGGINS

Let's move on to something
more tangible. We'll say
this is a piece of copper
wire. We know it has an
abundance of free electrons.
All we need is a force that
will move them. Where do
we get it?

ALLEN

I don't know.

55. CLOSE UP--HIGGINS

He smiles encouragingly.

HIGGINS

SURE you do. Where do you
get the power you need to
run your portable radio?

56. CLOSE UP--ALLEN

His face lights up as he
gets the idea.

ALLEN

A battery.

57. CLOSE SHOT--HIGGINS

As he sketches a battery
symbol near the long
thin rectangle repre-
senting the length of
copper wire. He labels
the negative and posi-
tive battery terminals
prominently.

HIGGINS

Right. I know you don't
like symbols--but it's
easier for me to use a
symbol than to draw a
battery that you could
recognize. That's one of
the advantages of the
symbol. (Slight pause)

He extends the rectangle
so that it joins with
the negative side of the
battery.

Now we'll connect the negative terminal of our battery
to our length of wire . . .

58. MED CLOSE SHOT--HIGGINS
    & ALLEN

With the blackboard
sketch between them.
Higgins lowers the
chalk, turning expec-
tantly to Allen.
Allen studies the
sketch. He points to
the negative terminal of
the battery.

HIGGINS

Now what's happening inside
our piece of copper wire?

ALLEN

Well . . . we've got a negative force pushing . . . er
. . . against the negative
electrons . . . so they

would move along this way.
I get it. The electrons are
flowing along——and that's
current flow.

Higgins points to the
end of the rectangle——
the unconnected end.

                    HIGGINS

Not quite. You're forget-
ting this point. The end of
the wire. We can't have
current flowing, because
there's no place it can flow
TO. What's needed now is
that second word you were
complaining about: a circuit.

CAMERA DOLLIES BACK TO
WIDER ANGLE

Higgins steps back to
the area of the black-
board on which he wrote
the four troublesome
words. He draws a
circle around the second
word: CIRCUIT. Then he
walks back to his
original spot.

                    HIGGINS
              (Resumes speaking)

The dictionary defines circuit as a passing or travel-
ing round——a revolution.
What we have here is just
one section of a circuit.
To make it a complete, or a
closed, circuit, we have to
connect our wire to the
other battery terminal.

He now extends the
copper wire line, form-
ing a rectangle and
joining the end to the
positive terminal of the
battery.

59. CLOSE SHOT--THE SKETCH

Higgins' finger points
out the various por-
tions as he mentions
them.

HIGGINS (OS)

Now we're applying what we
call an electromotive force.
At the negative terminal of
the battery, a negative
force--or voltage--is pushing electrons in this
direction--away from the
negative terminal. At the
positive terminal, electrons
are being attracted by the
positive voltage. And
throughout the length of the
wire, or conductor, elec-
trons are in constant
movement.

60. CLOSE SHOT--HIGGINS

He turns to face Allen.

HIGGINS

We have a circuit, and we
have current flow.

61. CLOSE SHOT--ALLEN

He nods his head
slightly, but he still
looks a bit puzzled.

ALLEN

But if they flow constantly,
won't it reach a point when
they're all used up?

62. CLOSE SHOT--HIGGINS &
ALLEN

Higgins smiles his ap-
preciation of Allen's
thinking process.

HIGGINS

No. You see, the battery is
emitting electrons at its
negative terminal and col-

lecting them at its positive
terminal. For every electron that leaves the wire at
the positive terminal,
another one enters at the
negative terminal. The
number of electrons in the
conductor remains constant
at all times.

                    ALLEN

It's like a parade . . .

                    HIGGINS

In what direction, in
relation to positive and
negative?

                    ALLEN

Well, electrons are nega-
tive, so they'll always
move away from the negative
terminal . . .

                    HIGGINS

Which means?

                    ALLEN

Negative to positive. Current flow will be from
negative to positive. . . .

                    HIGGINS

Good! Remember that point.
Electron current flow is
always from negative to
positive.

He picks up the eraser
and starts to erase the
sketches on the board.

63. WIDE ANGLE--HIGGINS &
    ALLEN

    At an angle holding the
    front area of the room,
    with the demonstration
    panel established in Sc
    1 partially visible in
    the f.g. Higgins com-
    pletes erasing the
    board, puts down the
    eraser and walks toward
    the demonstration
    panel, followed by
    Allen.

                                        HIGGINS

                              Now that we've covered some
                              theories, let's see if they
                              work out in practice.

64. MED CLOSE--HIGGINS &
    ALLEN

    They move in close to
    the panel. (NOTE: At
    this point there is a
    circuit which includes
    one battery and a small
    light bulb. The circuit
    is open.) Higgins looks   HIGGINS
    at the panel.
                              Let's trace this circuit . . .

65. CLOSE SHOT--PANEL

    Higgins' hand comes in   HIGGINS (OS)
    and traces the circuit.
                              When I close the switch to
                              complete the circuit, current
                              will flow from the negative
                              terminal of the battery--
                              through the light bulb--and
                              on to the positive terminal
                              of the battery. (Slight
                              pause) The fact that the
    Higgins' hand closes the light glows proves that cur-
    switch and the light   rent is flowing. But it also
    bulb glows.   raises another question.

66. CLOSE SHOT--HIGGINS &
    ALLEN

    Holding the panel be-   HIGGINS
    tween them, with the
    light bulb visible.   What causes the bulb to glow?

ALLEN

I remember that from school.
It's heat, isn't it?

HIGGINS

Yes, but what causes the
heat? (ALLEN SHRUGS) The
current in our circuit is
flowing through the wire and
through the filament of the
bulb. Now, the copper wire
is what we call a good conductor. Remember, it has
many free electrons. But the
material that makes up the
filament of the bulb is not a
good conductor. In fact, it
resists the flow of current.
This resistance causes fric-
tion--the friction creates
heat. Here you have the
three basic elements we'll be
concerned with.

67. FULL SHOT--THE PANEL

Higgins' hand comes in
and his forefinger
points to the various
components he mentions.

HIGGINS (OS)

An electromotive force--in
this case, provided by the
battery. Current flow,
through the circuit. And
resistance, in this case represented by the light bulb.

68. MED CLOSE SHOT--HIGGINS
    & ALLEN

The panel is between
them. Higgins removes
the connections to the
light bulb and selects a
resistor from the box of
resistors at the bottom
of the panel. He starts
to connect it into the
circuit. Allen follows

HIGGINS

Let's disconnect the light
bulb, and substitute a resistor in its place. (BRIEF
PAUSE) Actually, all materials have some resistance to
current flow, depending upon
the nature of the material,

Higgins' actions with
keen interest.

and its dimensions. Even
copper wire has some resistance, but the resistance in a
thin copper wire, such as
we're using here--(HE
POINTS)--is so slight it is
negligible. We can ignore
it. Resistors are com-
ponents manufactured of a
material that has a high resistance to current flow.

He completes the instal-
lation of the resistor.

69. CLOSE SHOT--HIGGINS

He looks offscreen to-
ward Allen, as he con-
tinues speaking.

HIGGINS

The circuits in any elec-
tronic device are designed to
serve a purpose. They make
use of the electromotive
force, the current flow and
the resistance. They control
and utilize these factors.
And, of course, they cannot
be haphazard. These three
elements must be calculated
and controlled. So, we need
some method of calibrating,
or measuring them.

He turns to face the
panel.

70. CLOSE SHOT--THE PANEL

CAMERA CENTERING on the
batteries, and the ad-
jacent voltmeter face.

HIGGINS (OS)

The electromotive force we
measure in terms of volts.

HIGGINS' HAND COMES in
and places a label,
VOLTS, on the panel
above the batteries.
(This can be a magnet-
ized label, or any other
suitable device.)

HIGGINS' HAND places a label VOLTMETER on the panel above the volt- meter.

The instrument we use to measure volts is called a voltmeter.

The CAMERA moves over to CENTER ON the ammeter at one side of the panel. Higgins' hand comes in and places a label AMPERES above the am- meter.

Current flow, we measure in amperes, or "amps" for short. (BRIEF PAUSE) The instrument used for this purpose is an ammeter.

HIGGINS' HAND places a label AMMETER underneath the ammeter.

CAMERA TILTS TO CENTER ON the ohmmeter, near the bottom of the panel. Higgins' hand comes in and places a label OHMS above the ohmmeter.

Resistance, we measure in Ohms. The measuring instru- ment is an ohmmeter.

Higgins' hand places a label OHMMETER below the ohmmeter.

71. CLOSE SHOT--HIGGINS & ALLEN

Higgins turns back to Allen.

HIGGINS

With these instruments, you can prove the existence of voltage, resistance and cur- rent flow. And you can measure them. Let's try the voltmeter first.

He reaches up toward the voltmeter leads.

72. CLOSE SHOT--PANEL

FEATURING the batteries and the voltmeter, as Higgins connects the voltmeter leads to the battery terminals. We

see the voltmeter needle
deflect, reading midway
between 1 and 2 volts.

HIGGINS (OS)

There we are--the voltmeter
reads one and a half volts.

73. CLOSE SHOT--PANEL

FEATURING the resistor
in the circuit, and the
ohmmeter. Higgins
reaches in and connects
the ohmmeter leads to
either side of the re-
sistor, and we see the
needle deflect, the
reading being 2 ohms.

HIGGINS (OS)

Now we'll measure the resistance by connecting the ohmmeter to either side of the
resistor. The resistance is
--two ohms.

74. CLOSE INSERT--PANEL

FEATURING the ammeter
and the switching ar-
rangement that will make
it part of the circuit.
Higgins reaches into
frame and points to the
ammeter face.
He throws the switches,
and we see the needle
deflect. Then he traces
the path of the current
with his finger.

HIGGINS (OS)

We made the voltmeter and
ohmmeter connections across
the battery and across the
resistor. The ammeter is
different. In order to measure current flow, we insert
the ammeter INTO the circuit.
The current flows through the
ammeter, and is registered
here (POINTS TO FACE OF
METER). We have point-sev-
enty-five amperes of cur-
rent.

75. CLOSE SHOT--HIGGINS &
ALLEN

HOLDING the full panel
between them. Higgins
turns to face Allen.

HIGGINS

Is it less of a mystery now?

ALLEN

Yeah . . . but you're deliberately keeping it very simple, aren't you?

HIGGINS

All right, then, I'll compli-
cate it. How would you go
about increasing the amount
of current flow?

76. CLOSE SHOT--ALLEN

He looks off at the
board, thinking.

ALLEN

It's the voltage that's moving the electrons . . . so I
guess that the thing to do
would be increase the voltage.

77. MED CLOSE SHOT--HIGGINS
& ALLEN

Higgins reaches up to-
ward the batteries and
starts to make the con-
nections.

HIGGINS

All right, we'll try that.

78. CLOSE SHOT--FEATURING
BATTERIES

Higgins connects the
jumper between the first
two batteries and then
changes the connection
to the circuit so that
both batteries are in
series. When he com-
pletes the connections,
we see the needle on the
voltmeter deflect to 3
volts.

HIGGINS (OS)

We'll connect two batteries
instead of one. This gives
us a total of three volts
. . . exactly double our previous voltage.

79. CLOSE INSERT SHOT--
AMMETER

We see that the needle
is now halfway between
1 and 2 amps. Higgins'
finger points to it.

HIGGINS (OS)

We do have an increase in
current flow. It's now one-
point-five amperes--exactly
twice as much as it was before.

80. CLOSE TWO SHOT--HIGGINS
    & ALLEN

Higgins turns from the
panel to Allen.

Allen's face wears the
happy expression of
someone who just made a
discovery.

HIGGINS

What does that tell you?

ALLEN

That I was right. And also
. . . that the current flow
increased the same as the
voltage . . . right?

HIGGINS
(Pleased with other's
progress)

You've got the idea. What
you mean is that the increase
in current flow is directly
proportionate to the increase
in voltage.

ALLEN

Double the voltage, double
the current flow.

HIGGINS

And vice versa. Now . . .
supposing I asked you to cut
the current in half . . .
without changing the voltage?
How would you do that?

ALLEN

Is it possible?

HIGGINS

Yes.

81. CLOSE SHOT--ALLEN

He looks off toward the
panel, studying it
thoughtfully.

ALLEN

Well . . . can I do anything
with the ammeter?

82. CLOSE SHOT--HIGGINS

HOLDING the ammeter to
one side of his head.
He shakes his head nega-
tive, pointing to the
ammeter.

HIGGINS

No . . . nor with the voltmeter or ohmmeter. And
that's an important point:
These are measuring devices
only. They're not used to
affect the circuit in any
way.

83. FULL SHOT--MEN AND PANEL

HOLDING the full panel
face, with Higgins and
Allen on either side of
it. Allen still studies
the circuit. He points
to various portions of
the circuit, as if work-
ing something out in his
mind. Finally, he
points to the resistor.

ALLEN

The only thing left is the
resistor. You said you
wanted the current cut in
half?

HIGGINS

That's right.

ALLEN

Well . . . if it works like
the voltage did, I think you
could do it by putting in a
bigger resistor.

HIGGINS

You mean one with a higher
resistance value. How much
higher?

ALLEN

I'm just guessing, of course
. . .

HIGGINS

All right, then, guess.

ALLEN

Double?

Higgins nods and starts
to fish around in the

box at the bottom of the
panel. He brings out a
resistor, offering it to
Allen.

HIGGINS

Double would be four ohms,
right? (ALLEN NODS) Well
. . . go ahead, take it.

ALLEN

What'll I do with it?

HIGGINS

Put it in the circuit. Go
ahead, you can do it.

84. MED CLOSE SHOT--ALLEN

(HIGGINS SUGGESTED)
He hesitates for a sec-
ond, then takes the re-
sistor. He disconnects
the two ohms resistor,
and hands it offscreen
to Higgins, then con-
nects the replacement
four ohm resistor. He
is slow and uncertain at
first, but picks up
speed quickly and is ob-
viously enjoying himself
by the time he has it
connected.

85. CLOSE SHOT--HIGGINS

He smiles as he is en-
joying watching Allen's
gradually building en-
thusiasm. We FRAME THIS
SHOT so that Higgins'
head is blocking the am-
meter face.

HIGGINS

All set?

ALLEN (OS)

Yep.

HIGGINS

We had one-point-five amperes
with the two ohm resistor.
If you guessed correctly, the
four ohm resistor should have
halved that to point-seventy-
five amperes. Let's see
. . .

He backs away, MOVING
OUT OF FRAME and clear-
ing the ammeter face.
WE ZOOM IN for a FULL
SHOT of the meter, which
now is back to its .75
amps reading.

HIGGINS

You were absolutely right!

86. FULL SHOT--HIGGINS,
ALLEN & PANEL

ALLEN

Allen is looking at the
ammeter. He turns to
Higgins, his expression
one of delight.

I was! You know, the only
reason I hesitated to say
double was because it seemed
just too obvious. I thought
it couldn't be that easy.

HIGGINS

It won't always be. Some of
the material we'll cover in
this course will be a lot
tougher than this. The point
is, though, that if you can
grasp these fundamentals, you
are capable of absorbing the
rest of the material . . .
including the formulas.

ALLEN
(His face suddenly sobers)

Oh, yeah . . . I forgot about
those.

Higgins reaches over to
the panel and discon-
nects the ammeter . . .
breaking the circuit.
He turns and walks to-
ward the blackboard, Al-
len following.

Despite his mild pro-
test, Allen sits down in
the front row. Higgins
picks up a piece of
chalk and stands in
front of the blackboard.

HIGGINS

Take a seat, Allen. I want
to give you a verbal test.

ALLEN
(Almost a groan of protest)

A test? Oh, no!

87. CLOSE SHOT--HIGGINS

He starts to draw a cir-
cuit on the blackboard
. . . the equivalent of
the circuit on the
panel, including a bat-
tery, resistor, and an
ammeter symbol.

HIGGINS
(As he sketches)

This won't be official . . .
relax. You know the battery
symbol. This one . . .
(DRAWS RESISTOR SYMBOL) . . .
represents a resistor. This
. . . (DRAWS AMMETER SYMBOL)
. . . is our ammeter. Your
first question is: What two
factors in this circuit determine the amount of current
flow?

88. CLOSE SHOT--ALLEN

He is looking off toward
the board.

ALLEN

The voltage and the resistance.

89. MED SHOT--HIGGINS &
CIRCUIT

He is looking over his
shoulder off toward Al-
len, but returns his at-
tention to the board at
once.

He writes "4 OHMS" below
the resistor.

HIGGINS

Correct. Now . . . how much
current flow would you have,
if this resistance was . . .
say . . . four ohms?

90. CLOSE SHOT—ALLEN

    He appears a little puz-
    zled.

ALLEN

That would depend upon what
the voltage was, wouldn't it?

91. MED SHOT—HIGGINS &
    CIRCUIT

    He turns away from the
    board and faces off to-
    ward Allen, putting down
    the chalk and moves to
    exit toward Allen.

HIGGINS

Right. There is a definite
relationship between voltage,
current and resistance in a
given circuit. Can you tell
me what that relationship is,
on the basis of what you've
learned thus far?

92. CLOSE SHOT—ALLEN

    He leans forward in his
    seat, looking off toward
    the blackboard and then
    toward the demonstration
    panel.

ALLEN

Hmm. I think I can. Not exactly, maybe . . . Let's see.
If you double the voltage,
without changing the resistance, you double the current.

As Allen speaks, we PULL
BACK TO A WIDER ANGLE AS
Higgins walks in from
the direction of the
blackboard.

He turns to Higgins.

ALLEN
(Continuing)

If you double the resistance
. . . without changing the
voltage . . . you decrease
the current by half.

HIGGINS

Good. Your statement is correct. It is also something
else. It is a formula.

ALLEN
(Surprised)

A formula?

HIGGINS

Exactly. A formula is simply
a guide . . . a method to
follow to achieve a result.
If I wanted to double the
current flow in my circuit
. . . (POINTS OFF TOWARD THE
BOARD) . . . I could do so by
following the formula you
just outlined, and doubling
the voltage. Now, I'd like
you to take a look at another
formula. One that's even
better than yours.

Higgins exits toward the
left end of the black-
board and the OHM'S LAW
CHART.

93. MED CLOSE SHOT--HIGGINS

He enters to one side of
the OHM's Law Chart and
gestures toward it. Al-
len shifts in his chair
to look off in the di-
rection in which Higgins
is pointing.

HIGGINS

This formula is well over a
hundred years old.

94. CLOSE UP--OHM'S LAW
CHART

Higgins' voice comes in
over the scene.

HIGGINS (OS)

It's called Ohm's Law, because it was first proved by
a German physicist named Ohm.

95. MED CLOSE SHOT--HIGGINS

He faces Allen who is
offscreen.

HIGGINS

With all due respect to Mr.
Ohm, it would be more accurate to call it Nature's Law,

for it describes how electrons will perform under a
given set of circumstances.
(PAUSE) You look puzzled
again.

96. CLOSE SHOT--ALLEN

He is looking off in the
direction of the chart.

ALLEN

I am. Just when I think I've
got it down pat, it gets complicated again. We were
talking about volts and current and resistance. Now,
all of a sudden, all I see
are symbols. What's "I" and
"E" and "R"?

97. MED CLOSE SHOT--HIGGINS

He picks up the chalk
and turns toward the
blackboard. He writes
the symbols I, E and R
on the board, one under
the other.

As he identifies each,
he writes the appropri-
ate word alongside the
symbol. Then he moves
over to a clear area of
the board and draws the
circular representation
of Ohm's Law as it ap-
pears on the chart.

HIGGINS

We haven't changed a thing
. . . just simplified a
bit. "I" stands for current
. . . "E" stands for the
electromotive force . . . and
"R" stands for resistance.

HIGGINS

The advantage of this formula
is that you only need know
the value of two factors in
order to determine the value
of the third.

We PULL BACK TO WIDER
ANGLE as Allen walks
into the frame and looks
at the blackboard.

ALLEN

I don't understand that at
all.

HIGGINS

Look at the chart . . .

They both turn to look
toward the chart.

98. CLOSE SHOT--OHM'S LAW
CHART

CAMERA FULL on the en-
tire chart.

HIGGINS (OS)
(Higgins speaks slowly)

Current equals the voltage
divided by the resistance,
resistance equals the voltage
divided by the current, and
the voltage is equal to the
product of the current times
the resistance.

99. MED SHOT--HIGGINS &
ALLEN

The OHM'S LAW circle is
on the board between
them. Higgins directs
Allen's attention back
to the board. He covers
the "I" on the circle
with his fingers.

HIGGINS

Let's assume you do not know
the amount of current flow
. . . but you do know that
the electromotive force is
twelve volts . . .

He writes the numeral 12
alongside the "E."

. . . and that the resistance
is six ohms.

He writes the numeral 6
alongside the "R."

E divided by R . . . or the
voltage divided by the resistance . . . will give you
the answer. In this case,
twelve volts divided by six
ohms is . . . ?

ALLEN

Two amperes?

HIGGINS
(Nodding in agreement)

Two amps of current.

He removes his fingers
from the "I" and writes
the numeral 2 alongside
it. Now he covers the
"R" with his fingers.

HIGGINS

To determine the resistance,
you divide the voltage by
the current, or twelve divided by two, which gives us
. . . (REMOVES HIS FINGER)
. . . six ohms.

ALLEN

Oh, I see . . . they're all
. . . they're all . . .
(GROPES FOR A WORD).

HIGGINS

Related. Current, voltage,
and resistance have a relationship, and that relationship is defined by Ohm's Law.

ALLEN

And if I can just memorize
that formula, I'll be in good
shape?

HIGGINS

Let's go back to our circuit
and see.

Higgins exits toward the
demonstration panel.
Allen remains behind,
staring intently at the
formula, as if trying to
memorize it. We HOLD on
him briefly.

100. MED SHOT--HIGGINS &
      PANEL

Higgins enters to the
panel and connects the

four batteries in se-
ries.

            HIGGINS
      (Speaking to Allen OS)

I'll connect all the batteries, which means we'll be applying six volts. We still
have the same four ohm resistor. Six volts, four
ohms. Can you tell me how
much current flow there will
be when I close the circuit?

101. MED CLOSE SHOT--ALLEN

At the blackboard, still
looking at the Ohm's Law
circle. He glances off
toward Higgins and then
picks up the chalk and
eraser.

           ALLEN

I'll try. You say we have
six volts . . . (HE ERASES
THE NUMERAL 12 NEXT TO "E"
AND REPLACES IT WITH A 6)
. . . and four ohms . . .

He erases the numeral 6
next to "R" and replaces
it with a 4. He erases
the numeral 2 next to
"I," then puts the
eraser down and studies
the board.

           ALLEN
       (Continuing)

Current would be equal to the
voltage divided by the resistance. That's six di-
vided by four . . .

He utilizes a clear
space on the board to
work out his problem,
six divided by four,
muttering to himself as
he does so. His prog-
ress is slow and delib-
erate . . . he can do
it, but it takes some
effort on his part.
When he finally arrives
at the answer of 1.5, he
writes that figure in

the Ohm's Law circle
next to the "I."

   . . . One point five. One
and a half amps. Am I right?

102. MED SHOT—-HIGGINS &
     PANEL

Higgins is looking off
toward Allen. He steps
back a bit and waves to-
ward the panel.

                      HIGGINS

Come see for yourself.

We PULL BACK TO WIDER
ANGLE as Allen walks in
and faces the panel. He
traces the circuit about
quickly with his finger.

                     ALLEN

Let's see now . . . to complete the circuit . . . I
have to close this switch.

103. CLOSE SHOT—-AMMETER

HOLDING the portion ad-
jacent to it, including
the switch. Allen's
hand reaches in and
closes the switch, and
we see the needle move
up to a poing midway be-
tween one and two.

                    ALLEN (OS)

One and a half amps. I'm
right!

104. MED SHOT—-HIGGINS &
     ALLEN

Allen now looking confi-
dent . . . even jubi-
lant. Higgins shrugs
off Allen's enthusiasm.

                    HIGGINS

Of course you are. You always will be—-if you follow
Ohm's Law.

Higgins turns and walks
toward the blackboard,
the CAMERA PANNING WITH

HIM. He picks up the
eraser and starts to
erase the board.

105. MED CLOSE SHOT--HIGGINS

As he continues erasing,
he works his way to the
four words he originally
wrote earlier . . .
Theories, etc. He wipes
them out, one by one,
starting from the top.
He pauses before the
word MATHEMATICS and
speaks off to Allen.

HIGGINS

Incidentally, the mathe-
matics in this course won't
get much more complicated
than what you just did. So
. . . (HE WIPES OUT "MATHE-
MATICS" WITH ONE STROKE)
. . . I think you can stop
worrying . . .

He puts the eraser
down and turns to look
offscreen toward Allen.
He does a "take" (Allen
isn't where he saw him
last), then looks about
the room. He reacts
when he sees:

106. CLOSE SHOT--ALLEN

Allen is frowning, look-
ing down, his head
shaking a slight nega-
tive. He looks up-and-
off toward Higgins . . .
a quick, skeptical look
--and then back down.
The CAMERA TILTS DOWN,
HOLDING ON a small
table. On it is a piece
of equipment, without a

dust cover. We have a
CLOSE ANGLE on a maze of
circuitry, tubes, resis-
tors, condensers, etc.——
a complex array.

ALLEN

CAMERA TILTS BACK UP TO
Allen as he looks off
toward Higgins and ges-
tures toward the equip-
ment on the table.

But what happens when I get
to something like this?
How can I figure it out? It
looks like a jungle!

107. MED LONG SHOT——HIGGINS

This is from Allen's
angle with Allen sug-
gested in the shot.

HIGGINS

You could find your way
around in a jungle, if you
had a good map, couldn't
you?

As Higgins refers to "a
good map" he comes
toward Allen.

108. MED CLOSE SHOT——ALLEN &
HIGGINS

Higgins enters to Allen
and picks up manual
from table.

HIGGINS

And you'll always have a
good map. (He picks up
manual and flips pages to
schematic) We call it a
schematic.

He holds up the sche-
matic for Allen to see.

109. INSERT——SCHEMATIC

This is very close on
the schematic in the
book.

HIGGINS (VO)

The most complicated cir-
cuitry is actually a com-
bination of many small
circuits, and once you've

learned how to read a schematic, you'll be able to isolate a problem to a small area of the circuitry.

110. MED CLOSE--HIGGINS & ALLEN

Same set-up as Sc. 108.

HIGGINS

You'll always have a manual to guide you. And you'll always have Ohm's Law. Equipment will vary, but Ohm's Law always remains constant. It's a dependable factor that will help you to repair the most complicated circuits you'll have to deal with.

111. WIDER ANGLE--HIGGINS & ALLEN

Higgins thinks a moment, then turns and walks back toward the demonstration panel followed by Allen, the CAMERA PANNING with them.

HIGGINS
(As he walks)

Let me make one thing clear, Allen. It isn't easy to become an electronics technician, and I'm not trying to give you the impression that it is. It requires intelligence, skill, and a lot of hard work. (Slight pause) The only point I wanted to make is that if you can understand this much of it--Ohm's Law, and the other basics I've explained--you can understand the rest.

The two men arrive at the panel and Higgins turns to face Allen as he continues speaking.

Higgins looks down in the small box containing the resistors. He selects one and holds it up and examines it.

(Pause while he selects resistor) This resistor is labeled two ohms. Think you could put it in the circuit and tell me in advance what the current flow will be?

There is a slight smile
on Higgins' face and we
get the impression that
he is up to something.

112. CLOSE SHOT--ALLEN

He nods his head con-
fidently.

                ALLEN

Sure. That's an easy one.
I equals E over R--the
voltage divided by the resistance. That's six
divided by two. Three amps
of current.

113. WIDER ANGLE TO INCLUDE
    HIGGINS

Same set-up as Sc. 111.
CAMERA PANS WITH THEM as
they move to place on
panel where Allen will
install the resistor.
Higgins hands the re-
sistor to Allen who
starts to connect it.

              HIGGINS

OK--show me.

114. CLOSE SHOT--HIGGINS

He is observing Allen,
still smiling faintly.

115. MED CLOSE SHOT--HIGGINS
    & ALLEN

Allen finishes the in-
stallation and reaches
up to the switch that
will close the circuit.

              ALLEN

Two amps . . .

116. INSERT--AMMETER

This is CLOSE on the
ammeter as Allen throws
the switch, closing the
circuit. The ammeter
needle fluctuates--but

it does NOT stop at two
amperes. It goes far
beyond that point--a
drastic differential.

117. MED CLOSE SHOT--HIGGINS
      & ALLEN

Same Angle as Sc. 115.
Allen's face drops. He
opens and closes the
switch again, but the
meter reading is still
wrong, and he looks dis-
mayed. He turns to
Higgins.

ALLEN

I don't get it. It should
be two amps, but it isn't.
(HE SIGHS) See what I mean?
I'll never make a tech-
nician. A simple circuit
like this and I did some-
thing wrong.

HIGGINS
(Calmly)

You didn't do anything
wrong.

ALLEN

But I must have . . . or
else Ohm's Law is wrong.

HIGGINS

Ohm's law is never wrong.
It is one of the things you
can always rely upon. Other
things can be wrong--com-
ponents can be defective.
But Ohm's law is never
wrong.

ALLEN

But . . . (PAUSE) . . . I
give up.

HIGGINS

Don't give up so easily.
Check things. You've got
other meters, haven't you?

118. CLOSE SHOT--ALLEN

He looks at the panel,
thinking.

119. CLOSE INSERT SHOT--
OHMMETER

HOLDING the portion of
the circuitry including
the resistor. We can
read the "2 ohms" mark-
ing on the resistor.

ALLEN

Well . . . I know the voltage is right . . . you
didn't change anything
there. The only thing I can
think of . . . (TRAILS OFF)

Allen's hands reach in
to attach the leads from
the ohmmeter to either
side of the resistor.
We see the needle fluc-
tuate, but it DOES NOT
read two ohms.

120. MED CLOSE SHOT--HIGGINS
& ALLEN

Higgins is smiling.
Allen turns to face him,
a trifle annoyed.

ALLEN

This darn thing isn't two
ohms! I don't care what it
says on it, it's not two
ohms. It must be bad, or
something.

HIGGINS

You mean defective. You're
right. It is defective.
You located a defective

component in a circuit, Allen. You used your meters, you used Ohm's Law, and you used your own intelligence.

Higgins quickly detaches the defective resistor. He tosses it up in the air and catches it. He has a happy expression on his face as he drops the resistor into his pocket. He glances at his watch.

HIGGINS
(Continuing)

I've got to get going. See you in class, Allen.

Higgins turns and exits, Allen's gaze following him off. Allen is smil- ing with gratitude to Higgins and with renewed confidence in himself.

ALLEN
(Calling after Higgins)

Thanks a lot, Sergeant.

FADE OUT.

FADE IN:

121. INT. CLASSROOM--DAY

FULL SHOT as new stu- dents start to filter in. They size up the classroom as they walk in slowly. Allen is in the b.g. at the panel.

122. MED SHOT--ALLEN

Allen is studying the panel with a great deal of interest. Private Matthews, one of the new students, enters and stands beside Allen. The newcomer looks at the demonstration panel and shakes his head.

MATTHEWS

Oh, man--here goes a couple of fuses. I'll never get through this course. Scratch one student!

ALLEN
(Smiles)

Don't worry about it. It's
not as tough as it looks.
If you take it in small
doses, it's pretty easy.

Allen turns and exits,
leaving Matthews still
staring at the panel.

DOLLY IN CLOSER ON
MATTHEWS as he does a
delayed "take" and turns
to look over his   MATTHEWS
shoulder in the direc-   Easy?
tion of Allen's exit.

123. FULL SHOT--CLASSROOM

Shooting across some
chairs toward the Ohm's
Law Chart. Several more
students are entering
the room. Allen walks
past them. As he exits,
we . . .

ZOOM SLOWLY TO A CLOSE
SHOT of the Ohm's Law
Chart. We hold briefly
on the chart before
we . . .

FADE OUT.

Analysis

The script of *Ohm's Law* is an excellent example of lean writing and clarity of expression. The audio and the visual are well synchronized; the visual depicts what the audio talks about and the audio specifically refers to what is being shown with the visual — a prerequisite to good audiovisual writing.

Since content is all-important with a technical subject, the script follows Format "B": the visual on the left, the matching dialogue on the right. This is the most practical way to present this subject, even though Format "A," or the Hollywood format, is more frequently used when there is dialogue. It is easier for the director and the film editor to follow in matching the audio with the visual.

Scene headings are specific. Camera angles are well defined, and focus attention on the center of interest at all times. Visual description leaves no doubt in the reader's mind just what he is going to see on the screen. The dialogue is simple, suited to the subject, and flows smoothly. The script leaves few unsolved production problems for the director or film editor. It can be shot substantially as written. It is good, solid professional audiovisual writing, reflecting imagination and craftsmanship.

For the sake of emphasis, attention is again directed to the introductory notes and technical material the writer furnished. The beginner should realize that such "packaging" makes his script more valuable to his director or producer.

The notes which precede *Ohm's Law* included several rough sketches, which were prepared by the script writer. Such drawings are not usually required, except for certain technical subjects, and are usually prepared for the writer by professional artists. For the sake of clarity, these have been redrawn for this book.

Part V: The Stock Film Documentary

Chapter 11: Making a Stock Film Documentary Series
Example Scripts: Army in Action, **Episodes 1, 2, 3, and 13**

Chapter 12: **Analysis of** Army in Action

11 Making a Stock Film Documentary Series

I have touched on the documentary made chiefly from film footage obtained from newsreels, commercial films, theatrical film libraries, government film libraries, and motion picture archives. These sources have provided producers of documentary films with great quantities of stock footage used in varying amounts in the making of commercial documentaries. Since stock film footage accumulates from day to day, the number of documentaries that can be made using this source of supply is vast. The filmed events of today provide evidence for tomorrow's record of history

The stock film documentary field can be a profitable one for the writer and can also present him with extremely interesting assignments. To create a fine motion picture script within the limitations of film that has already been shot, with all the unpredictable factors involved, is a challenge to the writer's inherent talent and to his acquired knowledge of his craft.

THE MAKING OF A DOCUMENTARY SERIES

A few weeks before this chapter was planned, I completed production of a documentary series of thirteen half-hour episodes, at the U.S. Army Pictorial Center, for television release in 1965, and wrote and directed the series as well. Producing, writing, and directing a complete film is seldom done by one person, but in this instance such an assignment provided me with the perspective to discuss here several scripts in that series.

The original title for the series was *Not For Conquest,* a phrase that is repeated throughout the narration. At the request of the sponsoring agency, the Office of the Army's Chief of Information, the title was changed to *Army In Action,* and the series was released on February 1, 1965. The first run was televised on more than three hundred and fifty stations in the United States and on forty overseas military stations. This series was released as part of the Army's public service

189

"Big Picture" program and won the Freedom Foundation Award—
the George Washington honor medal—in 1966. In addition to its
public release, the series has been made available to instructors of
military history (R.O.T.C.) in colleges and universities and to educational television stations. It is available for screenings in 16 mm prints
for fraternal, civic, veteran, and educational organizations. Requests
for prints may be directed to the information officer at any local army
installation. The Army maintains film libraries throughout the nation.

Students of motion picture and television writing and production
may be able to see the finished product, made from the scripts reproduced in this book, through the courtesy of the Office of the
Army's Chief of Information. Such an arrangement would offer the
opportunity to compare the working scripts with the final film version. Any request should refer to the "Big Picture" program and to
the television release numbers of the first three episodes and the last
episode of *Army In Action,* namely: TV 634, TV 635, TV 636, and TV
646. *Army In Action* is a compilation of fifty momentous years of
history from 1914 to 1964. The purpose of the series was to present
a dynamic perspective of those fifty years during which world events
and international crises forced the shaping, the building, and the
molding of the United States Army from its weakness of 1914 to its
strength of 1964.

Organization of Scripts for a Series

Four production scripts are reproduced in this book. The screen
treatment of the first episode is also presented for comparison with
the final production script of the same episode. The production
scripts of the first three episodes in the film were chosen as examples.
This gives the student and the inexperienced writer the opportunity
to follow the continuity sequentially, thus illustrating the development of the story line.

The first episode in the film series serves as the introduction, while
episodes two and three establish the theme of the main body of the
series. The script of the last episode is the summation. Space does
not permit reproducing in this book the nine middle episodes, which
deal with World War II, the years immediately following, the Korean
War, and the cold war years.

Transition through Optical Effects

The first three episodes are an abridged version of twenty-seven
years of history on only 7740 feet of 35 mm film running about ninety
minutes. To achieve this abridgment, only the most important his-

torical events could be included in the film; the problem was to avoid an episodic or staccato effect on the audience. In the final film version smooth transitions were made through the use of optical effects. In motion picture language optical effects are fades, dissolves, wipes, and pans, among others. Opticals are not always indicated in the script but may be decided upon during a screening of the rough print.

These scripts are examples of "lean" audiovisual writing. Words and phrases in the audio and in the description of the visual are kept to a minimum. In script form some of the narration may appear to be longer or fuller than it is in the finished film, but that is so only because the scenes to which the narration applies are briefly described. During the rough cut phase and in the polishing of the film, changes were made in the narration to adjust to the content and length of the scenes.

Selection of Stock Footage

In *Army in Action* it can be seen that the finished films follow the production scripts very closely. This was due in part to my knowledge of the existence, nature, and source of a great percentage of the stock footage selected and used. This knowledge was helpful, but lack of it would have been only a minor handicap. It was still necessary to use researchers for the actual job of finding and selecting the immense volume of stock footage used in the series. The stock film selected, from which the final films were cut, ran to about 180,000 feet of 35 mm film. It was also necessary for the researchers to work closely with the film editors and the writer-producer in coordinating the film.

In writing this type of documentary, scene numbers are used to separate and identify sequences which may include different but related scenes. The numbers, since they run in sequence, keep the film in order. This aids the researcher in his selection of footage and aids the editor in following the story line on film. It also preserves continuity in working toward the first rough cut of the film.

Sometimes the writer himself will select the stock shots he needs to tell his story—in the case of a short, for example. But the selection of stock footage required for an entire series would be time-consuming and impractical. Two of the responsibilities of the film maker are to maintain his production schedule and meet his release date.

Earlier in this book I emphasized the importance of noting on every scene in the script the source of the stock footage and the number of the can of film in which every reel of film is filed. However, for *Army in Action,* since I was both author and producer of the series, I devised a short cut. Each researcher worked from a copy of the completed script and made notations of the source for each scene as he selected and ordered the footage. The annotated copies of the script were then collated and given to the film editor for his guidance.

Narration and Timing

The release prints of *Army in Action* are in 16 mm. The running time of each episode is 28 minutes and 40 seconds. The original film used to manufacture the work print was in 35 mm. The answer print * of each episode was in 35 mm and 2580 feet in length. Eighty feet were devoted to the main and end titles. Eighteen minutes of narration was set as the maximum length per episode by the producer. Some episodes contain less than that and the first episode runs slightly longer. Finally, I used a tape recorder to time the narration of each episode. These recordings served as a controlling factor in determining the length of the narration, and also were an aid in audiovisual styling and quality.

When writing narration one should allow for footage without narration, so that what the audience sees on the screen carries the story, rounded out perhaps by music and sound effects. A good musical background, for example, can add dimension, mood, and excitement to a film.

Presentation of the Treatment

The production scripts which follow were developed from detailed treatments, of which the treatment for the first episode is representative. A fifty-five-page presentation established the story line, theme, purpose, and mood of the series. It stated the manner in which the subject matter would be treated and described the dynamic type of film editing which would be used. It stressed the need for special music and for highly skilled narrators. It included thumbnail synopses of all thirteen episodes and indicated the sources of stock footage. The presentation was approved by the sponsor.

* See Glossary.

ARMY IN ACTION *

A DOCUMENTARY SERIES

IN
THIRTEEN HALF HOUR EPISODES

EPISODE I

"WINDS OF CHANGE"

--TREATMENT--

ARMY IN ACTION

EPISODE I

"WINDS OF CHANGE"

In this introduction to the Series we must take time to
establish its premise and a forecast of the entire Series.
Preceding the Main Title* we open this introductory
episode with a teaser. In the background is the faint
throb of a primitive drum.
We Fade In on a big head Close Up of a Cro-Magnon man
and then Pull Back slowly to reveal a Full Shot of a
diorama painting, or we show life-like figures of pri-
mordial man, as the First Narrator says: "Man is Earth's
only creature who has learned and practices the arts of
war. The realities of war began when primitive man
was forced to defend himself against the aggressive attack
of others of his own kind." We Dissolve to another
still picture, or drawing, of primitive men in combat,
employing crude weapons--rocks, clubs, or spears--as the
narrator says: "He has fought his wars of aggression and
conquest from those misty reaches of Time and the feuds
between small tribal groups of the Dawn people . . ."
Dissolve to a classic painting of the battle between the
forces of the Duke of Wellington and Napoleon at Waterloo,
with the faint throb of the primitive drum changing to the
roll of a modern snare drum, as the narration continues
over, ". . . through the ages to the clash of mighty
armies."
A fast-moving montage of spectacular live action stock
combat footage from theatrical films which shows the
progressive development of armies and weapons and the
almost continuous succession of warfare from the distant
past to the present: Primitive men in close combat--giant
stone catapults (the first artillery) being used to attack
a fortified city with the defenders repelling invaders
using scaling ladders--the charge of Egyptian charioteers
--Roman Legions in action--the charge of Genghis Khan's
hordes--combat shots from the Crusades--English cross-

* See Glossary.

195

bowmen in action--medieval combat--the American Revolution
--the Civil War--WW I, II, and Korea.

Over this action montage is the following narration:
"The history of war is the history of the human race.
Wars of conquest for new lands and treasure. Wars to
build empires and to exploit vassal peoples--to capture
trade and commerce. Wars of suppression and rebellion.
Wars between opposing political and economic ideologies.
(Pause) Through all this immeasurable history of strife,
struggle and carnage, there shines forth a great light
. . ."

As the narrator says: "there shines forth a great
light" we Dissolve to a very impressive night shot of the
Statue of Liberty fully illuminated, this symbol of "the
light that burns in the night of man's darker hours." The
narrator continues: ". . . man's innate love and longing
for peace and freedom for all men everywhere." Dissolve
to Main Title.

From the Main Title, we Dissolve to: An outstanding
personality as the live narrator--the First Narrator--one
who can give proper emphasis to a dramatic reading and
lend stature to the Series (selection of the narrator or
narrators to await final development of the material and
other factors which will influence the choice of such a
personality, or personalities).

We discover the First Narrator sitting quietly reading
in a library set. (On one wall are photos of people to
whom we will refer later.) The narrator looks up from his
book and speaks: "The ideal of peace and freedom has
always caused men to defend themselves and their way of
life against the intruder, the aggressor, the oppressor.
If they were weak, they went down before the power of the
aggressor in the battle for survival. It is the story of
strength and weakness."

The First Narrator closes his book and places it on the
library table at his side as he continues speaking: "It
is an age-old story from which peaceful men of complacency
and good will have not always drawn an object lesson, but
the lessons of history must stand."

The Camera moves with him to another angle as he gets to
his feet: "If a nation is to live, it must be strong. If
it is weak, it, and its way of life, will perish before
the onslaught of the aggressor. We find this grim reality
throughout history. We are facing it again in our time.
One of the greatest deterring forces which gives the
modern aggressor pause is the combined military strength
of the United States. The United States Army is a potent

part of that military establishment--strong, ready, alert.
It has not always been so.

"The history of the Army's build-up during the past
fifty years from weakness to a strong, modern fighting
force is an epic story--the story of a mighty armed force
organized and maintained, NOT FOR CONQUEST, but for the
defense--not only of this nation, but of the entire free
world. Nothing like it has occurred in all the history of
man."

The First Narrator pauses and we go to another Camera
Angle as he continues: "For the first 133 years of its
history, the United States was isolated from European and
Asian wars by vast seas to the east and west. The
Atlantic and Pacific oceans were our protection. We had a
new and rich continent to develop--a mighty nation to
build.

"We did not wish to become embroiled in the quarrels of
remote and alien peoples. We wished to prosper in peace.
We took great comfort in our isolation--and our complacency grew until a leading role in world affairs, for
which we were ill prepared, was suddenly thrust upon us--
against our will and desires. It actually began in 1914."

As the First Narrator says "1914," through Special
Effects, the screen seems suddenly to explode to the
crashing accompaniment of German martial music (possibly
"The Watch on the Rhine") as the most effective Close Shot
of the Kaiser or the Kaiser surrounded by his spike-
helmeted General Staff (live or still) flashes on the
screen. (In contrast to the previous live narrator's
quiet reading, this scene with its sudden crash of music
is designed to startle the audience.) This is followed by
a montage of the best available and most impressive stock
shots of German armies of WW I advancing to attack France
through Belgium and Alsace-Lorraine.

We show scenes of frantic mobilization in France and
England, and, if possible, Russian footage of the time,
and Austria-Hungary and Emperor Franz Joseph. After the
first few moments, the blaring martial music fades to
background under the narration as the Second Narrator, in
more of a newsreel style of delivery, explains what is
happening as combat footage continues. We include scenes
of reinforcements being rushed by fleets of taxicabs from
Paris to the fighting front.

Following the dramatic establishment of the outbreak of
World War I in the Europe of August 1914, we cut back to
the United States to see American public and political
reaction through newspaper headlines, groups, and quotes

from prominent figures of the day, in simulated voices of
some of those personalities as they express their
opinions. These quotes and our narration reflect the
isolationist attitude of the time. To most typically
complacent Americans it was "just another of Europe's
interminable quarrels"--remote events "that we read about
in the newspapers." Among the great mass of Americans,
sideline sympathy was divided according to racial and
national origin. Our official position--strict neutrality
--was a policy proclaimed by President Woodrow Wilson.

Over suitable footage, the Second Narrator establishes
the fact that our own regular Army consisted of some
130,000 officers and enlisted men, scattered in small
units throughout the continental United States and our
possessions. No single unit was larger than a regiment.
None was combat ready. The Navy numbered 57,000 and the
Marine Corps about 10,000, for a total active defense
force of less than 200,000, while millions were being
mobilized in Europe.

There were a few men in our Army's small hard corps of
officers whose profession was to read signs of danger
which could jeopardize the security of our country. They
were dedicated men, little known to the American public,
especially in time of peace. They were professional
soldiers--Generals Hugh Scott, Tasker Bliss, and Peyton
March, who served successively as Chief of Staff from 1914
through our participation in WW I. (If there is no suitable newsreel coverage of these personalities, we will use
photos obtainable from West Point, newspaper archives, or
other sources.)

These were our top-level military planners, and they and
their staffs went to work, planning for a war they thought
might come, and if it did, wanted us to be ready. When
Woodrow Wilson learned that the General Staff was planning
for a possible war with Germany, he was greatly dis-
tressed. He thought such planning violated the spirit of
our declared neutrality. It was only after General Bliss
convinced the President that such planning was a routine
staff matter that Wilson abandoned his opposition to such
activities.

In newsreel style we span the years from 1914 to 1917--
a fast-moving chronology of highlights leading up to
declaration of war by the United States. We show the
agony of Europe during those years, the unrestricted
submarine warfare and the sinking of American ships by the
Germans that finally goaded the President to a declaration
of war. This was the first part of our answer to the

arrogant Prussian conviction that America would not
declare herself an active belligerent, but, if she did,
she was not prepared to fight. Our military weakness gave
comfort to the aggressor.

In his account of the events leading up to the U.S.
entry into World War I, the Second Narrator speaks of
Germany's far-reaching imperialistic ambitions--German
Foreign Minister Zimmerman's proposal to Mexico that she
not only declare war against the United States, but also
help persuade Japan to do the same. As a reward, Germany
promised to see that Mexico got New Mexico, Texas, and
Arizona. The uncovering of this plot further inflamed
American public feeling, already aroused by the sinking of
United States shipping by German submarines.

Continuing in the same style of newsreel coverage, we
show the response to the draft, the mobilization of our
military and industrial forces, the arrival in France of
the American Expeditionary Force. We stress the great
logistic problem in transporting a great army and mountains of supplies across three thousand miles of ocean,
much of it infested by enemy submarines.

Over matching footage (from the National Archives) the
narration: "More than two million United States Army
troops were convoyed to Europe without the loss of a
single transport--nearly eight million tons of the materials of war were shipped overseas--two billion dollars'
worth of food, 1800 locomotives, 27,000 freight cars,
423,000 tons of rails and fittings for the French rail-
roads, nearly 69,000 horses and mules."

Over brief shots of Russian and German forces, the
Second Narrator explains that the collapse of Czarist
Russia and the transfer of many German divisions from the
Eastern to the Western front enabled the Germans to launch
a great offensive in the West until, by the last of May,
1918, the Kaiser's armies were within fifty miles of Paris.

Using National Archives footage, we show and comment
upon the most impressive highlights of the American
Expeditionary Force in action, such as the American Second
Division and parts of two other divisions at Chateau
Thierry stopping the German advance on the Marne River;
the Second Division and a Brigade of Marines recapturing
Belleau Wood; the First Division capturing Cantigny; the
first big American operation, involving over half a
million men, attacking the St. Mihiel salient, capturing
thousands of prisoners and hundreds of guns; a million
more American troops in the Meuse-Argonne offensive;
finally, the Armistice and victory celebrations. The

narrator pays tribute to the WW I soldier, who fought in the finest traditions of the American fighting man, and to General Pershing and other U.S. military leaders.

The voice of our Second Narrator continues: "In the light of our more recent military history, World War I was a training ground for a small group of young American Army officers who, a quarter of a century later, became famous military leaders in the Second World War."

In the final Scene and Narration script, the backgrounds of these officers may be presented in much briefer form than that given below. (This montage of officers does not appear in the production script because it would interrupt the flow of the story line.)

"Dwight D. Eisenhower, graduate of West Point, in-structor of tactics in World War I. He became Supreme Commander of Allied forces in Europe in World War II, and later, President of the United States."

"George Catlett Marshall, professional soldier, graduate of the Virginia Military Institute, who later served brilliantly as Chief of Staff of the United States Army from 1939 to 1945. After that he continued to serve his country as Secretary of State and Secretary of Defense."

"Douglas MacArthur, West Point graduate, who became commander of the 42nd Infantry, the famous Rainbow Divi-sion of World War I. It was on the battlefields of Europe that Douglas MacArthur gained much of the experience, the knowledge, and the stature which one day enabled him to lead successfully another great American expeditionary force."

"Omar N. Bradley, graduate of West Point, served as a lieutenant of infantry in World War I. In World War II, as a field commander, he led the American forces in the invasion of France."

"George S. Patton, Jr., West Point, a young cavalry officer, learned about tanks as a captain in 1917 in command of the First Brigade, U.S. Tank Corps, using French-built tanks. He was wounded during the Meuse-Argonne offensive. Twenty-five years later he achieved spectacular success as the commander of armored divisions which smashed the enemy."

"Jacob L. Devers, West Point, served with the Field Artillery in World War I. He became an Army Group com-mander in World War II."

"Another West Pointer was Mark Clark, battalion com-mander in World War I, wounded in action, who fought in the bloody battles of St. Mihiel and the Meuse-Argonne offensive."

"Courtney Hodges saw action in France with the 6th
Infantry. He became a four-star general in World War II
as Commanding General, First Army."

"Walter Krueger, a non-commissioned officer in the
Spanish-American War who was later commissioned, served
with the 26th and the 84th Divisions in France in World
War I. He was detailed as Chief of the Tank Corps, AEF.
In World War II he commanded the U.S. Sixth Army in the
Pacific."

"Terry Allen, West Point, Battalion Commander of the
90th Division, AEF in World War I—in World War II commanded the U.S. First Division in the initial landings in
North Africa, followed by participation in the Tunisian
campaign and the invasion of Sicily. He then commanded
the 104th Infantry Division in the drive for the Maas
River in Holland, the drive to the Ruhr, and on to the
Rhine with the U.S. First Army."

"General Robert L. Eichelberger, West Point, served in
World War I as an infantry major and as Assistant Chief of
Staff of the American Expeditionary Force in Siberia in
1919. He distinguished himself in the vicious Pacific
island and jungle fighting in World War II."

"Henry H. 'Hap' Arnold, West Point, a pioneer army
aviator, whose World War I experience convinced him that
air power would be a decisive factor in future wars."

We return to a live shot of our First Narrator. (In the
production script and final picture the Second Narrator
continues the voice-over narration of action footage.) He
is standing near a wall of the library set on which we see
photos of the men featured in the montage. He speaks:
"These were men of destiny, young men who had learned the
hard, tough, and sober lessons of war—lessons which were
to serve them and their country in years to come. But in
1918 they returned home with their battle-weary troops.
The 'war to end all wars,' as Woodrow Wilson said, was
over. Peace would reign—for a while. But two great
soldiers of the time sounded a warning of things to come
which went largely unheeded."

The narrator turns to a photo of General Tasker Bliss on
the wall: "At the signing of the Treaty of Versailles,
General Tasker Bliss wrote a letter to the Secretary of
War in which he predicted that war would come again in
thirty years." The narrator turns to a photo of Marshal
Foch, who commanded all allied forces in WW I, and who
said, "This is not peace. It is an armistice for a
twenty-year period."

Over stock Archives footage the voice of the narrator

continues: "The Army of Occupation left the Rhine. We stacked our arms."

But there remained a few who refused to believe that the last great war was the "war to end all wars." They were our military planners who continued to evaluate the problems of mobilization and training. They studied the problems of how to improve weapons and fire power, of logistics, and of the strategic and tactical deployment of imaginary battalions—regiments, divisions, and armies engaged in paper warfare.

With appropriate comment we show the American people relaxing in peacetime. The soldier returned to his farm, his factory, his business, and his profession. A handful of regular troops fell into the monotonous routine of garrison duty, relieved only by an occasional desultory training exercise. Fort Benning, Fort Sill, and Fort Riley were quiet installations.

Over footage pertinent to the narration we continue: "At the United States Military Academy another generation of Americans studied the science of war. At the Virginia Military Institute others prepared themselves for leadership in civilian life as well as military life. At universities throughout the country, ROTC units trained a small number of citizens for leadership in times of national emergency. The National Guard trained in its armories and in the field during summer encampments.

"Yes, it was a time of peace. The military was not important in the general scheme. West Point was just another educational institution whose football team was all that interested the public. The General Staff, the War College, and the Command and General Staff School were vague terms in the public mind. The nation had fallen back into its old ways of isolation and complacency. It had just fought the war 'to end all wars.'

"But in Germany there was a shabby little man who had been a corporal in the German Army." At the start of this narration we Dissolve to a still photo of Hitler with his untrimmed mustache during his obscure years. At first, his image is in the distant background, as if seen at the far end of a telescope. As the narration continues, the image of Hitler moves very slowly toward the foreground, increasing in size. As the image slowly starts growing, German music (Götterdämmerung theme) fades in, its volume increasing almost imperceptibly with the slow advance of Hitler's image. "He was an impoverished, embittered painter, and not a very good painter at that. In his brooding, twisted mind was a growing hate and obsession.

He was a little man destined to become a monster. He
dreamed of many strange things, but there was one thing he
never dreamed of, that one day he would cause the mobilization of the mightiest United States Army in history.
His name was Hitler!"
The image of the shabby Hitler has advanced to almost
full screen. As the narrator says "Hitler!" the picture
of him is torn asunder revealing a dramatic head Close Up
of Hitler in his Nazi uniform, looking well fed and at the
climax of one of his harangues. Simultaneously, the
German background music suddenly comes up in a crashing
crescendo. We Freeze Frame as Hitler's burning eyes stare
out from the screen in their fanatic intensity.
Fade To:
A shot of the First Narrator as he addresses the Camera:
"You have just seen the introduction to a special Series
of BIG PICTURES--ARMY IN ACTION which presents highlights
of the history of the United States Army from World War I
to the present years of the Cold War. It portrays the
far-reaching events during the past fifty years which have
carried a nation from the complacency of isolation to
global responsibilities and commitments. It depicts our
country's struggle to defend its own way of life and that
of the free world as well. Military weakness is an invitation to the aggressor to attack. Only a strong United
States Army can fulfill the nation's role in meeting those
responsibilities for the preservation of freedom."

This example treatment presents a straightforward story line with
specific description of content. The critical reader can visualize what
he will see and hear in the end product. This treatment was approved
without change by the sponsor. Now let us see what happened when
the treatment was expanded into the final production script. A page-
by-page comparison will show the fuller development, the changes,
additions, and deletions made.

NOTE (This note appeared at the beginning of each script
as submitted for sponsor approval):

  Since this 13-episode Big Picture Series of Army in
Action presents only the highlights of United States Army
history during the past fifty years, it cannot feature in
detail the documentation of any single war, battle,
campaign, army group, or division. We use only the most
impressive highlights pertinent to the overall story we
have to tell. Such a condensation eliminates all ex-
traneous action and static material, and gives greater
pace, force, impact, and a freshness to the footage used.
Army in Action represents an entirely different approach
to the basic subject.

ARMY IN ACTION

EPISODE I
"WINDS OF CHANGE" (TV 634)
--PRODUCTION SCRIPT--

FADE IN:

1. SPECIAL EFFECTS STAGE   SOUND

   A SLOW FADE IN to the   THE SLOW, PULSING BEAT OF A
   throbbing of a primi-   PRIMITIVE DRUM IN THE B.G.
   tive drum in the b.g.
   First we see, in shadowy   (INSTEAD OF THE DRUM UN-
   outlines, a CLOSE SHOT   USUALLY APPROPRIATE MOOD
   of the sculptured head   MUSIC WAS USED.)
   and shoulders of a pre-
   historic man of the Cro-
   Magnon type. The background drop is the
   simulated wall of a cave
   upon which are paintings
   by primitive men--
   animals such as European
   Bison, deer, etc., as
   appear in the Lascaux
   Caves in France.

   In a SLOW DAWNING
   EFFECT, the figure is

lighted until it is more
plainly revealed, but at
maximum the lighting is
held down to <u>nearly</u> LOW
KEY. As the Narrator
says, "Man," the CAMERA
PULLS BACK. THE LIGHT-
ING COMES UP TO MORE OF
A NORMAL KEY.

MATCHED DISSOLVE:

CLOSE ON ONE OF THE
INDIVIDUAL CHARACTERS IN
A DIORAMA EFFECT PAINT-
ING or drawing of a
small group of Cro-
Magnon type men in
combat, using stone
axes, primitive spears
and small boulders.

DISSOLVE TO:

2. SPECIAL EFFECTS: The
   CAMERA PULLING BACK from
   a CLOSE UP to FULL SHOT
   of classic painting of
   battle between Napoleon
   and Wellington at Waterloo.

3. STOCK: A FAST MOVING
thru ACTION MONTAGE to be
9. made from clips from
   Hollywood productions,
   and from combat footage
   of Army Pictorial Center
   and other libraries, to
   present a dramatic recap
   of the history and
   progression of man's
   involvement in warfare.

The MONTAGE begins with
brief shots of primitive
men in close combat.
Attack on a walled city,

FIRST NARRATOR (VO)

Man, (very slight pause)
earth's only creature who
studies and practices the
science and arts of war.
(Slight pause) The realities of war began when pre-
historic man first launched
aggressive attacks against
others of his own kind.
Man has fought his wars of
aggression and conquest and
defense from those misty
reaches of time and the
feuds between small tribal
groups of the Dawn People
. . .

. . . down through the ages
to the clash of mighty
armies.

The history of war parallels
the history of the human
race. It is estimated that
since 3,600 B.C. some

invaders using giant
stone catapults, mobile
attack platforms and
scaling ladders. The
charge of Egyptian
charioteers. Early
Bedouin horsemen charg-
ing and in combat.
Roman Legions on the
march and in action.
Combat in the American
Revolutionary War.

14,500 wars, great and
small, have been fought.
Throughout more than 5,000
years man has known fewer
than 300 years of peace.
(This estimation does not
appear in the treatment.)
Instead, a succession of
wars of conquest for new
lands and treasure—wars to
build empires and exploit
vassal peoples—to capture
trade and commerce.

Brief cuts of combat in
the Civil War. Brief
cuts of U.S. Cavalrymen
of the West in the late
1860s and early '80s.

Wars of suppression and wars
of rebellion. Wars insti-
gated by power-hungry mad-
men. Wars between opposing
political and economic
ideologies.

Brief shots of combat in
trenches and the no-
man's-land of World War
I—U.S. troops, amphib-
ious landings and tanks
in action in WW II.

(FOOTAGE PLAYS FOR A FEW
BRIEF MOMENTS)
Through all this immeasurable history of strife,
struggle, and carnage, there
shines forth a great light.

DISSOLVE:

10. STOCK: Impressive night
footage of Statue of
Liberty with all lights
burning. Army Pictorial
Center Library. (Refer-
ence to source of foot-
age is made here and
there throughout the
scripts.)

. . . Man's innate love and
longing for peace and freedom.

FADE OUT:

FADE IN:

MAIN TITLE: "THE BIG PICTURE"

DISSOLVE TO:

SERIES TITLE: <u>ARMY</u> <u>IN</u> <u>ACTION</u>
               EPISODE I

DISSOLVE TO:

EPISODE TITLE: "WINDS OF CHANGE"

FADE OUT:

FADE IN:

11. INT.--STUDY.
    ESTABLISHING SHOT--
    FIRST NARRATOR.

    This set will be used
    throughout the series
    as the "study" of the
    First Narrator. It has
    bookshelves, a desk,
    leather couch or easy
    chair, and for this
    particular episode,
    photos on the wall, of
    military men to whom we
    will refer later. The
    First Narrator sits in
    the easy chair, reading
    a book. He looks up, as
    we ZOOM IN on him.

FIRST NARRATOR
(ON CAMERA)

The ideal of freedom has
always caused men to defend
themselves and their way of
life against the aggressor.
If they were weak, they went
down before the power of the
aggressor in the battle for
survival.

12. SEVERAL ANGLES on FIRST
thru NARRATOR as he speaks.
14.
    (In the actual shooting
    the narrator was "dis-
    covered" standing before
    a practical fireplace.
    The Director moved him
    from the fireplace,
    first to a desk and then
    to a wall map, the
    camera dollying with the
    narrator as he moved
    about. The camera was
    also moved in and out on
    the narrator--Med.
    Close to Close or Close-
    up--according to the
    relative importance of
    the narration. The
    Close-up was used for
    greater emphasis. The

We find this grim reality
throughout history. We are
facing it again in our time.

One of the greatest deterring forces which gives the
aggressor pause is the combined military strength of
the United States. The
modern United States Army is
a potent part of that
military establishment;
strong--ready--alert. It
has not always been so.

The history of the Army's
buildup during the past
fifty years--from weakness
to a strong, modern fighting
force--is an epic story.
The story of a mighty armed
force organized and main-
tained NOT FOR CONQUEST, but

opening and closing of
each episode were con-
tinuous shots—no cuts
were used.)

for the defense—not only of
this nation, but of the
entire free world, and
dedicated to win the ultimate victory. Nothing like
it has occurred in all the
history of man.

15. MS, DOLLY along with
narrator as he moves to
stand by a large wall
map showing the United
States and the Atlantic
and Pacific Oceans to
graphically illustrate
the geographic isolation
of the United States.

For more than a century, the
United States was more or
less isolated from large-
scale participation in major
European and Asian wars by
the vast oceans to the east
and west of us. Most Americans thought the Atlantic and
the Pacific were our protection. We had a new and rich
continent to develop—a
mighty nation to build. We
did not wish to become embroiled in the quarrels of
remote and alien peoples.
We wished to prosper in
peace.

16. MCS, narrator, then
SLOWLY DOLLY OR ZOOM IN
to CU.

(Reference to the Span-
ish—American War and the
emergence of the United
States as a world power
does not appear in the
treatment.)

The Spanish—American War saw
the United States emerge as a
world power, but we still
took great comfort in our
relative isolation—and our
complacency grew, until a
leading role in world affairs
—for which we were ill prepared—was suddenly thrust
upon us, against our will and
desires. It actually began
in 1914 . . .

(The First, or Host,
Narrator is used to
"editorialize." Actor-
Narrator George P. Gunn
brought convincing au-
thority and dignity to
the role. The incisive
off scene voice of Leon-

ard Graves took over the
Second Narrator's job of
more straightforward re-
porting of events as
they occurred on the
screen. Mr. Graves'
style of delivery lent
an added note of excite-
ment to the action on
the screen. He will be
remembered for his nar-
ration of the classic
"VICTORY AT SEA" TV
series.)

17. SPECIAL EFFECTS: The
screen seems suddenly to
explode, to the crashing
accompaniment of German
martial music--"The
Watch on the Rhine."
From the explosion
emerges a good close
shot (live or still) of
the Kaiser with his
staff, reviewing his
troops.

SECOND NARRATOR (VO)

In Germany, Kaiser Wilhelm
and his Prussian militarists
had built up a massive army
as an instrument of conquest
to expand the German empire.

18. STOCK: MONTAGE of German military might on
the move: men marching
in formation, guns being
moved by horses. Army
Pictorial Center Li-
brary and National Ar-
chives.

In 1914, Europe, and more
specifically the Balkans were
a powder keg with a short
fuse, awaiting the spark.

19. SPECIAL EFFECT: Mock-up
of headline of the time:
"Archduke and wife slain
by Assassin."

(This reference to the
immediate cause of World
War I does not appear in
the treatment.)

The fuse was ignited on June
28th of that fateful year.
During a visit to Sarajevo,
the Archduke Ferdinand of
Austria and his wife were as-
sassinated by Serbian nation-
alists.

19A. STOCK--Newspaper head-   Thirty days later Austria de-
thru lines, and specific ef-   clared war on Serbia. Serbia
23.   fects pertinent to nar-   appealed to her ally Russia.
      ration.   Russia ordered full mobiliza-
                                   tion. Germany did likewise.
      STOCK: German forces on   On the first of August German
      the move in mass--either   troops moved on France--send-
      marching or on trains.   ing a twelve-hour ultimatum
      Artillery firing, infan-   to Belgium. England, having
      try advancing. Army   guaranteed Belgium's inde-
      Pictorial Center Li-   pendence, honored her commit-
      brary, Newsreels.   ment. World War One was on.

      STOCK: Mobilization in
      England, France and Rus-
      sia.

      STOCK: German artil-
      lery fire, infantry ad-
      vancing.

      STOCK: French forces in
      combat or moving up--
      French artillery firing.

24.   STOCK: Massive German   By the 5th of September 1914,
      troop movement.   the swift German advance
                                   threatened Paris.

25.   STOCK: Shots of the re-   Thousands of French rein-
      inforcement of the West-   forcements were rushed to the
      ern front. We see Paris   front. Even the taxicabs of
      taxicabs carrying troops   Paris were used in a desper-
      to the front.   ate effort to stem the tide.

26.   STOCK: French artillery
      firing.

27.   SPECIAL EFFECT: Insert
      of actual or mocked up
      headline: "FRENCH HOLD
      GERMANS AT MARNE."

28.   STOCK: American people   To most typically complacent
      of 1914, on the streets,   Americans it was just another
      at home, going about   of Europe's interminable
      their work or play.   quarrels.

29. STOCK: Army Pictorial Center Library or Archives, of one or more Americans of the period reading papers.

Something we read about in the newspapers.

30. STOCK: The White House as it looked in 1914, then of President Wilson at desk or making speech.

Our official position—strict neutrality. A policy proclaimed by President Woodrow Wilson.

31. STOCK: Archives footage showing some general scenes of garrison life and military training in the U.S. Army of that period.

The entire United States Army consisted of less than 100,000 officers and enlisted men. No single unit was larger than a regiment.

32. STOCK: Archives, or Navy Pictorial Center footage—1914 era, U.S. Navy ships in port or at sea. Shots of Marines. Shots of Army troops.

With Navy strength at 57,000 and the Marine Corps about 10,000 America's total active military establishment was less than 170,000 men—

32A. Action Shots of heavy
&B. combat in Europe.

—while millions were mobilized and fighting in Europe.

33. STOCK: Scene from Archives or newsreels showing General Leonard Wood,
            or
SPECIAL EFFECT: Zoom in on still photo of General Wood. (The latter was used in the actual production.)

Retired Army Chief of Staff General Leonard Wood said: (Simulated voice of General Wood) "I believe our state of unpreparedness to be more dangerous than ever in history, except perhaps during the darkest moments of the Civil War."

34. STOCK: Footage in which the following personalities are seen: General Hugh Scott—General Tasker Bliss—General Peyton March. Best stock source probably Ar-

A few other professional soldiers read the signs of danger which could jeopardize their nation's safety. Dedicated men, little known to the unmilitarily minded American public in time of peace.

chives. If no stock ex-
ists, we may again have
to rely on SPECIAL EF-
FECTS shooting with
still photos. (Here
too, due to lack of live
footage, still photos
were used.)

Generals Hugh Scott, Tasker
Bliss and Peyton March, who
served successively as Army
chiefs of staff from 1914
through our participation in
World War One.

35. STOCK: Footage of WW I
    officers conferring
    around a map or confer-
    ence table, or consult-
    ing in the field on ma-
    neuvers. Army Pictorial
    Center Library,
    Archives.

Our top military planners and
their staffs went to work,
planning for a war they
thought might come, and, if
it did, they wanted to be
ready for it.

36. STOCK: Shots of Woodrow
    Wilson and General Tas-
    ker Bliss.

But so strong was the na-
tion's sense of neutrality
that President Wilson thought
such planning violated the
spirit of our neutrality.
General Tasker Bliss finally
convinced the President that
it was a routine staff function—a precautionary defense
measure. In those days we
were indeed a naive and ado-
lescent nation.

37. STOCK: Combat and bat-
    tlefield dead. French
    or British ambulances,
    or field hospital or aid
    station. Army Pictorial
    Center Library or
    Archives.

Meanwhile, Europe's agony
continued. By the end of
1915, the Allies had suffered
one and a half million casualties.

38. STOCK: French and Brit-
    ish troops in combat
    with Germans. Troops on
    the move, heavy artil-
    lery fire. Archives for
    battle footage.

    SUPERIMPOSE "THE MARNE"

During the first three years
of the war, great and historic battles were fought—
the first battle of the
Marne . . .

39. STOCK: Russian troops in battle.

    SUPERIMPOSE the word "TANNENBERG"

. . . On the Eastern Front, the Battle of Tannenberg, where the Russians suffered a disastrous defeat from which they would never fully recover.

40. STOCK: From National Archives of WW I. Scenes of typical World War I trench warfare, with no-man's-land, massive attacks "over the top"--and the use of the machine gun playing an important part. Over this footage, in synch with the narrator's words, we will super-impose the names of other well-known bat-tles, rounding out the summary of the 1914-1917 period of war before the U.S. entered the con-flict.

    SUPERIMPOSE "VERDUN"

    SUPERIMPOSE "THE SOMME"

Soon the Western Front was confined largely to trench warfare. (Pause) Here the machine gun came into its own as a defense weapon of great firepower.

The fighting at Verdun raged on from July through Novem-ber. There was--the Somme: Bloody, and indecisive bat-tles. On land, a massive stalemate . . .

41. STOCK: Shots of German submarines in action: torpedoings and sink-ings.

. . . while at sea, German submarines took a heavy toll of Allied shipping to choke off food and other vital sup-plies bound for England and France.

42. STOCK: Newsreel or Ar-chives footage, torpedo wakes streak through the water, ships explode.

Unrestricted submarine war-fare slowly pushed the United States toward war. In May of 1916, an American tanker was torpedoed.

43. SPECIAL EFFECTS: ZOOM IN on headline announcing the sinking of the Lusitania.

A week later the liner Lusitania was torpedoed. Twelve hundred civilians lost their lives—139 of them Americans.

44. STOCK: German submarines at sea, more torpedoings.

The United States government made strong protests. The Germans agreed to restrict submarine activities. The agreement was not kept. Within months, unrestricted U-Boat warfare was resumed.

44A. STOCK shot of President Wilson at desk, or speaking.

President Wilson ordered diplomatic relations severed.

45. STOCK: Newsreel footage from the time, showing Germany's Foreign Minister Zimmerman. If Newsreels did not cover the Zimmerman revelation, and if no general shots of his exist in Archives footage, then

SPECIAL EFFECT: Still photo of Zimmerman, with headline about his proposed deal with Mexico.

SUPERIMPOSE MAP of Southwestern U.S. with New Mexico, Texas and Arizona heavily outlined.

Anti-German sentiment flamed high when it was discovered that Germany's Foreign Minister, Zimmerman, had made a secret proposal to Mexico: that Mexico declare war on the United States and help persuade Japan to do likewise. As a reward, Mexico would be given a fat slice of the United States—New Mexico, Texas, and Arizona. So sure was Germany of winning the war.

46. STOCK: Shots of Kaiser and Staff. Newsreels.

The German warlords were convinced that America had neither the disposition nor the capability to wage war effectively. Our military weakness gave comfort to the aggressor.

47. STOCK: President Wilson addressing the congress, together with SPECIAL EFFECTS SHOTS using headlines of the day and additional still photos, if needed.

But on April 6th, 1917, President Wilson asked the Congress for a declaration of war.

48. STOCK: Wilson as he sits at desk in the White House, either motion or still photography. SUPERED over this is the text of the excerpt from Wilson's message to Congress, which appears at right, or Wilson's voice can be simulated.

(Live stock footage was used.)

His message reflected the feeling of the nation, when he said, "We have no selfish ends to serve. We desire no conquest, no dominion. We enter this war only where we are clearly forced into it, because there are no other means of defending our rights."

49. STOCK: Newsreel and National Archives footage of the punitive expedition against Pancho Villa, led by General Pershing along the Mexican border. Army Pictorial Center Library has limited footage on this.

(The treatment carried no mention of this punitive expedition into Mexico.)

We had an army of only 200,000 men--65,000 were National Guardsmen commanded by General John J. Pershing pursuing Pancho Villa who had been raiding our towns along the Mexican border.

50. STOCK: Newsreel coverage, and news headlines about the draft: shots of numbers being drawn.

For the European War we would need to raise an Army of four million men--and quickly. For the second time in the nation's history, manpower was drafted.

51. STOCK: World War I draftees being sworn in, arriving at training camps, starting training. Army Pictorial Center Library, and Archives.

Those millions had to be housed, fed, clothed, trained, armed and equipped—and transported. A seemingly insurmountable task faced fewer than nine thousand regular army officers and an equally small hard core of non-commissioned officers. But they met the challenge and molded raw citizen-soldiers into a fighting force that was to win the victory.

52. STOCK: American industry: steel, munitions plants at work. Army Pictorial Center Library.

   DISSOLVE:

Such a massive military operation required all-out support by American industry. Industry's response was magnificent.

53. DELETED

   (Deletions made in first draft script)

54. STOCK: Impressive shots of large ships leaving New York loaded with troops, and of convoys at sea, Newsreels, Archives, Army Pictorial Center stock.

More than two million United States Army troops were convoyed to Europe through submarine-infested waters, without the loss of a single transport. The United States Navy was on the job.

55. STOCK: Loading of equipment on board ships —heavy gear requiring cranes to lift it aboard. If possible, horses, mules, etc., being loaded and/or unloaded.

   DISSOLVE:

We transported nearly eight million tons of war materials: two billion dollars worth of food—1800 locomotives—27,000 freight cars—423,000 tons of rails and fittings for French roadbeds —and nearly 69,000 horses and mules.

56. STOCK: AEF troops un-
     load in France, with
     their packs, rifles,
     full field gear.

The words of a popular song
of the day seemed just right:
"We're coming over. And we
won't come back, 'til it's
over, over there." (Pause)
It was a brave song, to ease
the grim realities--but it
promised the victory.

56A. Brief shots of French
      welcoming the Americans.

57. STOCK: Archives. Stock
     of Russian and German
     troops in combat in
     WW I. Then shots of
     German Forces on the
     move to the Western
     front and their advance
     in combat.

Late in 1917 Czarist Russia
collapsed--enabling Germany
to transfer a large part of
her fighting forces from the
Eastern to the Western Front
for large-scale offensive
drives that carried them to
within 37 miles of Paris.

58. STOCK: Americans on the
     move, on foot and in
     vehicles or trains, to-
     ward the front in
     France. Archives and
     Army Pictorial Center
     Library.

To stop the massive German
offensive, General Pershing
sent the United States' 3rd
Division to Chateau Thierry.
The 2nd Division was rushed
up to the line on the west,
to hold the road that led
from Chateau Thierry to
Paris.

59. STOCK: Stock scenes
     from the National Ar-
     chives. Germans attack,
     Americans fire, using
     machine guns, rifles.
     German charge falters,
     breaks. The Germans
     turn and retreat.

For three days, the Germans
threw all they had against
the Americans, but the American line held. Despite what
the German soldier had been
told--he soon discovered that
the American soldier was a
tough fighting man.

60. STOCK: American troops
     advance, firing, jumping
     in and out of shell cra-
     ters, advancing. Na-
     tional Archives footage.

A few days before, a regiment
of the 1st Division had attacked strongly fortified
German positions at Cantigny
--over-ran them--and beat off
all counterattacks. The

American citizen—soldier had
taken the measure of the
much—vaunted German military
man and found that the German
was not ten feet tall.

61. STOCK: Troops reach
German trenches, and go
into them, bayonets
fixed. National Ar-
chives.

DISSOLVE:

62. STOCK: American troops
continuing the advance.
Intercut shots of artil-
lery at work. National
Archives.

DISSOLVE:

63. STOCK: American troops,   The first major all—American
vehicles, pack animals   offensive began on the 12th
on the move, to match   of September, 1918, to reduce
narration. Army Picto-   one of three big salients on
rial Center Library,   the Western front at St. Mi-
Archives.   hiel on the Meuse River.

64. STOCK: Pershing in the   The American First Army was
field in France, with   assigned the task of removing
staff officers, or   the bulge in the Allied line.
inspecting troops. Army
Pictorial Center
Library, Archives.

65. STOCK: U.S. Troops mov-   More than half a million
ing on road, in large   American soldiers were massed
numbers. Army Pictorial   for the attack.
Center Library or Ar-
chives preferred.

66. STOCK: World War I type   The big push called for all—
aircraft taking off and   out air support——the greatest
in the air. (Army Pic-   concentration of airpower yet
torial Center Library)   seen in warfare. More than
                                 1,400 aircraft.

67. STOCK: American artillery fires.

3,000 pieces of artillery blasted the enemy. (Artillery firing plays for a moment)

68. STOCK: Either Archives or Army Pictorial Center. Shots of large numbers of German prisoners.

In two days, the salient was smashed—15,000 prisoners taken—more than 250 pieces of artillery captured. The Americans moved on swiftly into the Meuse—Argonne area . . .

DISSOLVE:

69. STOCK: American troops on the move, but now by rail instead of on foot. Artillery on flatcars. Archives footage.

. . . A large-scale troop movement involving critical timing and utmost secrecy. First Army's G-3, Colonel George Marshall, worked out the intricate plans. (See Note—Scene 70.)

70. STOCK: George C. Marshall as a Colonel, with AEF in Europe—or

SPECIAL EFFECT: ZOOM IN on still photo of Marshall as a Colonel in Europe.

(This reference to Marshall was deleted as it interrupted the flow of the more overpowering account of the progression of the battle.)

Colonel Marshall's staff work was recognized as among the most brilliant of the war. Years later he would become Army Chief of Staff in the greatest of all wars.

71. SPECIAL EFFECT: Map, on which the movement of the fighting line is depicted, in a series of dissolves from one position to another. SUPERIMPOSED, Close Shots of advancing doughboys.

Large numbers of American troops were quickly shifted to pound the German forces already weakened by massive casualties and lack of supplies.

DISSOLVE:

72. STOCK: Close shots of   Now four thousand guns
    Artillery being moved,   blasted the enemy.
    being loaded, being
    fired.

73. STOCK: Pilots getting   More than 800 Allied planes
    into WW I airplanes.   went into action—some 600 of
    Planes take off.   them piloted by Americans.

74. STOCK: Air—to—Air shots
    of fighter planes in dog
    fights, of WW I bombers
    in the air, then bombs
    dropping. Air Force Li-
    brary Archives.

75. STOCK: From the Ar-   During the Allies' power
    chives. Shots of the   drive, those first primitive
    unwieldy, lumbering   tanks proved mobile armor
    British tanks, and the   would play an essential part
    lighter, beetle—like   in any future warfare.
    French design, on the
    move in battle, crossing
    trenches, etc.

76. SPECIAL EFFECTS: Photo   A young United States Army
    of Patton, 1918, along-   Officer, commanding one of
    side a tank, if possi-   the first tank brigades, was
    ble. If not, just the   wounded in the Meuse—Argonne
    man himself. Start the   action and awarded the Dis-
    shot as far out as pos-   tinguished Service Cross for
    sible, and slowly ZOOM   bravery. He had found his
    IN on his face as far as   element—the tanker's tank—
    possible, over narration   George S. Patton, Jr. A
    at right.   quarter of a century later he
                                     was to have a meeting with
    (This scene with its   destiny.
    narration was deleted
    principally because it
    interrupted the flow of
    the more important ele-
    ment—the battle. As a
    result, adjustments were
    made in the narration
    during the final editing
    phase.)

77. STOCK: Montage of combat scenes, footage
which has visual punch,
conveys the passage of
time, and shows both
German and American
troops in action.

The Meuse–Argonne offensive,
begun on the 26th of September 1918, was one of the last
great offensive actions of
the war. By the 7th of November, American troops had
driven through three major
German defense lines. The
Kaiser's legions fought on
stubbornly, but their supply
lines broke down and they
were unable to replace mount-
ing casualties. They sued
for peace.

78. STOCK: The emptiness of
No–Man's–Land. A long
PAN across the pits and
craters and torn wire
and splintered stumps of
trees––or else a series
of cuts which show no
movement, no explosions,
no smoke.

(In the final film ver-
sion Freeze Frame was
used to indicate sudden
cessation of all combat
action.)

(FROM THE SOUND AND FURY OF
THE COMBAT MONTAGE, WE SUD-
DENLY GO––WITH AN ABRUPT CUT
OFF––TO QUIET BACKGROUND MU-
SIC TO MATCH THE MOOD OF THE
SCENE OVER WHICH THE NARRA-
TION:)
At 11 o'clock on the morning
of November 11th, 1918, the
firing in World War I ceased.

79. STOCK: Armistice celebrations, crowds, waving
flags, cheering, Army
Pictorial Center Li-
brary, or Newsreels.

The "War to End All Wars"
was over.

80. STOCK: Close shots and
angles of WW I soldiers
in victory parade march-
ing past camera. Army
Pictorial Center and Na-
tional Archives footage.

The American citizen–soldier
had fought in the proudest
tradition of his nation's
military history.

81. STOCK: Showing General
Pershing, 1918.

The leadership of General
John J. Pershing established

an inspiring high standard
for future commanders to follow.

82. STOCK: Shots of Persh-   World War I was an invaluable
    ing with young officers.   training ground for a small
                                group of young American Army
                                officers who, a quarter of a
                                century later, were to be-
                                come famous military leaders
                                in the greatest of all wars.

83. Deleted from first
thru draft.
93.

     DISSOLVE:

94. STOCK: Shots of Persh-   They had gained experience
    ing and young officers.   which would serve them and
    Officers being awarded   their nation well, in years
    decorations, etc.   to come.

95. STOCK: Shots of WW I   But in 1918, they, too, wel-
    troops parading up Fifth   comed the Armistice, and re-
    Avenue.   turned home with their bat-
                                tle-weary troops. Peace
                                would reign--for a time.

96. Photo of General Tasker   But two great soldiers
    Bliss, or live footage   sounded a warning of things
    preferred.   to come, which few heeded.
                                General Tasker Bliss pre-
    (Only a still photo was   dicted that war would come
    available.)   again within thirty years.

97. Photo of General Foch,   Marshal Foch said: "This is
    or live footage pre-   not peace. It is an Armi-
    ferred.   stice, for a twenty-year pe-
                                riod." They were prophets of
    (Good live footage was   remarkable insight. (Pause)
    available.)

97A. Symbolic stock footage   But we stacked our arms.
     of Americans stacking
     arms.

98. DELETED.

DISSOLVE:

99. STOCK: Newsreel or Ar-   The American people relaxed,
chives, showing the   pursuing the arts and pleas-
American people of the   ures of peace. Our large
1920s; relaxing at   wartime army had disinte-
beaches and parks, heavy   grated. It became a memory.
traffic on roads.

100. STOCK: Farmer in field.   The citizen—soldier returned
Army Pictorial Center   to his plow . . .
Library.

101. STOCK: Workers entering   . . . his factory . . .
factory. (Army Picto-
rial Center Library)

102. STOCK: Office worker,   . . . his business, his pro-
or executive behind   fession.
desk. (Army Pictorial
Center Library)

103. STOCK: Bright night   Again—it was "business as
lights of a big city of   usual."
the 'twenties. Archives
footage, or Hollywood
stock.

104. STOCK: (OR STILL PHO-   Our troops engaged in peace-
TOS) of troops in fa-   time garrison duties . . .
tigues in the 1920s do-
ing some type of busy
work: painting, picking
up paper, or perhaps
peeling potatoes on K.P.

105. STOCK: Small—unit ma-   . . . and an occasional
neuver or exercise of   training exercise.
the 1920s. Army Picto-
rial Center or National
Archives footage.

109. STOCK: West Point as it
appeared in the 1920s:

the buildings, and ca-
dets in the uniform of
that time.

110. STOCK: Dress parade on   The United States Military
the Plain at West Point,   Academy at West Point—from
spectators watching,   whose gray walls and Plain
their clothes typical of   have come a host of men who
the time. Archives.   have made monumental
                                  contributions not only in
                                  war, but in the pursuits of
                                  peace—

111. STOCK: of early West   —was just another educa-
Point Football team of   tional institution in the
the 1920s or early 1930s   public mind, whose football
in action.   team evoked the principal
                                  interest.

112
thru DELETED.
114

115. STOCK: Hollywood stock,   Yes, it was a time of Peace.
or Newsreels. Something   The military was not impor-
typical of the '20s—   tant in the general scheme
people dancing the   of things.
Charleston, or a flag-
pole sitter, or the
increasing number of
rumble-seaters on the
roads, mirroring the
slight postwar hys-
teria.

116. STOCK: of man (civil-   The nation fell back into
ian) of the time, in   its old ways of blessed
shirt sleeves, relaxing   isolation and complacency.
and reading the sports   (Note: The following three
page of the paper.   items of narration, sup-
Other shot of the con-   ported by action matching
temporary American scene   visuals, were added during
—street traffic—people   the editorial coordination
at play.   phase.) We pursued fun
(Theatrical stock foot-   instead. Those were the
age covering the   days of prohibition.
"Roaring Twenties" was   Speakeasies and bootleggers
discovered and used to   did a thriving business.

portray something of the
mood of post—World—War—
I America.)

There were those who sought
relief from the backwash of
the recent great war. There
was the marathon dance craze
——it was a strange sort of
endurance contest——a
phenomenon of the times.

117. SPECIAL EFFECTS: Still
shot of Adolph Hitler,
mustache untrimmed, in
his shabby years. At
the start of the shot,
the photo is in the
distant b.g., as if seen
at the far end of a
darkened tunnel.
Throughout the narra-
tion, the image moves
toward us, increasing in
size. German music
(Goetterdaemmerung
Theme) fades in faintly,
and grows slowly in
volume; harsh and
militant.
At this point, the
slowly advancing photo
is almost FULL SCREEN.
Now it is suddenly torn
asunder to reveal a
dramatic head CU of
Hitler in full uniform
and at the height of his
power. As narrator
speaks his name, MUSIC
comes to crashing
crescendo.

ZOOM IN to ECU of
Hitler's eyes and their
intense hypnotic stare.

FREEZE FRAME.

FADE OUT:

FADE IN:

While in faraway Germany
there was a shabby little
man who had been a corporal
in the German Army. In his
brooding, twisted mind was a
hate and a growing Satanic
obsession. He dreamed of
many strange things——but
there was one thing he never
dreamed of——that one day he
would be the underlying
cause of activating the
mightiest United States Army
in history—— His name was
. . .

. . . Adolph Hitler!

(SOUND: VERY LOUD CHORUS OF
SEIG HEILS COME IN TO DROWN
OUT THE MUSIC WHICH FADES
UNDER.)

118. INT. STUDY--MS of First Narrator standing by library desk. Hold on MS for first part of this speech, then DOLLY IN SLOWLY to CS.

You have just seen the INTRODUCTION to a special documentary series of Big Pictures--presenting high-lights of the history of the United States Army from World War I to the cold war years of the 1960s . . . portraying the far-reaching events during fifty years which carried a nation from isolationist complacency to immense global responsibili-ties and commitments, in a struggle to defend its own good way of life and that of the Free World as well.

119. CLOSE UP of the First Narrator.

Only a strong, modern United States Army with the capa-bility and the will to fight and win the final victory can fulfill its role in meeting those great respon-sibilities and commitments in the preservation of those freedoms to which we--as our forefathers before us--have pledged our lives and our fortunes.

FADE OUT:

ARMY IN ACTION

EPISODE II
"THE THREE FACES OF EVIL" (TV 635)

FADE IN:

1. SPECIAL EFFECTS (Drawing No. 1)
A TIGHT CLOSE SHOT OF the helmeted head of a brutal Roman soldier, modeled after the familiar image of Mars, the God of War, shown in a stylized drawing. CAMERA immediately begins DOLLYING BACK to disclose the object of his brutality; a frail-bodied shepherd youth only half the soldier's size. The shepherd is armed only with a traditional shepherd's crook, while the soldier carries a heavy short sword and shield.

FIRST NARRATOR (VO)

Aggressive men bent upon conquest have always overwhelmed the weaker peoples they would conquer, plunder, and enslave by their superior strength and force of arms.

2. (Drawing No. 1)
TIGHT CLOSE SHOT of shepherd's terrified face.

MATCH DISSOLVE TO:

3. (Drawing No. 2)
TIGHT CLOSE SHOT of shepherd's face. His former fearful expression has changed to one of grim determination and self-confidence. CAMERA PANS to face of helmeted soldier and we

Yet the defender's will to fight has always given the aggressor pause.

227

see that <u>his</u> expression has changed to a mixture of dismay and fear.

CAMERA DOLLIES BACK to reveal that the soldier is backing away from the shepherd, who now stands taller than the other, has dropped his shepherd's crook to the ground and holds instead an English longbow with arrow ready to let fly.

Time and again, the will to resist, together with equal or superior weapons, has driven the aggressor back . . . has vanquished him. The answer to the sword and spear, to the primitive bow and arrow, was the deadly English longbow . . .

4. (Drawing No. 3)
FULL SHOT of a helmeted early Spanish soldier firing his harquebus from a forked rest at enemies seen fleeing in the far background.

. . . just as the advent of gunpowder and the first primitive firearms sounded a thunderous end to the era of the longbow.

5. (Drawing No. 3)
TIGHT CLOSE SHOT of the barrel of the Spanish harquebus.

MATCH-DISSOLVE TO:

6. (Drawing No. 4)
TIGHT CLOSE SHOT of bar-rel of World War I ma-chine gun. CAMERA DOLLIES BACK to reveal that it is a machine gun and that it is being fired by two WWI Ameri-can soldiers from an en-trenched position. Four or five German soldiers are seen falling in background.

The machine gun came into its own as a weapon of deadly firepower in World War I. That same war saw two other new and potent weapons make their first appearance in combat . . .

7. (Drawing No. 5)
FULL SHOT of World War I French or British tank

. . . the tank, first designed to break the stale-mate of trench warfare . . .

advancing on battle-
field. It appears to
be under heavy fire
from the trench it is
approaching, but is
obviously impervious.

8. (Drawing No. 6)   . . . and the airplane that
    TIGHT CLOSE SHOT of WWI   carried the war into the air
    airplane with U.S. in-   and, through bombing and
    signia. PULL BACK--   strafing, created confusion
    and we see that it is   behind enemy lines. The
    engaged in mortal com-   plane was to revolutionize
    bat with a German   warfare and, in so doing,
    Fokker.   change the world and the
                                lives of men.
    CAMERA DOLLIES BACK
    still farther and we see
    an entire battle scene.
    The sky is filled with
    dueling aircraft, while
    below on the battle-
    field, American troops
    are going over the top
    to advance to the attack
    with several primitive
    tanks leading the way.
    Shells are exploding.

    FADE OUT:

 9.
thru Deleted.
13.

    FADE IN:

    MAIN TITLE: "THE BIG PICTURE"

    DISSOLVE TO:

    SERIES TITLE: "ARMY IN ACTION"
                    EPISODE II

    DISSOLVE TO:

    EPISODE TITLE: "THE THREE FACES OF EVIL"

    FADE OUT:

    FADE IN:

14. STOCK: Polish and Russian troops of WW I era in combat, if possible, otherwise moving toward the front with mules, wagons, etc. (Screen direction should be watched in these scenes. If Polish troops are moving generally from screen left, the Russian troops should be moving from screen right. The same consideration applies to the scenes which follow.)

SECOND NARRATOR (VO)

Less than two years after World War I—the end of the "war to end all wars"— Poland, backed by France, attacked Soviet Russia and tiny Lithuania to reclaim ancient boundaries.

15. STOCK: A CUTTING MONTAGE of French, Belgian, Greek, Italian, Czech, Polish and Roumanian troops (WWI) era in combat as suggested by the Narration. (Note: Since it is extremely unlikely that appropriate footage can be found for all these events, Newspaper headlines of the times will be intercut with the combat scenes. The purpose is a brief, fast-moving montage conveying the chaotic series of "little wars" which prevailed at the time.)

Roumania invaded Hungary and occupied Budapest . . . Czechoslovakia clashed with Poland in a border dispute . . . Greece and Italy attacked Turkey . . . Belgium and France, over British protests, occupied the German Ruhr.

DISSOLVE TO:

16. STOCK: LONG SHOT—Riots in Bologna, Italy, in May 1922 as Fascists battle Communists in the streets.

A far-flung series of seemingly unrelated events was beginning to weave a web that eventually would enmesh nearly all mankind.

17. STOCK: (or Special Insert), FULL SHOT of newspaper headline reading in effect, "Fascists seize Milan." (This would be a newspaper dated May 3, 4, or 5, 1922.)

18. STOCK: LONG SHOT-- Americans walking along a busy street (circa 1922).

As far as most Americans were concerned, those small wars and foreign political turmoils were far from our ocean-guarded shores--remote from the American way of life . . .

19. STOCK: FULL OR MEDIUM CLOSE SHOT of a news- stand or newsboy as pedestrians pause to buy papers.

20. STOCK: FULL OR CLOSE SHOT of pedestrian scanning front page of his newspaper.

. . . Something to read about in the newspapers.

21. STOCK: CLOSE SHOT-- Front page of a news- paper (1922) with a headline dealing with some international military or Fascist- Communist crisis. Ex- ample: "ITALIAN TROOPS OCCUPY FIUME AFTER FASCIST COUP."

22. STOCK: MEDIUM OR LONG SHOT of circa 1922 pedestrian as he glances at headline, puts paper under arm and continues down busy street.

22A. STOCK: LONG OR MEDIUM   The old maxim, "The price of
     SHOT of circa 1922   freedom——and peace——is
     Americans enjoying   eternal vigilance," was for-
     themselves at a dance,   gotten in the roaring
     football game, etc.   twenties.

     DISSOLVE TO:

23. STOCK: ESTABLISHING   During the years immediately
     SHOT——German General   following World War I, the
     Staff officers of the   chauvinistic Prussian mind,
     immediate post—World—   stunned and humiliated by
     War—I period, possibly   defeat, began planning for
     including Von   the next war. The German
     Hindenburg.   militarists planned ex-
                                 ceedingly well. They would
                                 become masters of the
                                 blitzkrieg——lightning war.
                                 All they awaited was a
                                 political leader and the
                                 coming of the next war.

24. STOCK: INTERCUTS OF
     CLOSE of post—World—
     War—I German officers.

     (Actual footage of
     post—World—War—I Ger-
     man civilian type of
     "Homeguard" was shown
     in training.)

     SLOW DISSOLVE TO:

25. STOCK: ESTABLISHING
     SHOT Fascist street   (MUSIC: UP FULL DURING RIOT
     demonstrations (newsreel   SCENES.)
     footage) in Italy in
     1922. These demonstra-
     tions occurred as fol-
     lows:
     a) Fiume, March 3.
     b) Bologna, entire month
        of May.
     c) Milan, August 3—4.

26. STOCK: INTERCUTS OF
     CLOSE ANGLES on Fascist

rioting in the Italian
cities mentioned above.

27. STOCK: Mussolini at
thru Fascist Congress in
28. Naples, Oct. 24, 1922.
INTERCUT CU of
Mussolini.

Nineteen twenty-two--the
bombastic newspaper editor
with a gladiator's jaw led
his blackshirted legions in
a march on Rome: a bold,
Fascist thrust for power.

29. STOCK: WIDE ANGLE--
Fascist march on Rome,
October 28, 1922.

30. STOCK: Shots of
Mussolini stirring up
Fascist mobs, waving his
fist, tilting his head
to display the famous
jaw to best advantage.

Benito Mussolini was a flamboyant reincarnation of the
Caesar-god image. He made
good copy for the inter-
national press. (Slight
Pause) He ordered large
doses of castor oil forced
down the throats of those
who disagreed with him.

31. STOCK: Nazi mob in
Munich streets, circa
1923. (No authentic
footage of the November
1923 Beer Hall Putsch,
but any mob scenes oc-
curring in Germany not
later than, say, 1924
will serve here.)

A maniac of ferocious
genius, as Winston Churchill
was later to describe him,
led a beer-hall putsch in
Munich and was thrown in
jail.

32. STOCK: CLOSE OR MEDIUM
CLOSE SHOT of Hitler in
1920s. Close insert of
Mein Kampf.

While in prison, he wrote a
book--Mein Kampf--which told
the world exactly what he
planned to do.

33. STOCK: MEDIUM SHOT--
American of 1920s read-
ing a newspaper.

34. INSERT SHOT--Newspaper
with date line obscured
and the following head-
line: "POLITICAL STRIFE
IN MUNICH."

Adolph Hitler was merely a
rabble-rousing part of the
political turmoil in Germany
--that we read about in the
newspapers.

34A. STOCK of Munich riots.

DISSOLVE TO:

35. INSERT SHOT--Another newspaper front page, this one dated September 19, 1931. The headline reads: "JAPS INVADE MANCHURIA."

September 1931--an explosion on the Japanese-operated South Manchurian Railroad resulted in the invasion and occupation of Manchuria by a Japanese army.

36. STOCK: MEDIUM OR MEDIUM CLOSE SHOT of an American, circa 1930, scanning newspapers laid out on a newsstand.

It was a faraway Asian event --that we read about in the newspapers.

DISSOLVE TO:

37. STOCK: Japanese troops landing at Shanghai on January 28, 1932.

January 1932--Japan invaded the International Settlement at Shanghai.

38. STOCK: Japanese troops in International Settlement of Shanghai. (If possible, a shot of U.S. Consulate with U.S. flag.)

DISSOLVE TO:

39. STOCK: Von Hindenburg and Hitler at time of Hitler's ascension to the Chancellorship. (January 30, 1933)

January 1933--Adolph Hitler became Chancellor of Germany, sharing power with the aging President, Von Hindenburg.

DISSOLVE TO:

40. STOCK: BRIEF SHOT of Von Hindenburg's funeral procession.

August 1934--President Von Hindenburg died . . .

41. STOCK: Hitler addressing a huge crowd (circa 1934) after his ascension to complete power.

. . . Hitler became absolute ruler of Germany. Now he could do what he had spelled out in _Mein Kampf_ for all to

see. In substance, it was:
"Today, Germany; tomorrow,
the world!"

42. STOCK: Mass Nazi rally
with crowd rhythmically
raising arms in "Seig
Heil" salute.

DISSOLVE TO:

(SOUND EFFECTS: Crowd
voices giving the notorious
Nazi "Seig Heil" salute,
over and over again.)

43. STOCK: Italian aircraft
making bombing-strafing
attacks in Ethiopia.

October 1935--Mussolini's
Fascist Army invaded and
conquered Ethiopia in seven
months, using the weapons of
modern warfare against a
people who still fought with
spears and primitive firearms.

44. STOCK: Italian troops
with steel helmets,
etc., moving to the
attack.

45. STOCK: Ethiopian troops
and tribesmen with
spears and ancient
rifles. Include shot of
Haile Selassie and his
wild tribal chieftains
in war-like demonstra-
tion.

DISSOLVE TO:

46. STOCK: German troops
moving into the Rhine-
land in 1936.

SECOND NARRATOR

March 1936--Hitler, in
defiance of the Versailles
Treaty which, only 17 years
earlier, had ended World War
I, sent troops to occupy the
Rhineland. Amazingly, the
French did not resist.
Ironically, the German
troops had secret orders to
withdraw--if the French
Army did resist.

47. STOCK: Hitler (circa
1935) with other members
of German Government.
Their demeanor is
serious.

48. STOCK: Combat footage   July 1936--the Spanish Civil
    from Spanish Civil War.   War became a proving ground
                                   for Nazi Germany, Fascist
                                   Italy, and Soviet Russia--
                                   they furnished men and
                                   weapons to the opposing fac-
                                   tions.

49. STOCK: INTERCUT CLOSE
    SHOTS of typical
    protagonist in Civil
    War. If possible, the
    last of these Intercuts
    should show a Spanish
    insurgent in the turret
    of a German-made tank.

50. STOCK: TWO SHOT--Hitler   October 1936--the Rome-
    and Mussolini in con-   Berlin Axis was formed. An
    versation, circa 1936.   unholy alliance of aggres-
                                   sors consolidating their
                                   forces for greater con-
                                   quests.

51. STOCK: CLOSE UP of
    Mussolini.

52. STOCK: CLOSE UP of
    Hitler.

53. STOCK: SHOTS of the   December 1937--the Japanese
    PANAY bombing, close   invaders of China bombarded
    shots wounded U.S. Navy   and sank the United States
    men, Army Pictorial   gunboat "PANAY" on patrol in
    Center and National   the Yangtze River.
    Archives.

54. STOCK: TWO SHOT--Secre-   We protested angrily. The
    tary of State Cordell   Japanese apologized. The
    Hull and Jap diplomat,   apology was accepted.
    circa 1937.

55. STOCK: CUTTING MONTAGE   World events were beginning
    SHOWING: to move with ever-increasing
    a) Hitler reviewing Ger-   momentum toward a cataclysm
       man troops,   of blood. The point of no
                                   return was fast approaching.

b) Mussolini reviewing
   Fascist troops,
c) Japanese soldiers
   herding a long line
   of beaten Chinese
   prisoners, circa
   1937.

56. STOCK: SHOT of an
American reading a news-
paper--preferably in
some tranquil setting
such as a park bench.

While the aggressors were
either building up their
armed might and working toward war--or were actually
at war--we Americans read
all about it in our news-
papers . . .

57. STOCK: A family--
mother, father, children
--gathered around a
1937-style radio.

. . . heard all about it
over our radios . . .

58. STOCK: 1930s movie
audience watching a
newsreel of the period.

. . . watched the violence
and the carnage in the newsreels, in the safety and
comfort of our movie
theatres.

59. STOCK: LONG SHOT--
breakers rolling in from
the Atlantic from screen
Right to Left.

It was all so far away from
the shores of our great protective oceans--the Atlantic
on the east . . .

60. STOCK: LONG SHOT--
waves rolling in on
Pacific beach, from
screen Left to Right.

. . . and the Pacific to the
West.

(Note: Scene direction
is specified in the
above two scenes to keep
the viewer oriented.
Think of the motion pic-
ture screen as you would
a map. The top of a
map, as you look at it,
is always to the north
with east to the right
and west to the left.

Under this orientation
the waves of the Atlan-
tic would naturally roll
in from screen right.
The Pacific waves would
roll in from screen
left. It is a good and
important orientation
device that the author
has used for years in
maintaining proper
screen direction.)

61. STOCK: SHOT of a fac-   Besides, we had our own
    tory gate with sign,   troubles. The United States
    reading "CLOSED" or "NO   was in the grip of a para-
    HIRING."   lyzing depression.

62. STOCK: MEDIUM SHOT—Men   Millions were unemployed—on
    on depression bread   some form of relief.
    line.

63. STOCK: A dust-bowl   A great drought had des-
    farmstead with dust cov-   troyed hundreds of thousands
    ering fence post, piled   of acres of farmlands on the
    up against buildings,   Great Plains, creating an
    etc. A farmer is seen   arid dust bowl. Thousands
    gazing at the desola-   of families were impover-
    tion.   ished—made homeless. It was
                                   a tragic time of domestic
                                   travail affecting millions of
                                   Americans.

64. STOCK: SHOTS of line of
    old cars piled with
    household belongings
    during "Okie" migration
    to California.

65. STOCK: CLOSE SHOT—
    Okie family jammed into
    an old tin-lizzie
    filled with mattresses,
    kitchen utensils, etc.

66. STOCK: MEDIUM SHOT of   The Federal Government had
    President Roosevelt   taken emergency measures to

addressing Congress,   meet the growing internal
circa 1937.   crisis.

67. STOCK: FULL SHOT iden-   Among the many relief
tifying sign on building agencies it established was
or camp entrance. It   the Civilian Conservation
reads: "Civilian Con-   Corps . . . The CCC . . .
servation Corps."

68. STOCK: CUTTING MONTAGE   . . . it provided work and
of young CCC workers   training for unemployed
planting trees, digging   young men in a program of
ditches, etc. Archives. conservation of the coun-
                          try's natural resources of
                          timber, soil, and water—in
                          reforestation and soil
                          erosion control.

69. STOCK: An Army officer   The United States Army was
addressing a group of   given the responsibility of
CCC youths in camp.   operating and administering
                          1,600 CCC camps with 300,000
70. STOCK: CLOSE SHOT—   enrollees throughout the
the officer.   continental United States,
                          Alaska, Hawaii, Puerto Rico,
71. STOCK: REVERSE ANGLE— and the Virgin Islands.
the boys in audience.

72. STOCK: An interior,   Educational facilities were
classroom scene with CCC provided from elementary
youths at desks.   through high school, as well
                          as college courses.

73. STOCK: TWO or THREE   Each camp was commanded by
SHOTS of officers in CCC an Army officer, usually a
camp office gathered   captain with two lieuten-
around desk or table, as ants, one as Adjutant and
though in planning ses-   the other as Supply and Mess
sion.   Officer.

74. STOCK: SHOTS of Army   It was invaluable experience
officers with CCC youth, in leadership for Army
as available. Scenes   officers. Military law and
should FEATURE the Army   discipline did not apply to
officers.   the CCC camps. To gain
                          respect and authority, young
                          officers had to learn to

rely on the personal characteristics of leadership.
More than 4,500 regular and
reserve Army officers on
active duty were engaged in
this work during the years
preceding our entry into
World War II.

75. STOCK: A high ranking   While this goodly percentage
    U.S. Army officer, with   of our officer corps was
    members of his staff,   engaged in the peacetime
    inspecting a CCC instal- pursuits of making democracy
    lation.   work at home . . .

    DISSOLVE TO:

76. STOCK: Combat scenes   . . . the officers in the
    from Ethiopia, FEATURING aggressors' armies were
    Italian officers.   being trained, conditioned,
                              and blooded to combat tough-
                              ness by the brutal war in
                              Ethiopia . . .

77. STOCK: Combat footage   . . . as military advisors
    from Spanish Civil War   and so-called "volunteer"
    FEATURING German or   participants in the vi-
    Italian Officers.   ciously fought Spanish Civil
                              War . . .

78. STOCK: SHOTS of massed   . . . and in Japan's war of
    Japanese troops of Sino- conquest in China. (Slight
    Japanese War period. A   Pause) While the aggressors
    Jap battle flag appears   were flexing their mighty
    in shots.   muscles . . .

79. STOCK: U.S. troops,   . . . our Army could muster
    circa 1937, in close   only 180,000 officers and
    order drill on parade   enlisted men, including the
    ground.   Army Air Corps. And they
                              were far from combat read-
                              iness.

80. STOCK: CLOSER ANGLE--
    Drilling troops, em-
    phasizing their anti-
    quated weapons and
    uniforms.

81. STOCK: Sailors—circa 1937—lined up at rail of battleship. (Wearing whites.)

The Navy had less than 114,000 men.

82. STOCK: Marines, circa 1937, in training situation.

. . . The Marine Corps, 18,000. A total defense establishment of a little more than 300,000 men.

83. STOCK: Hitler entering Vienna in his armored Mercedes, March 14, 1938.

The aggressor nations continued their march of conquest. In 1938 Nazi Germany seized Austria in a lightning-like coup.

84. STOCK: Chamberlain and other delegates signing Munich agreement.

85. STOCK: CLOSE SHOT of Hitler as he signs Munich agreement.

At a parley in Munich, in a desperate bid for peace, Britain, France, Italy and Germany agreed to the dismemberment of democratic Czechoslovakia. Hitler got the spoils without firing a shot.

86. STOCK: Mussolini and massed Italian black-shirts.

Nineteen thirty-eight was a year of triumph for the ever stronger and more belligerent aggressors.

87. STOCK: German Brown Shirts raiding a Jewish shop.

Drunk with power and blood lust, the Nazis turned upon a large segment of their own German citizens, perpetrating their greatest abomination—

88. STOCK: German-Jewish civilians as they are herded into trucks or RR cars.

89. NEWSREEL SHOTS of Nazi riding a Jew through the streets in a cart—a classic shot from "Why We Fight."

German Jews were herded into concentration camps. A mass "fine" of 400,000,000 dollars was imposed, holding them collectively responsible for the assassination of one German diplomat.

90. STOCK: SHOTS of prison-   The concentration camps were
    ers in concentration   a brutal prelude to a
    camp. Army Pictorial   ghastly program of mass
    Center, National   extermination.
    Archives.

91. STOCK: LONG SHOT--Hit-   Now the greatest of the
    ler addressing a Nurn-   aggressors had brazenly come
    berg rally, seen over   forth in full view of the
    the helmeted heads of   world to reveal not only his
    troops.   evil purpose and design, but
                                 the abysmal depths of his
92. STOCK: Hitler in Nazi   ruthless character as well.
    uniform addressing
    rally.

93. STOCK: SHOTS of Cham-   At Munich, Britain believed
    berlain at airport after   she had "gained peace in our
    return from Munich as he   time."
    makes famous "peace in
    our time" statement.

94. STOCK: LONG SHOT of row   France sat behind her
    of pillboxes in pre-war   Maginot Line, confident of
    Maginot Line.   its impregnability.

95. STOCK: CUTTING MONTAGE   The United States reacted
    of Army, Navy and Marine   feebly to the threatening
    personnel from im-   holocaust-- While our mili-
    mediate pre-World-War-II   tary planners were con-
    period. (Training   sidering defense measures
    scenes rather than   which involved mobilization
    formal reviews)   of the National Guard and
                                 the reserves for a total
                                 defense force of about a
                                 million men, actual regular
                                 army strength was increased
                                 by only 5,300 men. The
                                 Navy added 5,400 and the
                                 Marine Corps--the combat-
                                 ready shock troops--in-
                                 creased their strength by a
                                 pitiful handful--133 men.
                                 We were little better off
                                 than in 1917, and the flames
                                 of an even greater con-
                                 flagration were already

licking at our feet. We had yet to learn the lessons of history.

96. STOCK: SHOTS of Hitler and Goering.

97. STOCK: Tojo and high-ranking Japanese officers, if possible, in conference situation.

The aggressors drew their own logical conclusions: the United States was an isolationist nation——a nation struggling to recover from the grip of a great depression . . . 19% of . . .

98. STOCK: TWO SHOT——Hitler and Mussolini, their heads together in serious conference.

its work force unemployed in that year of 1938 . . . a total defense force——Army, Navy and Marine——of less than 320,000 . . .

99. STOCK: CUTTING MONTAGE of Army training activities, circa 1938. All scenes should emphasize the scarcity of equipment.

It was the false and fatal economy of unpreparedness—— the age-old invitation to an aggressor.

100. STOCK: SHOT——General George Marshall in official meeting, if possible _before_ he became Chief of Staff.

But through those years of the gathering storm, United States military leadership remained alert to the defense and security of their country.

101. STILL PHOTOS of old War Department Building, the Army War College and Command and General Staff School, in synch with narration.

102. STOCK: High-ranking officers in pre-WW II uniforms gathered around a table, or at a wall map.

WIPE TO:

At the War Department, the War College and the Command and General Staff School, our dedicated military planners studied the implications of the fast moving events. _They_ were not deaf to the triumphant shouts of the arrogant aggressors.
M U S I C (A thunderous drum roll and clash of cymbals)

103. STOCK: LONG SHOT--
Hitler with massed Nazi
troops.

LIVE SOUND
(massed chorus)

Seig Heil! . . Seig Heil!
. . Seig Heil!

104. STOCK: LONG SHOT--
MUSSOLINI on balcony,
arm raised in Fascist
salute as crowd chants
the standard "Duce!
. . Duce! . . Duce! . ."

LIVE SOUND
(massed chorus)

Duce! . . Duce! . . Duce!

105. STOCK: Japanese troops.
Rising Sun flag in back-
ground, as they raise
their weapons in Banzai
salute.

LIVE SOUND
(massed chorus)

Banzai! . . Banzai! . .
Banzai!

FADE OUT:

FADE IN:

106. INT. STUDY--DAY--MEDIUM
thru CLOSE--First Narrator,
108. standing beside his
library table.

FIRST NARRATOR

A frightening display of
ruthless power and evil purpose by the Nazi, Fascist
and Japanese militaristic
bully boys. Time was running out fast for the Free
World. Human liberty was in
deadly peril. (Slight
Pause)

CAMERA DOLLIES IN TO
CLOSER ANGLE

You have just seen the
Second Episode in a special
documentary series of Big
Pictures--presenting highlights of the history of the
United States Army from
World War I to the years of
the Cold War, a history
which has been dictated by
the far-reaching events
which have carried this
nation from isolationist
complacency to immense

(In the actual shooting the director gave the camera more movement than is indicated in the script.)

global responsibilities and commitments in a titanic struggle to defend its own way of life and that of the rest of the Free World as well. We know now that military weakness is an invitation for the aggressor to attack, and in the light of that great lesson—that we have finally had to learn the hard way, at tragic cost in blood, lives and re-sources—we have good cause to wonder if World War II with all its carnage would have happened, if the free nations had remained mili-tarily strong—if the Armed Forces of the United States had at that time been as strong and as ready as they are today.

CLOSE UP—FIRST NARRATOR

FADE OUT:

It is a good and significant question.

<u>ARMY</u> <u>IN</u> <u>ACTION</u>

EPISODE III
"FLAMES ON THE HORIZON" (TV 636)

FADE IN:

1. STOCK SHOT——a city
   in flames——large belch-
   ing fires, with <u>no</u> fire-
   fighting equipment
   showing.

2. STOCK: A major forest
   fire.

   <u>FIRST</u> <u>NARRATOR</u> (VO)
   Fire is a destroyer of lives
   and property and precious
   natural resources.

3. STOCK: A dramatic LONG
   SHOT of a once-healthy
   forest, now completely
   burnt out, a desolate,
   smouldering, and flat-
   tened wasteland.

4. STOCK——BRIEF CUTS of
thru artillery fire——cap-
7. tured <u>enemy</u> <u>footage</u>.
   Nazi and Japanese.
   CLOSE-UPS of guns fir-
   ing. Gun crews reload-
   ing and firing. Buildings of Chinese city in
   flames as result of
   bombing in WW II.

   War, when launched by a
   pyromaniac aggressor bent
   upon conquest and the sub-
   jugation of peoples, can be
   a still greater destroyer.

8. STOCK: LONG SHOT to
   parallel Scene 3, only
   now we are looking at
   devastated ruins created
   by artillery fire and
   aerial bombings from WW
   II stock.

9. Scenes of Nazi troops thru collecting a large num- 10. ber of European civilian prisoners, marching them off toward vehicles or prison camp.	War can destroy the freedom and liberties of free men, if they are not sufficiently manned, armed, and equipped to halt the spreading flames and beat them out.
11. STOCK: A raging forest thru fire, with men in fore- 12. ground starting up a backfire.	Fire is used to fight fire. "Back-firing," it's called.
13. STOCK SHOTS of American thru artillerymen quickly 14. moving their weapon into firing position. An effect of quick re- sponse to enemy aggres- sion. Action ends, after narration, with a dramatic firing of the gun, seen in CLOSEUP.	In war, armed force must be met by armed force. There is no other choice for free men who would remain free.
15. Scenes of European ci- thru vilians being herded 19. into a German concentra- tion camp, with emphasis on the anguish and fu- tility on the drawn faces of the prisoners.	Personal property lost in a fire can be replaced. Free- dom and personal liberty, once crushed under the ag- gressor's ruthless heel, may never be regained.

FADE OUT:

FADE IN:

MAIN TITLE: "THE BIG PICTURE"

DISSOLVE TO:

SERIES TITLE: <u>ARMY</u> <u>IN</u> <u>ACTION</u>
               EPISODE III

DISSOLVE TO:

EPISODE TITLE: "FLAMES ON THE HORIZON"

FADE OUT:

FADE IN:

20. INT. STUDY—MEDIUM SHOT FIRST NARRATOR: (ON CAMERA)
    Host narrator, speaking.
    He stands near a picture   A modern military force is
    of George Washington in   as vital to the safety of
    characteristic pose.   the nation as are modern
                                fire departments for the
                                protection of our towns and
                                great cities. But we, as a
                                peace-loving nation, have
                                been slow to learn that
                                lesson . . .

21. INSERT PICTURE OF GEORGE   . . . to follow the admoni-
    WASHINGTON.   tion by George Washington in
                                1790, in his first annual
                                address to Congress. "To be
                                prepared for war," he said,
                                "is one of the most effec-
                                tual means of preserving
                                the Peace."

22. MEDIUM CLOSE SHOT of   Soon after World War One and
    narrator.   the demobilization of our
                               armed forces, we quickly
                               fell back into our old com-
                               fortable ways of isolation
                               and complacency. Any les-
                               sons we might have learned
                               from the "war to end all
                               wars"—the war that was
                               waged to "make the world
                               safe for Democracy"—were
                               soon forgotten, as was the
                               great truth that the price
                               of freedom is eternal
                               vigilance. Even then, it
                               was later than we knew or
                               cared to admit.

23. SPECIAL EFFECTS SHOT   SOUND EFFECTS: The crash of
thru still on narrator, as   harsh brassy music: This is
24. screen explodes into   followed by appropriate ef-
    raging flames. The nar-   fects of flames bursting
    rator is "flamed out" as   forth, in synch with accom-
    we see the numerals,   panying visuals. At end of
    1939, ZOOM UP FAST from   scenes, flame EFFECTS blend

infinity, filling
screen. (May have this
in stock.)

DISSOLVE:

25. Stock newsreel coverage
thru of Sino-Japanese War,
27. with flaming buildings
everywhere in evidence.
MOVIETONE 20/74.

28. STOCK similar to that of
thru Scenes 25-27, now featur-
29. ing war orphan scenes,
from newsreel coverage
in MOVIETONE 21/1
(Hankow).

30. STOCK of Hitler's entry
thru into Prague—cut to
32. crowd—then a LONG SHOT
of Hitler speaking at
podium. MOVIETONE 21/3-
21/4, 5/21/57.

33. STOCK establishing
thru scenes of Danzig seaport
34. —MOVIETONE 21/101
(Danzig).

DISSOLVE:

35. STOCK of Nazis MOVING
thru INTO POLAND, beginning
41. CLOSE ON armor moving
forward. MONTAGE of the
most spectacular scenes,
heavy artillery firing,
one big gun or battery
after another, and air
strikes—to be selected
from STOCK MOVIETONE
21/103; 22/4; 22/6; ADC
1196; MID 6158; MID
6209.

into similar effects of Sino-
Japanese War scenes.

SECOND NARRATOR:

1939, and the fires of war in
China were still raging.

Half a world away, Czechoslovakia, dismembered by the
Munich Pact, fell to Hitler
without a battle.

Hitler demanded that Poland
surrender the Baltic seaport
of Danzig with its strategic
corridor to the sea—a prize
lost by Germany in 1920 at
the signing of the Treaty of
Versailles. Poland did not
yield.

SECOND NARRATOR:

September 1st, 1939—in defiance of British and French
warnings, the Nazis, after
making a secret non-aggres-
sion pact with Russia, invaded and conquered Poland,
with their smashing blitz-
krieg tactics.

42. STOCK: Dramatic shots thru of the Fall of Warsaw, 44. with Nazi legions moving into the city. MID 6209, Army Pictorial Center.	The fiery curtain to Act One of World War Two was raised.
45. STOCK representing Brit- thru ish and French declara- 46. tions of war on Germany --brief scenes of deter- mined British and French diplomats. Dramatic shots of British and French mobilization-- military activities of the time.	Britain and France declared war. (BRIEF PAUSE) The die was cast. Now British Prime Minister Chamberlain knew there would be no peace "in our time."
47. STOCK GROUP SHOTS of thru U.S. officials deliber- 48. ating over neutrality papers. MOVIETONE 22/12.	The United States proclaimed its neutrality, just as it had at the beginning of World War One. Three thousand miles of Atlantic Ocean, it seemed, were still an ample safeguard for the immediate defense of our nation.
49. STOCK of German and Rus- thru sian officials at the 50. negotiating table, with quick cut to Russian forces moving into Fin- land.	In a cynical agreement, Ger- many and Russia had parti- tioned conquered Poland. (BRIEF PAUSE) Soon, Russia attacked little Finland.
51. STOCK of the Sino–Japa- thru nese War, from OF–6, 53. BATTLE OF CHINA: MOVIETONE 20/74.	In China, the two Asian gi- ants continued their struggle to the death.
54. STOCK newsreel scenes of thru the World's Fair in 1939 59. at New York. MOVIETONE 21/67. We begin with establish- ing scenes of Pres. Roosevelt opening the Fair, then we cut to	With the rest of the world exploding into violent war, the New York World's Fair opened serenely to throngs of

most dramatic, but brief scenes of Fair.

peaceful and pleasure-loving Americans.

60. STOCK MONTAGE showing
thru Americans reading pa-
63. pers, listening to radio newscasts; we cut to movie house, for brief shot of people watching newsreel—we hear background effects of Movietone report about the war in Europe.

The wars in Europe and Asia were still far away. We read about the battles in the papers, heard about them over the radio, and watched some of the destruction and carnage in the newsreels.

64. STOCK: A squad or platoon of U.S. soldiers, circa 1939, as they march on a parade field, with cuts to small group undergoing small weapons firing at a training center. Action ends with a CLOSEUP of soldier firing a rifle. There should be an almost complacent effect to the action here—no sense of urgency. MOVIETONE 22/1; 22/11 as well as other film at Army Pictorial Center.

The strength of our regular Army was less than one hundred ninety thousand—for the protection of one hundred thirty million people of a great nation in a time of growing peril.

SOUND EFFECTS: Match sound of weapon firing in preceding scene with popgun firing in Scene 65.

65. STOCK CLOSEUP of happy
thru American civilian at
69. World's Fair (or similar 1939 affair), as he takes aim and fires popgun at moving targets of carnival-type stand. Cuts to targets being hit and missed, face shots of the proud and satisfied "marksman." We follow with brief cuts of Fairgoer popping grotesque balloon, another is seen pounding

Again, as at the beginning of World War One, we had proclaimed our traditional neutrality.

the "Strong Man" mallet
down against the gong-
inducing device. Most
of action here plays si-
lent except for effects.
MOVIETONE 21/57 and ad-
ditional footage.

70. STOCK action of young   We danced the Jitterbug.
    Americans dancing. OF-
    FICIAL 8357, 8482.

71. STOCK of '39 World's   Millions of Americans were
    Series, featuring Joe   more interested in Joe Di-
    DiMaggio home run. At   Maggio and the New York Yan-
    end of sequence, we see   kees taking four straight
    mass shot of the sta-   from Cincinnati in the
    dium crowd responding   World's Series, than they
    to home run: gigantic   were in the deadly games be-
    roar.   ing played in Europe and
                                 Asia, where aggressors were
                                 "out to take all."

    WIPE TO:

72. STOCK of Nazis en masse,   SOUND EFFECTS: Baseball au-
    shrieking, "SEIG HEIL!"   dience cheers cross-matched
    SCPC, OF-1.   with the fanatical chorus of
                                 Nazi forces seig-heiling
                                 their leader.

73. STOCK of massed Fascists   SOUND EFFECTS: Fascists in
    in Italy, shrieking,   Italy,
      "VIVA IL DUCE!"   "VIVA IL DUCE!"

74. STOCK scene of massed   SOUND EFFECTS: Massed Japa-
    Japanese troops,   nese shouting,
      "BANZAI!"   "BANZAI!"

75. Captured enemy footage.   In the grim international
thru German and Japanese   game of war, the aggressor
78. troops in the attack.   teams were pitching and run-
    CAMERA featuring foot-   ning the bases in what then
    troops scurrying along,   looked like a shutout.
    as a parallel to run-
    ning-the-bases in Scene
    71. A shot of a pitcher
    as he throws the ball.

MATCH DISSOLVE to a German soldier throwing a hand grenade.

The effect of a rapid advance of the conquering dictators; one shot of troops running matched with another and still another of movement across Europe and Asia.

But the World's Series in *that* big league had yet to be played.

79. CUTTING MONTAGE of shots of that period, identifying . . .

Gen. MacArthur

Three years before, General Douglas MacArthur had retired from active duty to become military advisor to the Philippines.

80. Shot Gen. Eisenhower.

Dwight D. Eisenhower, then a field grade officer, was a member of MacArthur's staff.

81. Shot Gen. Marshall.

By coincidence, General George C. Marshall was appointed Acting Chief of Staff the same day the Nazis invaded Poland.

82. Shot Gen. Bradley.

Omar N. Bradley was a member of the War Department's General Staff.

83. Shot Gen. McNair.

Lesley J. McNair was a colonel, Executive Officer in the office of the Chief of Field Artillery.

84. Shot Gen. Somervell.

General Brehon Somervell was head of the depression-born Works Progress Administration in New York City.

85. Shot Gen. Arnold.

It would be another year before General Henry "Hap" Arnold would become Deputy Chief of Staff of the Army Air Corps.

86. Shot <u>Gen. Eichelberger</u>.   Robert L. Eichelberger was
                                        still a colonel, commanding
                                        the 30th Infantry at the Pre-
                                        sidio of San Francisco.

87. Shot <u>Gen. Patton</u>.   George S. Patton, Jr., a
                                        colonel then, was Post Com-
                                        mander of Fort Meyer in
                                        Virginia.

88. Shot <u>Gen. Mark Clark</u>.   Mark Clark was a member of
                                        the staff of the 3rd Divi-
                                        sion at Fort Lewis, Washing-
                                        ton.

89. Shot <u>Gen. Krueger</u>.   General Walter Krueger com-
                                        manded the 2nd Division at
                                        Fort Sam Houston, Texas.

90. Shot <u>Gen. Hodges</u>.   Courtney Hodges was then a
                                        colonel, Assistant Com-
                                        mandant of the Infantry
                                        School at Fort Benning.

91. Shot <u>Gen. Patch</u>.   Alexander M. Patch was serv-
                                        ing as a Lieutenant Colonel
                                        on the Infantry Board at
                                        Fort Benning.

92.
thru DELETED.
93.

94. STOCK sequence of Pres.   Their Commander-in-Chief,
thru Roosevelt's Embargo   the President of the United
97. Speech.   States, took the first step
     <u>NOTE</u>: May have to   that was to make America the
     precede this with brief   "Arsenal of Democracy." In
     scenes of Congressional   November, 1939, Roosevelt
     action on the Embargo   signed a bill removing the
     legislation, as well as   Arms Embargo Act. Now we
     bill-signing of the   could supply the implements
     President. <u>MOVIETONE</u>   of war to England and France
     <u>22/17</u>.   on a cash-and-carry basis.

98. STOCK of the early war thru effort, especially that 102. of items to be sent to Britain and France, assembly line motion. OWI Footage, Archives Short Subjects.

Full-scale Lend Lease was still in the future, but our neutrality was starting to crack. The wheels of our industrial complex were beginning to turn. The slumbering, complacent giant among nations was awakening.

103. STOCK of the beginnings thru of our military buildup. 107. We see U.S. soldiers alertly on guard in Puerto Rico, MOVIETONE 22/15.

Slowly we began to increase our military manpower. The Army was authorized to recruit some 83,000 men . . .

Shot of Marine Ground Forces.

The Marine Corps 10,000 . . .

Mass SHOTS of our armed forces, Army Day, 1940. MOVIETONE 22/61. Featuring Naval Units.

. . . the Navy 42,000. But our combined military establishment was still less than half a million men—hardly a token force in light of world events. Only a small handful of our forces was adequately equipped and partially trained for combat.

108. SPECIAL EFFECTS SHOT. thru Nazi troops invading 110. Denmark, entering Norway. The numerals "1940" zoom up full frame from infinity. Numerals hold briefly then FADE OUT as action of invasion continues. MOVIETONE 22/62.

In the spring of 1940, the Nazi war machine rolled into Denmark—and into Norway.

111. Cutting Montage—Most thru dynamic scenes to be 122. selected . . .

Holland was brutally crushed.

—Heavy bombing of Holland. MOVIETONE 22/71.

--Est. Shot, Nazis into
Belgium, MOVIETONE
22/71, 22/73, 22/74.

In one deadly swoop, the
Nazis over-ran Belgium . . .

--Nazis into Luxembourg,
MOVIETONE 22/71.

. . . Luxembourg . . .

--Nazis into France,
Captured enemy footage,
Army Pictorial Center.

. . . and smashed across the
French frontier.

--CLOSE ON Nazis fighting
in Belgium. MOVIETONE
22/71 plus other footage
at Army Pictorial Center.

It was blitzkrieg--lightning
war. The aggressors struck
with massive airpower . . .

--Heavy German bombing
in Holland and other
countries. MOVIETONE
22/71, other Army
Pictorial Center foot-
age.

--Dramatic STOCK of Ger-
man armor moving forward
in attack, MOVIETONE
22/68, other Army Pic-
torial Center footage.

. . . with armor--with
mobile artillery. (PAUSE)
Strike fast, strike hard
with overwhelming, ruthless
force!

--Captured enemy film,.
German artillery fire
with cuts to cities
being torn apart by Nazi
guns and bombs.

Destroy entire cities,
reduce them to ashes and
rubble, along with the
charred bones of their in-
ferior civilian population!
Show no mercy! Destory the
will to fight! Show them the
hopelessness of resistance.
Those were Hitler's orders.

123. STOCK of Hitler in one
of his most violent
harangues.

124. STOCK of British and
thru French troops fighting
126. against the Germans in
France.

The British rushed in what
combat-ready troops they
had, to try to help the
French stem the German tidal
wave that was sweeping the
Continent.

127. STOCK of Sir Winston
thru Churchill, touring
130. Thames. Action ends
with him giving a
"thumbs-up" sign,
MOVIETONE 23/9.

In Britain Winston
Churchill, an indomitable
man of the century—born
of an English father and an
American mother—took over
the reins of government.

SOUND EFFECTS: Sir Winston
Churchill's
voice comes
up full.

SIR WINSTON CHURCHILL (VOICE
OVER)

"I have nothing to offer but
blood, toil, tears and
sweat!"

131. STOCK of Pres. Roosevelt's defense speech,
1940, using voice-over
narration here, but
changing to voice-over
FDR speech in following
scenes.

In America, another great
leader put before Congress
and the Nation the urgent need
for one billion eight hundred
million dollars, and fifty
thousand aircraft for de-
fense.

132. NEW SHOOTING
thru
137. MEDIUM GROUP SHOTS of
families and other small
groups listening to FDR
speech, via the Nation's
radios. We hear the
speech voice-over. We
see concerned faces—the
effect of a nation
waking up. We see
people seated around
radio sets, at the
kitchen table, the gen-
eral store, the barber
shop. We see a boy of
21 in one of the family
settings (to be used
later as the "Why Me?"
boy). As he and his
family listen to the

PRES. ROOSEVELT (VOICE-OVER)

"The brutal force of modern
offensive war has been
loosed in all its horror.
New powers of destruction,
incredibly swift and deadly,
have been developed; and
those who wield them are
ruthless and daring. No old
defense is so strong that it
requires no further
strengthening and no attack
is so unlikely or impossible
that it may be ignored . . .

radio speech, mother
registers silent concern
for the boy. Perhaps we
also see a young child,
on a living room floor,
playing with a toy tank
or soldiers, as we hear
the President's words.

138. STOCK LONG SHOTS of thru the most dramatic action 140. of evacuation at Dunkerque, <u>MOVIETONE</u> <u>22/78</u>.	<u>SECOND NARRATOR</u>: The French Army was fast disintegrating. British forces were saved from annihilation or capture by their miraculous evacuation at Dunkirk.
141. STOCK of Mussolini's declaration of war on France & Britain.	Italy declared war against France and Britain.
142. STOCK of German troops thru entering Paris--CAMERA 143. featuring LONG SHOT of Nazi columns marching by the Arc de Triomphe. STOCK SHOTS of French troops moving toward the south of France and evacuation to North Africa.	Paris, undefended, fell like a ripe plum into the Nazi basket of conquest. What remained of the French Army retreated to Mediterranean ports for evacuation to North Africa to live to fight another day and help win the victory.
144. thru DELETED. 145.	
146. STOCK of German and thru French officials signing 147. an armistice, emphasis on Hitler, who was at Compiegne at the time. <u>SCPC, ADC 1735-36</u>. SPECIAL EFFECTS: As narrator says "England!" the screen seems to ex-	Hitler signed an armistice with France and became mas- ter of all western Europe. He could now concentrate on the destruction of his greatest adversary--England!

plode to match bomb
explosion as it hits.

148. STOCK of the most dev-
thru astating German bomb-
150. ings of England. Plays
without narration, only
effects.

Actually a continuation
of the action in #148–
150, now with effects
under narration. More
now on British anti-
aircraft firing—the
effect of a country
fighting for her life.
For scenes #148–154,
MOVIETONE 22/101,
22/103, 23/1, 23/3, 23/8.

Only Britain, fighting for
her life, and the Atlantic
Ocean, stood between the
United States and what was
then the most powerful conquering armed force the
world had ever known.

151
thru DELETED.
154

DISSOLVE:

155. STOCK: Roosevelt at
thru desk. Shots of National
157. Guard response to the
mobilization order.
Boarding trains, etc.

On the First of September,
1940, in response to the
growing peril, President
Roosevelt called up 60,000
National Guardsmen from 26
States for one year's service.

158. STOCK establishing
thru scenes of U.S. Congress,
159. OFFICIAL 9894. Action
centers on the signing
of the Selective Service
Bill.

In the same month—for the
third time in its history—
Congress enacted a Selective
Service Bill.

160. STOCK: Last film refer-
thru ence refers to climax
165. scenes of men registering for the draft—pref-
erably shots showing
long lines of men.
OFFICIAL 9894 MOVIETONE
23/4.

Sixteen million Americans
registered for the draft.

166. STUDIO SHOTS—CLOSEUP of
thru the familiar sign of
167. Uncle Sam pointing his
     finger at "You."

MEDIUM SHOT of the young
man of 21, established
in scene #137. He re-   There were some who asked,
acts to the Uncle Sam   "Why me?" But the majority
poster, pointing to   knew why . . .
himself as his lips form
the words, "WHY ME?"

168. More representative   . . . and—despite any inner
thru STOCK scenes of men emotional conflicts—they
171. registering for the   responded in the same spirit
     draft.   as had their forefathers.
                         They knew that the gutty men
                         who made and preserved this
                         nation never asked, "Why
                         me?"

172. STOCK LONG SHOTS of long These were men who could
thru lines of inductees being look anyone in the eye and
176. supplied with uniforms,   say, "I'm proud to be an
     others out on drill   American and to serve my
     fields attempting to   country in its time of
     march in a proper mili-   need."
     tary manner. OFFICIAL
     C—34, 35.

177. MONTAGE, to be selected From the cities, the towns,
thru from STOCK—best scenes   the villages, the farms, the
182. depicting the procession plains and the mountains
     of inductees from every   they came—citizens from
     corner of the nation,   every walk of life, who
     to the training camps.   would soon prove themselves
                             to be soldiers in the finest
                             traditions of the American
                             Fighting Man.

183. BRIEF CUTS of large-   Within a year our Army grew
thru scale troops movements. to a million five hundred
186. OFFICIAL C—100, 256,   thousand men. It would con-
     659, other feature foot- tinue to grow to a peak
     age.   strength of eight million.

187. STOCK of the most rigor-
thru ous training in 1940--
191. men under barbed wire,
with machine guns firing
close overhead--bayonet
training--road march,
airborne style--weapon
firing. OFFICIAL C-100,
256, 659.

They had to be trained to
combat hardness, if they
were to meet and destroy an
enemy already toughened and
blooded by combat.

192. STOCK: SHOTS of the
thru then most up-to-date
195. Army weapons--armor in
action--fighting planes
in action--mortars
firing--artillery.
OF-7, SCPC, additional
Army Pictorial Center
STOCK. (This from shots
of training only.)

A new and mighty Army was
being forged along new lines
to meet the challenge of
improved enemy weapons--new
tactics--new stratagems.

196. STOCK GROUP SHOT with
General Marshall fea-
tured among other high-
ranking officers, in a
tactical area if pos-
sible, THE GEORGE
MARSHALL STORY, from BIG
PICTURE.

At last our top military
leaders were being given the
wherewithal to implement
plans they had made for the
defense of America--under
direction of George C.
Marshall, Army Chief of
Staff.

(Following scenes to be
either live or stills,
vintage 1940, 41 or 42.
But do not mix stills
with live footage--must
be one or the other.)

197. Gen. McNair

General Lesley McNair was
charged with directing the
gigantic training program.

198. Gen. Somervell

General Somervell was ap-
pointed Assistant Chief of
Staff in charge of Supply.
His was to be a superhuman
task.

199. <u>Gen. Eisenhower</u>	Soon Dwight D. Eisenhower was to have a "meeting with Destiny."
200. <u>Gen. Arnold</u>	General Hap Arnold, Deputy Chief of Staff of the Army Air Corps, stepped up the training of much-needed pilots.
201. DELETED.	
202. CUTTING MONTAGE selected thru from STOCK showing am- 207. munition, weapons, etc., coming off the assembly lines. OF-7, SCPC, other STOCK. The most dramatically <u>moving</u> <u>shots</u> we have with an overall effect of the supplies of war moving steadily to military users.	America was rising up out of the rut of her apathy. She was beginning to understand the hard fact that she was an integral part of the world—a world that suddenly had become one of violence and brutality—one in which America would have to fight to the death if she were to survive.
208. STOCK night scenes in thru Britain, as Nazi planes 212. fly over—framed in anti-aircraft spot- lights. We see de- struction of towns, Coventry in ruins, the noble defenses of the British anti-aircraft crews, the RAF counter- force chasing a Nazi plane out of the sky.	While we were marshaling our resources, England was being given the blood bath Hitler had promised.
213. A continuation of pre- thru ceding sequence, again 215. showing the bombings and the countering anti-air- craft firing. Scenes play without narration, only effects. For Scenes #208-215 <u>BRITISH</u> <u>INFORMATION SERVICE</u>	SOUND EFFECTS: Night bomb- ing and anti-aircraft counterfire.

FILM, "TARGET FOR TO-
NIGHT."

DISSOLVE:

216. STOCK SHOT--family at   Americans knew what would
     radio, very serious as   happen to the United States
     news of Britain's plight   if Britain fell. Our re-
     is reported.   sponse to the desperate plea
                                     for help came late, but not
                                     too late, in 1940.

217. STOCK of Pres. Roose-   PRES. ROOSEVELT: (ON
thru velt's "Arsenal of   CAMERA)
219. Democracy" speech.

                              (NOTE: That portion of the
                                     Aid-to-Britain
                                     speech in which the
                                     President calls for
                                     "all aid to Britain
                                     short of war." Also
                                     that portion in
                                     which he refers to
                                     the U.S. as Arsenal
                                     of Democracy.)

220. STOCK to establish   SECOND NARRATOR:
thru British-Italian fighting
221. in North Africa--an   In North Africa, British
      Italian push in clear   forces were fighting an
      evidence. SCPC "THE   Italian drive upon Egypt.
      BIG PICTURE" TITLE:
      BATTLE OF NORTH AFRICA,
      PT 1."

222. STOCK. Est. Shots of   Nazi and Fascist troops
thru Germans driving into   smashed into the Balkans--
224. Greece--motorized move-   into Greece--1940 was a
     ment to give the feel of   black year for what was left
     a still very pronounced   of the free world.
     enemy attack. SCPC, MID
     6147 OFFICIAL C-102.
     Will be effective to show
     prominent historical
     landmark in Greece, as
     Nazis pass.

225. CUTTING MONTAGE from
thru STOCK, showing the
227. three-axis onslaught,
      LONG SHOT of Nazi troops
      in a mass tactical
      formation, OF-2 "THE
      NAZI STRIKE."

      LONG SHOT of Italian
      forces fighting en
      masse, SCPC, OF-1

      LONG SHOT, Japanese
      forces fighting en
      masse against China.
      OF-10, "KNOW YOUR
      ENEMY: JAPAN."

1941 was to be an even
blacker year during which
the aggressors attacked the
only two remaining major
powers not yet at war,
Russia and the United
States. For the aggressors
it was to be the world or
nothing.

228. STOCK scenes quickly and
thru dynamically depicting
231. the Nazi attack on
      Russia.

      Nazi artillery fire,
      SCPC, OF-5.

      Nazi armor moving for-
      ward on the Russian
      front, SCPC, OF-5.

      Nazi infantry crossing
      rugged terrain, firing,
      SCPC, OF-5.

      Nazi fighter planes
      swooping down on Russian
      lines, SCPC, OF-5.

In June, 1941, Hitler suddenly unleashed his forces
against Soviet Russia.

SOUND EFFECTS: Up full.

232. STOCK representing
thru Russian withdrawal, an
234. artillery piece slowly
      turning and making its
      way homeward; troops
      scurrying to the rear; a
      tank raking in one side,
      moving off in new direc-
      tion; at least one
      dramatic scene of
      smoldering scorched
      earth, flames still

Sorely wounded, the Russian
bear retreated--falling back
before the onrushing Nazi
legions.

visible, as the with-
drawal continues.

235. LONG SHOT of the Statue
of Liberty. Perhaps new
shooting will be neces-
sary if present stock
shots are considered
inadequate.

There was only one major
power in the free world to
go--the militarily weak
United States. Now she
stood alone, but how long
could she stand?

236. STOCK: LONG SHOTS--
thru Japanese mass demon-
237. strations, an atmosphere
of hate. Shots of
Japanese staff officers,
Jap carriers at sea.

The Asian Axis partner
thought she had an answer
to that, one that would complete the aggressors' pattern
for conquest of the entire
world.

238. Scenic LONG SHOTS of
thru peaceful Oahu in early
240. morning.

It was a quiet Sunday morning in Hawaii. A newly
risen sun shone on beautiful
Oahu. It was symbolic.
(Pause) It was the last time
we were to be caught napping
by a Rising Sun!

241. EXTREME LONG SHOTS, from
thru STOCK, BRIEF CUTS of
246. Japanese planes in
formation coming in high
over the Pali, bound for
Pearl Harbor. The
insignia on one of the
wings, the Rising Sun.
The bombing attack on
Pearl Harbor begins. No
narration, only effects.
As bombs begin falling,
we . . .

SOUND EFFECTS: Plane engine
hum builds as planes come
nearer.

SOUND EFFECTS: Bombing attack on Pearl Harbor begins.

247. SUPERIMPOSE, faintly, a
CLOSE UP of the flag of
the Rising Sun, which
ripples from a breeze.
The image of the bomb-
ings fades until the
flag, now rippling fills
the screen momentarily.

SOUND EFFECTS: Bombing,
anti-aircraft fire, machine
gun fire with a disjointed
background chorus of tri-
umphant "BANZAI'S!"--as flag
becomes clear on screen,
sounds intensify.

Then suddenly the center
of the flag—the Rising
Sun—burns away, and we
see . . .

248. The most dramatic STOCK   The surprise attack was a
     LONG SHOT of the ruins   staggering blow to our Navy
     of Pearl Harbor im-   at Pearl Harbor.
     mediately after the at-
     tack.

     NOTE: Film source for
            scenes #241-249
            U.S. NAVY FILM
            "DECEMBER 7TH"
            for Pearl Harbor
            action.

249. For the Rising Sun
     insignia on plane wing,
     TF 1-3302, SCPC,
     "RECOGNITION OF JAP ZERO
     FIGHTER."

250.
thru DELETED.
253.

     DISSOLVE:

254. STOCK of the President's   PRES. ROOSEVELT: (ON
thru Declaration of War   CAMERA)
256. speech, in which he   (Essential content as noted
     refers to the "day that   in screen description.)
     shall live in infamy."
     OFFICIAL C-1515.

257. BRIEF CUTS of "last   Soon—the fall of Bataan and
thru stand" fighting during   the never-to-be-forgotten
260. the fall of Bataan,   Death March of thousands of
     climaxed with the most   American and Filipino
     startling LONG SHOT of   troops. Many would never
     the Bataan Death March,   reach the prison 65 miles
     SCPC, OF-10.   away. Hundreds met death
                                       along the way.

261. DELETED.

     DISSOLVE:

262. INT—STUDY—DAY—MED.
     SHOT of host narrator.

<u>FIRST NARRATOR: (ON CAMERA)</u>
                (QUIETLY)

A terrible price to pay for
unpreparedness, for com—
placency, for apathy—for
the military weakness that
invited the aggressor to
attack. (Pause briefly in

DOLLY INTO CLOSE SHOT.ˑ   reflection) Does anything
                          more need to be said?

SLOW FADE OUT
                          <u>NO MUSIC</u>
END

ARMY IN ACTION

EPISODE XIII
"THE FINEST TRADITION" (TV 646)

FADE IN: FADE IN MUSIC:

1. STOCK--Series of warmly
   beautiful shots in which
   there is no evidence of
   man or his works.

2. CS--Deer: perhaps a doe MUSIC FULL
   and fawn grazing peace-
   fully.

3. ELS--Wild grass rippling MUSIC CONTINUES
   in the wind.

4. MS--A beaver gnawing a
   tree or swimming toward
   his dam, busily pushing
   a good-sized piece of
   wood ahead of him.   MUSIC BEGINS TO FADE UNDER

5. HIGH LS--A dense forest   FIRST NARRATOR (VO)
   of first-growth timber.   (Speaking SLOWLY AND
                                      QUIETLY)

                              This was the raw land . . .

6. LS--Verdant, wild   a wilderness . . . a virgin
   shrubbery.   land of rich soil . . .

7. LOW ANGLE--A vast, high   . . . great forests . . .
   stand of virgin timber.

8. FS--A powerful water-   . . . mighty rivers.
   fall.

8-A. FS--River with an immense flight of water-
   fowl rising toward the
   skies.

   DISSOLVE TO:

268

9. LS—Vast prairie land   . . . vast plains and end-
   with buffalo grazing   less, fertile prairies . . .
   peacefully.

   DISSOLVE TO:

10. FS—Rocky Mountains, the   . . . towering mountains
    most impressive shots   that had stood in silent
    obtainable.   majesty for long centuries
                                 . . .

11. LS—Snow and glaciers,   . . . as if they were giant
    a very majestic view.   guardians holding in trust a
                                 land in which a new idea was
                                 to be conceived and ex-
                                 pressed.

    DISSOLVE TO:

12. STOCK—Theatrical foot-
    age, early scenes of
    pioneer life in New
    York, Pennsylvania or
    Kentucky.

13. MS—Several men clearing   . . . the proposition that
    the land—cutting trees   all men are created equal
    or removing rocks.   and have an inherent right
                                 to govern themselves . . .

14. CS—Pioneer plowing a   . . . and to pursue happi-
    field.   ness in an atmosphere of
                                 liberty and freedom . . .

15. Early settlers building
    a log cabin.

16. CS—One of the men   . . . the ultimate dream of
    building the cabin   free men of good will and
    pauses to wipe the sweat   men who would be free
    away, then goes back to   everywhere. But first, the
    work.   great human dream had to be
                                 conceived . . .

    DISSOLVE TO:

17. STOCK—Theatrical foot-
    age of the conflicts of
    the American Revolution.

18. LS—Minute men of 1775   . . . born in the travail of
    in conflict with the   violent conflict . . .
    British Redcoats.

19. MS—Minute Man firing   . . . between the forces of
    his rifle.   those seeking freedom . . .

20. Redcoat wounded by a   . . . and the oppressive
    rifle ball, falling to   forces of tyranny . . .
    the ground.

    DISSOLVE TO:

21. A meeting of the Found-   . . . then given life and
    ing Fathers.   expression by the wisdom of
                                 those men who wrote the
    SUPERIMPOSE: The Decla-   Declaration of Independence
    ration of Independence.   . . .

22. Another Angle—The
    Founding Fathers.

23. ELS—Constitutional
    Convention.

24. DISSOLVE IN: The Con-   . . . the Constitution of
    stitution of the United   the United States . . .
    States.

25. DISSOLVE IN: The Bill   . . . and the Bill of Rights
    of Rights.   . . .

    DISSOLVE TO:

26. STOCK—Theatrical battle
    scenes of Civil War.

27. MS—Union Cavalry   . . . and further con-
    charge.   secrated by their sons . . .

    DISSOLVE TO:

28. World War I Infantry   . . . and grandsons to save
    charge.   those same principles and
                                 ideals—
    DISSOLVE TO:

29. World War II Armored   Otherwise the great American
    Units moving up and   dream could never have been
    firing.   perpetuated as a reality.

    DISSOLVE TO:

30. INT. STUDIO--DAY:
    Series of MED. CLOSE
    SHOTS of individual
    American soldiers from
    different periods of
    American history--all
    bearing arms.

    (Same as in last se-
    quence of this same
    episode)

31. MCS--A member of Rogers'   The tradition of the Ameri-
    Rangers, wearing buck-   can fighting man began when
    skin. Dolly with   men in buckskin first fought
    soldiers.   to protect the Colonies in
                               the French and Indian Wars
                               some 200 years ago . . .

32. CS--Minute Man.   . . . later, the Minute Man
                               at Lexington and Concord
                               . . .

33. CS--A Continental   . . . the Continental
    soldier, under arms.   soldier . . .

34. CS--A soldier of 1812.   . . . the soldier in the
                               War of 1812 . . .

35. CS--A Union soldier.   . . . the Union soldier
                               . . .

36. CS--World War I Infantry   . . . the World War I
    soldier.   doughboy . . .

37. An American Infantry   . . . GI Joe in World War
    soldier of World War II   II . . .
    under arms.

38. CLOSE ANGLE on soldier   . . . and the Korean War
    in combat in the Korean   soldier . . .
    War.

    DISSOLVE TO:

39. INT BARRACKS DAY MS--   . . . the citizen-soldier
    Modern soldier of voting   who served no aggressive
    age marking a ballot,   dictator or oppressive

then folds the ballot   police state, but his free
carefully.   country and the ideals for
                               which it stood . . .

40. INT BARRACKS DAY CS--The   . . . the citizen-soldier
    soldier inserts his   who, by his right to vote
    ballot in an envelope,   . . .
    licks it to seal the
    envelope and puts it
    down.

41. INT BARRACKS DAY ECU--   . . . could even choose his
    The sealed envelope. We   own Commander-in-Chief.
    can see the words,
    "Absentee Ballot."

    FADE OUT.

    FADE IN:

    MAIN TITLE: "THE BIG PICTURE"

    DISSOLVE TO:

    SERIES TITLE: ARMY IN ACTION
                    EPISODE XIII

    EPISODE TITLE: "THE FINEST TRADITION"

    FADE OUT.

    FADE IN:

42. INT. STUDY.   CLOSE   FIRST NARRATOR:
thru ANGLE on First Narrator.
48.   The very title of citizen-
                                 soldier is symbolic of the
                                 country which he has been
                                 called up to defend . . .

                                 . . . for history shows that
                                 the United States of America
                                 never has been by nature, by
                                 free choice, or in practice,
                                 militaristically minded.

(As noted in comment in   In 1775, the original
First Episode, no cuts   Thirteen Colonies had no
were used in the actual   ready military strength of
shooting--the Camera   their own with which to
DOLLIED with the Narra-   fight for their freedom.

tor as he moved about
the set.)

They had to acquire a
strength slowly. It took
them six long years of
fighting to win the Re-
volutionary War.

MOVE IN TO CLOSE UP

In the War of 1812, we were
too weak militarily to pre-
vent invading British forces
from burning the White
House.

In the Civil War, many of
our foremost military men
were Southerners who went
over to fight for the Con-
federacy. It took the
North years to train and
equip the Army that finally
won the war.

MOVE BACK TO WIDER ANGLE
AS NARRATOR GETS TO FEET
TO STAND BY DESK FOR A
MOMENT.

Upon our entry into World
War I in 1917, our regular
Army stood at 130,000. It
took us a year to hastily
raise a citizen-soldier Army
of four million.

. . . and just as hastily to
train, arm, equip, and
transport two of those four
million men as quickly as
possible to the aid of our
exhausted and desperate
Allies in Europe.

NARRATOR moves to corner
of desk and sits on its
edge.

We and our Allies won that
war of conquest that had
been launched by the German
militarists and, having won
what was said to be "the
war to end all wars," we
stacked our arms and
quickly returned to the
pursuits of peace and
prosperity.

MOVE INTO MCS

The strength of our Army
dropped from four million in
1918 to a little over

137,000 by 1934. In 1939 when World War II broke out in Europe, less than 200,000 men comprised our regular Army.

The German and Japanese militarists were convinced that the United States was too weak to wage a successful war--that the American was no soldier.

MOVE IN TO CU--Narrator

Our military unpreparedness invited the aggressors to attack. We had failed to heed George Washington's admonition: "To be prepared for war is one of the most effectual means of preserving peace." But continuing world events were to finally convince us of the great truth of that pronouncement made by the Father of our Country more than 170 years ago.

DISSOLVE TO:

49. STOCK--World War II inductees learning to be soldiers.

50. MS--Line of recruits being issued uniforms.

SECOND NARRATOR: (VO)

No, we were not a military-minded nation . . .

51. LS--Squads of recruits learning close-order drill.

. . . but like the strong man of peace, we did not know the extent of our strength until we had to muster our forces . . .

52. CS--recruits on the firing range.

. . . fight and win the biggest war in the history of the human race . . .

DIAGONAL WIPE TO:

53. STOCK--Highlights of
    U.S. troops in action in
    World War II.

54. North Africa landings.   . . . from the shores and
    All shots are <u>very</u> fast   desert sands of North
    moving.   Africa.

55. Combat in the North
    African desert.

56. The landings and land   . . . through Sicily . . .
    phase of the Sicilian
    campaign.

57. The advance through   . . . up through Italy . . .
    Italy.

58. The liberation of Rome.   . . . the liberation of
                                 Rome . . .

59. High point of the Nor-   . . . over the Normandy
    mandy landings. The   beaches . . .
    first of the big build-
    up on the beaches.

60. The breakthrough at
    Avranches.

61. LS--the advance of   . . . the Liberation of
    Patton's forces across   Paris and all of France
    France.   . . .

62. The penetration into   . . . and into the heart of
    Germany.   Germany itself . . .

63. Combat--Guadalcanal.   . . . to the far islands of
                                 the Pacific . . . Guadal-
                                 canal . . .

64. Action in New Guinea.   . . . the jungles of New
                                 Guinea . . .

65. Fighting in Burma.   and Burma . . .

66. Combat in the Philip-   . . . the Philippines--<u>this</u>
    pines.   by the nation the aggressors
                                 had said was too weak to
                                 wage war successfully--

67. MCS--American troops, battle-seasoned, bringing in Japanese prisoners.

--this by the American fighting man the aggressor had said was no soldier--

68. CS--A single soldier, from the above sequence --selected to stand for all Americans in combat.

but there he was, winning the victory, but not for conquest.

DISSOLVE TO:

69. STOCK--Carefully selected shots from both European and Pacific theaters of continuing combat action--interspersed with very brief glimpses of the wounded and the dead--avoiding too much agony and the too macabre.

70. MLS--one brief shot each of U.S. soldiers in combat in Europe and in the Pacific-- They are advancing.

Here were the American fighting men who gave of their blood . . . their suffering and their lives . . . that this nation, under God, as Abraham Lincoln once said, shall not perish from the earth. (Pause) These men lived up to their heritage as Americans. They fought in the best tradition of the American soldier--

71. MS--Walking wounded heading toward the rear areas, trying to look unconcerned and cheerful.

. . . to win against all odds and obstacles--and so they, with the same guttiness as their Forefathers had displayed . . .

72. Shots of combat in the Pacific--of our troops advancing.

73. CS—An individual
    soldier, tired, dirty,
    grinning in victory.

achieved victory and pre-
served us a free nation.

74. STOCK—Korean War

    Highlights from Korean
    combat footage from
    Episode X.

In Korea the American fighting man beat back armed aggression by the Communist
North Korean Army . . .
. . . and then fought
against the sudden massive
attack of Chinese Com-
munist Armies plus North
Korean Forces to a stand-
still at the 38th parallel,
in a war that served notice
on the Communists that we
will fight aggression anywhere, and at any time when
such aggression threatens
our own security and that of
our Allies, and of the rest
of the Free World of which
we are a part.

DISSOLVE TO:

75. STOCK—Berlin East-
    West Wall.

76. Shots of Russian tanks
    moving toward the Wall.

And in the Cold War crisis
when Russian tanks . . .

77. MS—the Russian tanks at
    the Wall.

. . . rolled up to the West
Berlin Wall . . .

78. American and Russian
    tanks—gunpoint-to gun-
    point.

. . . our American tanks
faced them at point-blank
range . . .

79. CS—An American soldier
    in a tank-turret—
    Berlin Wall.

. . . as the American fighting man again demonstrated
. . .

80. CS—Another soldier at
    the Wall.

. . . his fine sense of
discipline and cool courage

81. CS—Still another   . . . in the midst of a
    soldier—Berlin.   dangerous, highly explosive
                                    situation.

82. LS—American and Russian   He would not be bluffed.
    tanks confronting each   Here was strength and deter-
    other.   mination—the only language
                                    the aggressors understood
                                    and respected.

83. MS—Infantry moving up   We were ready and had the
    to the Berlin Wall in   will to fight—if we were
    trucks.   forced to fight.

84. CS—Individual soldier—   It is this man upon whom our
    Infantry.   freedom depends—

85. CS—Another Infantry   the same breed as those
    soldier.   others . . .

86. MS—Several other sol-   . . . who made and preserved
    diers.   us a nation.

    DIAGONAL WIPE TO:

87. MS—A platoon of crack   The American soldier has come
    troops at inspection—   a long way since the early
    with arms.   beginnings of our Army in
                                    1775.

    DISSOLVE TO:

88. STOCK—Theatrical shots
    of Continental Army sol-
    diers, winter of 1777.

89. MLS—Ragged soldiers   In winter quarters at Valley
    huddled around a small   Forge, through the long, bit-
    fire.   ter winter of 1777, he suf-
                                    fered from cold, hunger, dis-
                                    ease.

90. MS—an individual Con-   He was ill-clothed, ill-
    tinental soldier, eating   equipped, as yet untrained,
    a scanty, unappetizing   but, despite the hard-
    bit of food.   ships . . .

    DISSOLVE TO:

91. MLS--A line of these men   . . . his fighting heart car-
    marching through the   ried him through four more
    snow.   years to win the victory.

92. CU--A pair of rag-bound
    feet advancing through
    the snow.

    MATCH DISSOLVE TO:

93. CU--Well-shod feet of a   Today, the American fighting
    present-day American   man is the best fed, clothed,
    soldier advancing   and equipped soldier in the
    through snow or ice--   world . . .
    to contrast with pre-
    vious shot.

94. MS--Party of fully   . . . in whatever clime he
    equipped American sol-   may be . . . from Arctic
    diers advancing over   cold . . .
    Arctic terrain as above.

95. MS--Infantrymen on a   . . . to tropical jungle. He
    realistic exercise in   is also the best combat-
    the tropical jungle.   trained soldier the United
                                  States Army has ever pro-
                                  duced.

96. FAST CUTTING MONTAGE--
    American troops in
    training; close order
    drill; firing mortars--
    range; firing individual   Where once an infantryman
    weapons--on the range;   needed only a knowledge of
    range-firing, bazooka;   the rifle, bayonet, and hand
    bayonet exercise; class-   grenade . . . today he is the
    room work; ranger train-   master of a large family of
    ing; firing recoilless   weapons of great and rapid
    weapons.   firepower.

97. STOCK--Simulated combat
    from "The Rifle Squad in
    the Attack" and "The
    Platoon in the Attack."
    Army Pictorial Center.

98. CU--Squad leader signal-   He is well versed in tactics.
    ing to his men.

99. MS--Squad sprinting to
    new position.

100. Another angle--platoon
     deploying.

101. Another angle--platoon
     moving up.

     DISSOLVE TO:

102. STOCK--Theatrical foot-
     age of Union Cavalry ma-
     neuvering.

103. CS--Cavalry officer sig-   Our ground forces have come a
     naling "charge."   long way since the horse cav-
                                       alry days.

104. LS--Cavalry charging.

     DIAGONAL WIPE TO:

105. STOCK--World War I.   In World War I, the horse
     Footage of U.S. Infantry   cavalry was replaced by the
     advancing, led by French   first armored vehicles--they
     and/or British built   were primitive tanks then--
     tanks. Several brief   built by the British and the
     shots.   French--for we had no armor
                                       of our own at that time.

     DISSOLVE TO:

106. STOCK--Most impressive   And the advent of the tank
     shots of U.S. Armor in   changed warfare from trench
     action and/or Armor com-   stalemate in World War I to
     bined with Infantry--   one of fast maneuver in World
     best footage from World   War II.
     War II.

107. Brief shots of an entire
     U.S. Armored Division
     moving out. (4th Ar-
     mored) Army Pictorial
     Center stock.

108. FS--Entire column of
     armor.

109. MCS—An officer riding
     in a tank turret.

110. LS—Tank platoon.

111. FS—Another angle as the
     Division continues to
     move out.

Today, our armored force is
one of the most potent of our
ground forces with greatly
increased firepower and ma-
neuverability.

112. STOCK—Aircraft in World
     War I.   Aerial combat
     action—U.S. and German.

World War I saw the airplane
bring a new dimension to warfare.   The soldier was no
longer earthbound.
Several hundred United States
Army planes were engaged in
the St. Mihiel drive.   They
represented just about our
entire Air Force.

DISSOLVE TO:

113. STOCK—Most impressive
     shots of U.S. Air Force
     in World War II.   Massed
     B-17's on a bombing run
     over Europe.   Fighter
     action—Army aircraft.
     Strafing—Army aircraft.
     B-29's over Japan.

Air power was to be a de-
cisive factor in World War
II.   From July of 1940 to
August 1945, the Army Air
Corps acquired nearly 160,000
military aircraft of all
types.   This was an air ar-
mada to stagger the imagination.

114. STOCK—paratroop drops.
     Hooking up.   Jumping.

     Masses of 'chutes open-
     ing as many troops para-
     chute down toward the
     enemy.

The airplane had given wings
to the infantryman to carry
him long distances . . .

. . . to be dropped behind
enemy lines, to take an objective, or to quickly rein-
force a beleaguered unit.

115. STOCK—Most modern air-
     craft.   Paratroop land-
     ing.   Men and equipment
     parachuting down, vehi-
     cles, supplies landing.

Today, the plane can drop the
infantryman not only where he
needs to go, but supplies him
with immediate ground transportation, weapons, and other
supplies.

116. STOCK--Heavy artillery firing. Several <u>good</u> shots, World War II.

DIAGONAL WIPE TO:

In World War II, the 155 mm gun, the 8-inch howitzer, and the 240 mm howitzer represented our heavy and long-range field artillery.

117. STOCK--Firing a ground-to-ground missile.

Today modern ground-to-ground missiles with a greater range and devastating fire power . . .

118. STOCK--A ground-to-ground missile striking its target and exploding.

. . . with nuclear capability have revolutionized the artillery's mission.

119. STOCK--WW II anti-aircraft footage. CU--Recoiling action of a 105. Anti-aircraft battery firing at enemy planes.

In World War II our anti-aircraft weapons took a heavy toll of enemy planes; but like the old tube field artillery, they too have been replaced . . .

120. STOCK--Ground-to-air missiles, repeat from Episode XI--an Honest John missile fired, hit and destroyed by a Hawk missile.

. . . by modern ground-to-air missiles capable of knocking down not only supersonic aircraft but deadly short-range incoming enemy ballistic missiles in flight before they can reach their target area.

121. STOCK--STRAC troops pouring from their transport plane.

DISSOLVE TO:

Today, the American soldier is ready and able to go anywhere at any time, when emergencies arise and with firepower he never possessed before.

122. STOCK--Massed shot of many, low-flying helicopters landing.

123. STOCK--Troops pouring from the helicopters.

DISSOLVE TO:

124. STOCK--Shot of "Big Lift" planes and activi-

In October of 1963 our capability of moving potent

ties, readying for take-
off at Ft. Hood, Texas.
Troops loading, etc.

strike forces anywhere in the
world in a remarkably short
space of time was dramati-
cally demonstrated in a joint
Army-Air Force maneuver ap-
propriately named "Operation
Big Lift."

125. STOCK--Shots of "Big
Lift" planes taking off
--in flight--interior
plane--shots of troops
relaxing, reading, play-
ing cards, as they are
being flown to Europe--
shots of refueling by
tanker plane while in
flight.

"Big Lift" involved 116 combat aircraft and more than
200 Air Force troop carriers
in transporting the Second
Armored Division of fifteen
thousand combat-ready troops
based at Fort Hood, Texas, to
Germany in the biggest trans-
oceanic Army-Air Force deployment ever made.

126. STOCK--Shots of "Big
Lift" planes as they
near and start to land
at their destinations,
Rhein-Main, Sembach and
Ramstein Air Force Bases
in Germany, and Chambley
and Toul-Rosieres Air
Bases in France.

A deadline for this monu-
mental transfer was set at 72
hours. It was accomplished
in 63 hours and 10 minutes--
more than eight hours ahead
of schedule. Off-load bases
for the Army troops were
Rhein-Main, Sembach and Ramstein Air Force Bases in Germany, and Chambley and Toul-
Rosieres Air Bases in France.

127. Other "Big Lift" shots
to match narration as
troops leave planes.
Shots of their movement
to the areas containing
their prepositioned
equipment--tanks, ar-
mored vehicles, moving
out of the areas with
their vehicles, etc.

From terminal points in Europe, the troops were moved
to areas containing prepositioned combat equipment and
moved to an assembly area
near Darmstadt, Germany, to
be deployed in NATO training
exercises. "Big Lift" was an
impressive achievement in
planning, coordination, performance, and successful ac-
complishment of a gigantic
operation.

DISSOLVE TO:

128. CU Radarscope

129. MS—Enlisted technician   Today's American soldier, in
     in a radar tracking van.   a fast-moving technological
                                age . . .

130. MS—Enlisted men oper-   . . . is a fighting man pos-
     ating a fire-control   sessing greater knowledge and
     center.   more technical skills than
                                any soldier in history . . .

131. CS—Enlisted man servic-   . . . from the operation of
     ing a piece of elec-   weapons of great fire-power
     tronic gear, perhaps for   to the complexities of elec-
     a Nike-Hercules missile.   tronics which control both
                                defensive and offensive sys-
                                tems.

     DISSOLVE TO:

132. CS—Squad leader—STOCK   The quality of his leadership
     from "Rifle Squad in the   is second to none, from squad
     Attack."   leader . . .

133. CS—Platoon leader in   . . . to platoon leader . . .
     action—STOCK from "The
     Platoon in the Attack."

134. STOCK—MS of General   . . . to those who comprise
     Bruce Clarke about to   his top military leadership.
     review the 4th Armored   They, too, have had to master
     Division of the 7th Army   the more complex problems of
     in Germany.   modern warfare . . .

135. STOCK—A series of the   . . . in building and main-
     most effective shots—   taining a modern combat-ready
     with emphasis on troops   Army in the Cold War years
     —as President Kennedy   with their constantly recur-
     reviews Third Army units   ring crises.
     —SPX 476. Massed
     troops; Organic trans-
     port; Mechanized weap-
     ons.

     DISSOLVE TO:

136. ELS—Cadets in parade at   Since its founding in 1802,
     West Point. STOCK—from   the United States Military
     recently shot scenes in   Academy at West Point . . .
     the Army Pictorial Cen-
     ter Library.

137. MS—Officers and staff   . . . has been the principal
     taking the review.   fountainhead of professional
                                    military leaders who have
                                    distinguished themselves in
                                    three of the greatest wars in
                                    history.

138. STILL PICTURE—CUTTING
     MONTAGE—General Offi-
     cers. Use fast diagonal
     wipes—alternating from
     right to left—left to
     right, etc.

139. Grant.   Grant . . .

140. Lee.   . . . Lee . . .

141. General John Pershing.   . . . Pershing . . .

142. General Dwight Eisen-   . . . Eisenhower . . .
     hower.

143. General Douglas Mac-   . . . MacArthur . . .
     Arthur.

144. General Omar Bradley.   . . . Bradley . . .

145. General George Patton.   . . . Patton . . .

146. General Mark Clark.   . . . Clark . . .

147. General Maxwell Taylor.   . . . Taylor . . .

148. STOCK—One or two shots   . . . and many others who
     of field-grade officers   distinguished themselves not
     leading troops in com-   only in war, but in peace—
     bat.

149. STOCK—MS of a young of-   soldiers all—who preserved
     ficer leading troops un-   the finest tradition of the
     der fire.   American fighting man—

150. STOCK—LS—troops mov-   devotion to duty and the de-
     ing forward under heavy   termination to win the vic-
     fire.   tory regardless of the odds
                                    against which they fought.

151. STOCK—CUTTING MONTAGE

In this advanced technological age, much emphasis is given the machines of modern warfare.

152. LS—As the 4th Armored of the Seventh Army moves out en masse.

All this scientific achievement is remarkable and most impressive

153. Nike—Hercules missile being fired.

. . . but the actual ultimate weapon is not found among them . . . for the

154. Hawk missile firing.

actual ultimate weapon is

155. Nuclear detonation.

. . .

156. CU—The finest type of young infantryman in ready combat posture. Centered in spotlight.

. . . Man himself.

DISSOLVE TO:

157. INT. STUDY—CS of a detailed, plastic model of the human brain.

FIRST NARRATOR—(VO)

No machine or complex electronically controlled weapon, equipment, or computer possesses this . . . an imaginative and creative brain.

DOLLY OUT TO INCLUDE THE FIRST NARRATOR IN MED. ANGLE. He speaks to CAMERA.

And it is more than a brain that makes man himself the ultimate weapon, for, together with his brain, he has a fighting heart, and a soul —something that no man-made machine can possess. A machine knows no ideals, no loyalty, no devotion to duty, no sense of self-sacrifice. As he did in the not-too-long ago, man could still live his life without machines—but machines could not and would not exist without man. Per-

MOVE IN TO CLOSER ANGLE ON NARRATOR.

haps today, we have become so preoccupied with the marvels of our technological progress that we tend to neglect the preeminence and genius of individual man himself. The man with the brain, the fighting heart, the soul and the conscience which have made of him a very special creature with an individuality and a God-given destiny to fulfill. To express the best that is in him, he must be free to think as he pleases, to pursue a good way of life in freedom, according to the highest social and moral instincts and within the codes and mores of a free Democratic society.

MOVE IN TO CU.

And the American soldier is given every encouragement to express himself as a free citizen of the country he stands ready to defend.

Yet there have been and still are men and ideologies of evil purpose who have tried to make machine-like robots of masses of other men to serve as virtual slaves, to think what they are told to think, and to subjugate whole nations under the tyrannical concept of dictatorships and police states—the very opposite of the American concept of life under liberty and democracy. And it is that freedom . . .

DISSOLVE TO:

158. REPEAT SCENE 156. MED CLOSE—The finest type of clean-cut, young infantryman in ready combat posture.

FIRST NARRATOR—VO:

. . . that this man symbolizes—and stands ready to defend—the American fighting man who, for two hundred

years, has never failed to
protect his country and the
freedom under which he was
born, lives, and has his being.

DOLLY IN TO CLOSER   During those two hundred
ANGLE.   years he has never failed to
                        answer his country's call in
                        time of need. His is a rich
                        heritage and a fine tradition
                        to which young Americans add
                        luster in the discharge of
                        their daily duties around the
                        world.

DISSOLVE TO:

159. INT. STUDIO--DAY

MED CLOSE SHOT--Buckskin   It began in the French and
clad and armed member of   Indian Wars when Rogers'
Rogers' Rangers standing   Rangers fought to protect the
at ease. Behind him is   Colonies. They were among
a sky and cloud back-   the first to answer the Roll
drop.   Call.

(Roll Call voices were
recorded after scene was
shot and then synchro-
nized with lip movement
--lip sync. This scene   SNEAK IN MUSIC
was shot as a continuous   (Specially selected inspira-
DOLLY SHOT with the cam-   tional theme)
era DOLLYING down the
line of Roll Call sol-
diers.)

                              OFF SCENE VOICE
                        (This is given as a military
                        command)

The Ranger snaps to at-   Hawkins!
tention in response to
roll call.
                                RANGER

The CAMERA DOLLIES ON   Here, sir!
TO:

A Minute Man of 1775 as   OS VOICE
he comes to attention.

SUPERIMPOSE '1775'

The CAMERA DOLLIES on to:

A Continental Soldier as he comes to attention in response to roll call.

SUPERIMPOSE '1776'

The CAMERA DOLLIES on to:

A soldier of 1812 as he snaps to attention.

SUPERIMPOSE '1812'

The CAMERA DOLLIES on to:

A soldier of the Mexican War as he snaps to and reports.

SUPERIMPOSE '1846'

The CAMERA DOLLIES on to:

A Union soldier as he comes to attention.

SUPERIMPOSE '1861-65'

The CAMERA DOLLIES on to:

A cavalryman of the western plains Indian campaigns. He is a sergeant who speaks with a distinct Irish brogue. He snaps to attention as his name is called.

Prescott!

MINUTE MAN

Here, sir!

OS VOICE

Adams!

CONTINENTAL SOLDIER

Here, sir!

OS VOICE

Taylor!

1812 SOLDIER

Here, sir!

OS VOICE

Rutledge!

MEXICAN WAR SOLDIER

Here, sir!

OS VOICE

Perkins!

UNION SOLDIER

Here, sir!

OS VOICE

O'Reily!

CAVALRYMAN

Here, soir!

SUPERIMPOSE '1866-76'

A soldier of the Span-   OS VOICE
ish-American War as he
responds to roll call.   Bancroft!

SUPERIMPOSE '1898'   SPANISH-AMERICAN WAR SOLDIER

CAMERA DOLLIES on to: Here, sir!

A World War I soldier as   OS VOICE
he comes to attention.
                                   Jones!

SUPERIMPOSE '1917'   WORLD WAR I SOLDIER

CAMERA DOLLIES on to: Here, sir!

A World War II soldier   OS VOICE
as he responds, smartly.
                                   McCloskey!

SUPERIMPOSE '1942-45'   WORLD WAR II SOLDIER

                                   Here, sir!

CAMERA DOLLIES on to:

An American Negro sol-   OS VOICE
dier, a sergeant, of the
Korean War. He snaps to   Jackson!
attention.

SUPERIMPOSE '1950'   KOREAN WAR SOLDIER

                                   Here, sir!
CAMERA DOLLIES on to:

A soldier of the Cold   OS VOICE
War as he comes smartly
to attention.   Allen!

SUPERIMPOSE '1964'   COLD WAR SOLDIER

                                   Here, sir!
DISSOLVE TO:

160. EXT. ARLINGTON--DAY,
      CS--the soldier on guard
      at the Tomb of the Un-
      known Soldier.

      MS--PAN WITH the soldier
      as he marches across his

post from screen left
and exits screen right
as camera holds on the
tomb.

FIRST NARRATOR--(VO)
(SPEAKING THOUGHTFULLY
AND SLOWLY)

He who is called the Unknown
Soldier is the best known
soldier of them all . . . for
the spirit of him is the em-
bodiment of the eternal image
of the American fighting man
and the echoing words of another young American who, in
1776, voiced an immortal

SLOW ZOOM IN ON CLOSE
ANGLE OF INSCRIPTION.

creed: "I only regret that I
have but one life to lose for
my country." (PAUSE) Whatever his name, race, color,
or religion matters not, for,

CAMERA SLOWLY TILTS UP
TO SUN SHOT CLOUDS IN
SKY.

if his immortal soul is, as
the inscription on his monu-
ment states, "known but to
God," it is certain that when
he reported in for his final
tour of duty he could proudly
face his Supreme Commander
and say, "Sir, I am an American soldier who fought for
the freedom and dignity of
Man."

FADE OUT.

Unity and Form in the Stock Footage Film

After reading and studying the preceding example scripts you can see that almost all the basic principles of writing for original shooting can be applied equally to writing for stock footage. Extensive research and thorough knowledge of the subject are of paramount importance in writing the historical documentary. Events must be in chronological order and their relationships clearly established. Naturally, having to use stock footage is an obstacle to the achievement of unity and form, but it is not insurmountable. Unity and form demand the joining of ideas in their proper relationship in *time, place,* and *mood.* In other words, the goal is the right thing in the right place at the right time.

Sound Effects and Music

In the scripts reproduced in this book few sound effects are specified. A duplicate work print was given to the sound editor, as well as to the music arranger and editor, as soon as the work print was in final form. The sound editor then put in the proper sound effects on separate tape to be synchronized with the master work print at the final recording session. The producer made the choice as to where sound effects would be used. In the final episode of the series, music was used throughout with no sound effects.

The use of music is seldom indicated in the example scripts. That is a separate production phase altogether. The writer, producer, and musical director may have ideas about choice of music. However, in a predominantly stock film, such as *Army in Action*, it is impossible to score a picture until the work print is ready.

A writer certainly may indicate the kind of music he would like in his script, but he must realize that this can only be a suggestion. Music for a motion picture involves problems that only a good music editor can solve.

In my capacity as producer of the *Army in Action* series, I brought

292

A re-recording or "dubbing" session at the console, in which all sound tracks for *Army in Action* were mixed. The author, as Producer of the Series, is seated between Recording Engineers Thomas F. Hanlon and Leslie W. Guile, Jr. U.S. Army Photo.

in the music director and editor as soon as the work prints were ready for the voice-over narration. Unless the writer is working on a film *about* music, he should not concern himself too much with the music track.

Stock Footage and Original Shooting

It might be helpful to refer back to the production script of *The Making of a Champion* for a direct comparison between the predominantly stock film documentary and a documentary script written for original shooting. Each script is a blueprint of what the writer wants to see on the screen. In writing the script for original shooting he has almost unlimited opportunity to get exactly what he wants on the screen. In writing for stock film footage he has to adjust himself to the unavailability of specific shots he needs. Or, if they are available, they may not be suitable for one reason or another, such as poor photography or damaged film.

Another problem in making a picture with stock film arises when desired footage is of insufficient length to support essential narration. In many such instances Freeze Frame is the only answer to gain necessary additional footage.

Special Effects

Special Effects are also useful in making the stock documentary. In the treatment of Episode I, it was planned to use a diorama painting or life-like sculptured figure of a Cro-Magnon man which was believed to be available. No such figure or painting could be found. Finally a studio artist fashioned a Cro-Magnon head and shoulders. It was shot in Special Effects with a backdrop simulating the painted wall of the Lascaux Caves in France.

Paintings and stylized drawings lend themselves well to the stock footage documentary, as used in the openings of Episodes I and II of the Army series. Statues can be used with good effect if shot at interesting angles and with good camera movement.

The Challenge of the Stock Footage Documentary

The new writer should welcome the opportunity to work on a stock footage film. It is an experience that will make him aware of the art of pictorial relationships which applies to all audiovisual presentations. It will demand ingenuity and inventiveness. And it will involve a close working relationship with the film editor. It is in the editing room that a film takes on its final form. The problems that arise in the cutting room and the way they are solved are of great instructional value. It is here that the beginner will realize the necessity of thinking in audiovisual terms, with heavy accent on the *visual*.

Part VI: Conclusion

 **13** **Back to Fundamentals**

In all forms of craftsmanship there is no substitute for experience. Experience is the accumulation of knowledge put to use. This book represents an accumulation of knowledge gathered, not just by one person, but by many others who have tested basic principles and techniques. You can save yourself time and avoid mistakes if you familiarize yourself with those basic principles and techniques. Once you have learned them, your success depends on how you employ them.

To bring into focus the fundamentals of writing for audiovisual presentations, the following summary may be helpful:

1. Aptitude is a prerequisite.
2. You must understand the scope — the possibilities and the limitations — of the visual in communicating ideas.
3. An audience understands and remembers much more of what it sees than what it hears. The primacy of the visual in audiovisual presentations is all-important. You must learn to think and write in terms of visual action.
4. Before you begin your writing assignment, familiarize yourself with the film's subject matter, its purpose, and its intended audience.
5. The accuracy and quality of the research behind a script determines its value. As an audiovisual writer, you must be a good reporter and a persistent brain-picker, able to extract all the information you need from technical advisors and other authorities on the subject of your script assignment.
6. Organize your material so that it has unity and form — unify your ideas by placing them in their proper relationship in time, place, and mood to form a coherent, well-integrated production script.
7. The treatment is a detailed narrative, sequence by sequence, of your shooting script. It should be well developed and informative so that the reader, producer, director, and sponsor will have no doubt about *what* you want to show and say in the film and

how you will show and say it. In addition, a well-developed treatment will be of immeasurable value to you in finishing the shooting script.

8. The shooting script is the blueprint of the picture. It is a scene-by-scene description of the action as it will appear on film. Each scene must relate to the preceding and following scenes. Never jump about with your scenes, but follow a steady, smooth progression of events as they would occur logically. The shooting script must be written in terms of audiovisual action—not in a "literary" style. It must give primacy to the visual. The audio must be closely integrated with the visual and closely synchronized in time. The visual should carry as much of the message as possible. Develop the visual first, then write the narration to match, explain, or complement the visual. Be sure the body of your script keeps the story or message moving. A little overwriting is more desirable than underwriting, since it is far easier to cut footage than to pad inadequate material.

9. Scene description is the director's guide, and must describe fully what he is to shoot and substantially how he is to shoot it. Write in a lean, straightforward style. Write the scene so that it can be photographed effectively and economically. Evaluate the content and purpose of each scene as you write it.

10. Proper script format is indispensable to the director, cameraman, and film editor, and to those who break down the script for cost and budgeting. A good script aids those who plan the shooting schedule and arrange for location shooting, casting, props and wardrobe, crew, and the many other production requirements of a motion picture.

11. Avoid conflict between the audio and the visual. Where the subject matter is chiefly abstract and dependent on the narration for explanation, do not write visual support which requires concentration on that visual. Write visual support which is pertinent, but do not permit the viewer-listener to be distracted from understanding and absorbing what the audio has to say. Do not indicate use of heavy, distracting sound effects or background music.

12. When you indicate the camera angles in your script, keep the camera focused on the center of interest and its related aspects. Although the use of camera angles is one of the director's responsibilities, the writer must think and write with the requirements of the director in mind. Select the camera angle that will emphasize the importance of each scene's content. The camera angle used is always relative to the size of the object being

photographed, whether it is a man or a mouse. Your story can be told only by the camera. Use it to create mood, emphasis, and impact.

13. The reestablishing shot is most important in many instructional films. In Part III an example was given using a large automatic telephone switchboard: In an establishing shot the entire panel is shown; the camera then moves in to a close angle on a particular area of the board—the center of immediate interest. If the camera kept moving about the board in a series of close shots without moving or cutting back to a reestablishing shot, the viewer would become confused as to what part of the panel was being shown. Use the reestablishing shot to keep the viewer oriented.

14. Instructional or training films, especially those concerned with the operation of machinery, mechanical devices, or equipment, need clear, direct treatment. The instructional or training film is intended to teach, as clearly and simply as possible. What do you want to show? What is it? How does it work? Its function, its structure, and its operation are the core of your film.

15. Tempo, or pacing, can determine a film's effectiveness. Whether it is shot with a motion picture camera, a TV camera, or recorded on tape, the audiovisual presentation is a moving picture to the viewer-listener. Therefore, keep it moving. Avoid static scenes and sequences. Keep the audio moving along with the visual and keep them integrated. The instructional film must move more slowly than other films since it must clarify and emphasize each teaching point before moving on to the next.

16. At the end of the instructional film, and in certain types of orientation films, recapitulation is essential to sum up and review the major teaching or information points. It should not be presented as a fast-moving montage of quick cuts. Instead, each of the principal points must be given sufficient running time to be absorbed by the viewer-listener. However, too much repetition can either bore the viewer-listener or make him impatient. If the subject matter in an instructional or orientation film cannot be understood at a single screening, it should be shown again a day or two later.

17. Do not crowd your script. Concentrate on its basic message. Your viewer-listener can absorb only so much knowledge or information at a single viewing. If, for example, the film is specifically on repair and maintenance, operational factors should not be introduced. They are different subjects and should be made as separate films.

18. Lean audiovisual writing is neither too succinct nor too wordy. An audiovisual presentation should not be an illustrated lecture with stuffy, ceaseless narration.

19. Audience identification is most important in a film designed to influence a selected audience. It must speak the language of that audience to be convincing. Characterizations, narration, and dialogue must be written so that viewer-listeners can identify with the characters in your film.

20. Audience participation is closely related to audience identification. The use of a device which encourages audience participation enhances the effectiveness of the film. The personal approach should be used whenever possible, as opposed to cold, impersonal narration. In most instructional films, use the direct approach: "When you do this, do it thus-and-so." Empathy between audience and film is the goal in audiovisual communication.

21. Memory retention devices are necessary in instructional films. Good ideas along these lines are hard to come by, but whenever possible try for some idea which will serve as a recall device. Something with solid impact makes the audience remember the film. The British instructional film on mines and booby traps mentioned in Part III used such devices admirably.

22. Do not crowd the footage with narration, but let the visual carry as much of the message as possible. Narration should be used only to explain, or complement, that which the visual cannot by itself convey. Some scenes may be entirely without narration when the visual is self-explanatory. Scenes may run many feet, yet require only a few words of narration. A few seconds of running time without narration usually should be allowed at the beginning and the end of each scene. The exception is the overlapping of continuous action from one scene to the next, requiring continuous explanation in the audio. Narration should never be used over scenes in which there are heavy sound effects. Avoid conflict between background music and narration.

23. Good narration has a quality of human conversational warmth to encourage rapport. It must be lean writing, with emphasis on the salient points. Give the narrator words and phrases which he can read easily and which can be understood by the listener. The subject matter and the intended audience will, of course, determine the vocabulary.

24. In using a live narrator, avoid keeping him on camera for long stretches. If a narrator remains on the screen for too long, you have a lecturer being photographed instead of a motion picture.

25. Dialogue should be lean, since the time element is so important in instructional films. When the lines are spoken, they must sound like natural conversation. The narrator says what is necessary and no more.

26. Be conscious of costs. Do not write in huge casts, crowds, expensive sets, locations, background, and unnecessary special effects. Avoid single scene sets (a set in which only one or two relatively unimportant shots are played) if the same action or effect can be achieved by other and simpler means.

This book is devoted almost exclusively to the fundamentals of writing for the audiovisual medium. The audience for nontheatrical films is immense. Films have been sponsored by very large corporations, with productions budgeted as high as $500,000. One outstanding example is *Louisiana Story*, produced by Robert Flaherty in 1948 for Standard Oil of New Jersey at a cost of more than $300,000. It tells the charming, true story of a Cajun family in the Louisiana bayou country and the impact which the discovery of oil has upon their lives. While it was intended to be a public-relations documentary film, its excellence brought it commercial distribution; it was enjoyed by millions, and is now regarded as a classic.

The good film, no matter what its budget may be, results from the application of fundamental and basic techniques of film writing.

The Practical Side

Writing Fees

In the nontheatrical film industry, freelance writing fees may run from approximately $400 a reel to $2,000 a reel, depending on the subject matter and the production budget. Generally, the longer the picture, the smaller the fee per reel. The average fee is probably $500 to $750 per reel for established writers on productions with ample budgets. Producers and sponsors with large production budgets pay top prices to professional writers. For films of high quality, the established writer may get $1,000 or more per reel. But the inexperienced writer cannot expect to receive the same fees as the established professional. You, as a beginner, must serve your apprenticeship, since it is important for you to gain experience and accumulate writing credits. You should be willing to accept a small fee and thus earn your living while you learn your craft.

Manner of Payment

The writer is usually paid one-third of his fee after the producer's approval of the treatment. The second third is paid after approval of the initial shooting script, and the final payment is made after approval of the final shooting script. When a writer works with the film editor and writes narration to fit stock film, or to fit previously shot footage, final payment is usually made after approval of the executive screening.

Writing Time

The time it takes to write a three-reel thirty-minute nontheatrical film naturally varies. Subject matter is a governing factor. Very simple presentations of simple subjects may take only a few days. The fees for such scripts are proportionately low.

Writing demands time enough to come up with ideas, to develop them, and to work up their presentation. Developing and thinking through an idea or story line can take up more time than the actual writing. Constant revisions, additions, and deletions are made by the craftsman as he progresses with his rough draft, until he has shaped it into a polished piece of work. A writer may take four to seven weeks to write the average nontheatrical three-reel film. This includes time for conferences, for research, and for writing the treatment, the initial shooting script, and the final shooting script. Time may also be needed to make whatever changes and revisions result from conferences with the producer and sponsor.

If the subject matter is more elaborate, requiring extensive research and frequent consultations with technical advisors, you may have to give the project more time. This can mean a higher fee. Extensive travel to gather research material may also prolong the writing assignment. Under such circumstances the writer may be allowed transportation costs and expenses in addition to his writing fee.

Writing assignments which require the delivery of a finished script of high quality within a week or ten days are not uncommon. To meet such a close deadline obviously requires fast thinking, fast writing, and long, exhausting working hours. Only craftsmanship and a high degree of professionalism can deliver the goods satisfactorily and on time. Premium fees are usually paid for such exacting assignments. A writer may be paid a thousand dollars or more for a week or ten days of such high-pressure work.

Producers and Sponsors

Some producers are creative and provide their writers with imaginative as well as practical help, while others need guidance from the writer. The same is true of sponsors. The people who hire an experienced craftsman, who pay him well, and who rely on his taste and judgment usually leave things almost entirely in his hands. However, the writer may be engaged by a sponsor who insists on dominating the scene by interfering with the writing, the directing, and the editing. In such cases you have one of two choices: either give him what he wants, or part company. If you have the skill and the stamina, you may be able to guide such a sponsor to a reasonable point of view. Quite often, you may find that your sponsor does not understand how to read an audiovisual script, or may not understand the technical terms in a script. It is part of your job to explain these things to him.

Accuracy and Authenticity

In writing documentary and instructional films, strict adherence to the facts is essential. Poetic license and deliberate distortion of facts are ruled out by the very nature of documentation and instruction.

However, the persuasion film allows you greater freedom of imagination in your writing.

Career Opportunities

Some writers of entertainment films have become directors, producers, and executives of motion picture studios. The same opportunities exist in the growing nontheatrical film industry. In fact, there probably may be greater opportunities in nontheatrical films because the field is growing so rapidly and needs top-level writers.

There are a few qualified people in the nontheatrical field who work as writer-directors, following through from script-writing to film editing. Others write, direct, and produce their own films. These versatile people have a distinct advantage over those restricted to one phase of film-making. Many writers do not choose to become involved in areas which require executive or supervisory ability and responsibility. They prefer to devote themselves to creative writing, as most writers probably should. However, some directorial experience can be of immense value to the writer. If your ambition is to become a director or producer, you must learn the business inside out. Script writing may well offer that opportunity. Remember that, in the audiovisual field, talent and craftsmanship, harnessed by disciplined professionalism, are the keys to a satisfying and exciting career.

Selective Glossary of Film Terms

Any glossary in the film field, with its many technical and working terms, is necessarily derived from a variety of sources. Everyone in the field is indebted to predecessors and contemporaries, and the present author is no exception. He is deeply indebted not only to colleagues, but also to printed sources, among them Raymond Spottiswoode's *Film and Its Techniques* (University of California Press, 1966), a work of a quite different orientation in the world of the film. A number of the definitions which follow have been checked against and rendered conformable to the Spottiswoode volume, but the present author is responsible for any differences of expression and meaning. The reader should bear in mind that the glossary which follows is designed, specifically and particularly, for a purpose somewhat different from that of any of its predecessors.

This Glossary contains some terms that do not directly pertain to script writing. They are included to acquaint the new writer with terminology in common use throughout the motion picture industry.

Words in *italics* are defined in the Glossary. The term *film* is italicized when it refers to photographic film, but is not italicized when it refers to a motion picture.

Abbreviations

SC	Scene	MLS	Medium Long Shot
BG	Background	FS	Full Shot
FG	Foreground	MS	Medium Shot
OS	Off Screen	MCS	Medium Close Shot
EXT	Exterior	CS	Close Shot
INT	Interior	CU	Close Up
SFX	Sound Effects	ECU	Extreme Close Up
SS	Stock Shot	POV	Point of View
ELS	Extreme Long Shot	VO	Voice Over (Scene)
LS	Long Shot	ZI	Zoom In

Academy leader

A standardized length of *film* at the beginning and end of reels of *release prints* that contains identification and threading information for the projectionist; named after the Academy of Motion Picture Arts and Sciences. See *Universal leader*.

Action

The moving pictorial content of a film as distinguished from the *sound;* the *action* which takes place in front of the *camera* during the filming of a *scene*.

"Action!"

An order given by the *director* when the *sound* and/or *picture cameras* are running at proper *speed;* a cue to begin the *action* in the *scene* being shot.

Ad lib

Lines of dialogue not in the *script,* spoken spontaneously by an actor.

Animation

Bringing inanimate objects to apparent life and movement by the use of art work, cells, cutouts, or puppets, and a highly specialized photographic process.

Answer print

A laboratory print reviewed for *negative cutting*, timing, and print quality.

Assembly

The putting together of the *scenes* and sequences of a film into approximately the right order or *continuity* as they appear in the script. See also *editor, fine, cut,* and *rough cut.*

Assistant director

An assistant to the *director.* He is responsible for immediate supervision of the *production* crew, coordinating the many factors involved in maintaining the shooting schedule. He acts as liaison with suppliers of services, and sees that actors, technicians, and equipment are present at the right time and place.

Audio

The term "audio" is synonymous with *sound* and is used more in TV production than in motion picture production; as in "audio-video" ("sound-and-picture").

Background projection.

See *process projection.*

Barn doors

Hinged doors mounted on a studio lamp, which may be swung to block off light from an area where it is not wanted.

Blow-up

An optical printing process by which a *picture image* is increased in size, such as "blowing up" a 16 mm image to a 35 mm image.

Boom, Camera

A mobile *camera* mount, usually of large size, on which the *camera* may be projected over the *set* and/or raised above it. Provision is made for counterbalancing, raising and lowering, rotating, and bodily moving the *boom*, these motions being effected either by electric motors or by hand. See *crane shot.*

Boom, Microphone

A pole-like device used to project the microphone over a *set*, and out of *camera* range, to pick up the *sound* of dialogue. It can be quickly lengthened or shortened according to need, and pointed in any direction as required. See also *fishpole*.

Boom man

The operator of the *microphone boom* or *fishpole* who manipulates and adjusts the *boom* and *microphone* as required by the sound man or *mixer*.

Cameo shot

A type of *limbo shot* in which the action is photographed against a black background with an absolute minimum of stage dressing. See *limbo*.

Camera angle

The *camera's* field of view. The terms "high angle," "low angle," and "wide angle" are based on an imaginary norm which roughly corresponds to a 35 mm *camera* with a 2-inch *lens* pointed at a *scene* from about eye level with the actors; the angle at which a *scene* is photographed.

Camera, Motion picture

An instrument for making a series of intermittent exposures on a strip of sensitized *film* which, after development, can be projected in such a way as to produce an illusion of movement.

FIELD CAMERA: A battery-powered *camera* for use in the field where commercial power is not available.

HAND-HELD CAMERA: A *camera* light enough to be held in the hand for emergency shooting. Used for newsreel coverage and by the military in combat.

STUDIO CAMERA: A fully soundproofed *camera* designed for studio use, capable of shooting both sound and silent motion pictures. Synchronous motors can be used for *sound recording,* and the *camera* incorporates many features necessary for interior shooting.

Cameraman

A motion picture *cameraman* is distinguished from other photographic technicians by his title of Cinematographer. The *first cameraman* is frequently called Director of Photography. He has an *assistant cameraman* who is responsible for operation of the *camera* and its accessories, such as lenses, magazines, film, and power source. Large production units may employ a *second cameraman* and a *first* and *second assistant cameraman*.

Close shot

A *close shot* of a human roughly encompasses his upper torso and head, from approximately the waist up. Every *camera angle* must be relative to the size of the object being photographed. See *shot*.

Close up

A *close up* of a man shows only his head and shoulders. It is not as close as an *extreme close up*, which shows only the eyes and mouth. See *shot*.

Code numbers

Identical numbers printed by a coding machine along the edges of synchronized positive *picture* and *sound tracks* prior to *editing*, thus providing sync marks at intervals of one foot from the start to the end of a *reel*. See also *edge numbers*.

Composite

The presence on one piece of *film* of corresponding *sound* and *picture images*, either in editorial, camera, or projection *synchronism*.

Composite dupe negative

A *composite dupe negative* is a *composite negative* which, after exposure and processing, produces a *dupe negative picture* and *sound-track image*.

Composite master positive

A *composite master positive* is a *composite print* usually made for the purpose of producing *composite* or *picture* and *sound dupe negatives* which would be used for printing *release prints*.

Composite negative

A *composite negative* is a *negative* film which is exposed and processed to produce both *sound track* and *picture negative images* on the same *film*.

Composite print

A composite print is a *positive film* having both *picture* and *sound track images* on the same *film* which is in projection *synchronism*.

Continuity

The uniform and logical development and progression of *actions* or *scenes* or *sequences* in a *script*.

Crane shot

A *shot* made with the *camera* mounted on a mobile crane or *boom* which can be raised or lowered and moved in and out over the *set* to photograph a continuous *action* or series of continuous related *actions*. See *shot*.

Cue

The line or signal upon which an actor starts his performance.

Cut

The direct cutting from one *scene* to the next without the use of an *optical effect* (*dissolve, wipe,* or *fade*). See also *editor* and *shot.*

"Cut!"

The order given by the *director* when the *action* in a *shot* is completed to his satisfaction, to indicate that the *sound* and/or *picture cameras* are to be shut off.

Cutaway shot

A *shot* depicting *action* related to the main *scene*, or to objects which are significant to the main *scene*. It can be used as a time lapse device; see page 75 for an example to cover a time lapse while the service station attendant fills a gasoline tank. Also see Scene 116 of *The Making of a Champion*, which is more than a *reaction shot*, since it also covers a time lapse. In editing a film, the film *editor* may use a pertinent *shot* to *cut* into a main *scene* in order to eliminate a piece of unsatisfactory footage. A *cutaway shot* can be used when a group is listening to music by "cutting away" to a radio which is the source of the music. See also *editor* and *shot.*

Cutter

In modern usage the term *cutter* has largely been replaced by *editor*, with the exception of the term *negative cutter.*

Cutting outline

A guide for the film *editor* in assembling in rough *continuity* a film being made from *stock footage*. A *cutting outline* is prepared by the writer, who indicates and briefly describes the *scenes* he has selected from *stock footage.*

Dailies

The *prints* delivered daily from the laboratory of *negative* shot on the preceding day. Also called *rushes.*

Diffusers

Pieces of a cellular diffusing composition placed in front of studio lamps to soften the light; also called jellies. See also *scrim.*

Director

The person who has complete responsibility for translating the *shooting script* to *film*. He controls all that takes place in front of the *camera* to obtain optimum quality of photography, *action*, dialogue, and artistic concepts in consonance with the intentions of the *pro-*

ducer through the medium of the *shooting script*. See also *assistant director*.

Dissolve

An *optical effect* between two superimposed *shots* on the screen in which the second *shot* gradually begins to appear, the first *shot* at the same time gradually disappearing. Also called *lap dissolve*.

Documentary

A type of film marked by its interpretative handling of realistic subjects and background. A filmic record of historical events. Sometimes the term is applied so widely as to include all films which appear more realistic than conventional commercial pictures; sometimes so narrowly that only short films with *off-screen* (or *voice over*) narration and a background of real life are included.

Dolly

A light and compact wheeled mount for a *camera*, used for making *dollying shots*, and for moving a *camera* from place to place on a *set*. See also *boom, camera,* and *shot*.

Dollying or dolly shot

The continuous, uninterrupted movement of the *camera* closer to or farther away from the *action* or the object being photographed, whenever it is necessary or more effective to obtain a *closer* or a *wider angle* on the *scene* without *cutting* to a closer or a longer *shot*. Sometimes called *trucking* and tracking. See *shot*.

Double exposure

One image superimposed on another when some *special effect* is desired. Successive exposure of a light-sensitive emulsion to two *scenes*, so that two images are visible on the same piece of *film* after development, one superimposed on the other.

Double-system sound recording

A method by which the *sound* is recorded on a piece of *film* or magnetic tape separate from the *film* which carries the *visual*. See *single-system sound*.

Dubbing

Synchronization with the lip movements of an actor of a voice not originally recorded in *synchronism* with the picture *track*. The voice may or may not be that of the original actor, and it may or may not be in the same language. *Dubbing* is usually accomplished by means of *loops*, consisting of short sections of the dialogue in *composite print* form, while the actors are guided by *playback*. *Dubbing* is used to record musical *scores* and songs, and to prepare foreign-language versions of films.

Dupe (duplicate) negative

A *dupe (duplicate) negative* is a *negative film* that is produced by printing from a *positive*.

Echo chamber

A means of *sound recording* which gives *sound* a hollow effect, such as that of a ghostly voice speaking.

Edge number

One of a series of numbers, combined with key lettering, printed at intervals of a foot along the edge of *raw stock*. These numbers, incorporated in the *film*, print through to *positive* stock for the purpose of exactly matching *positive* to *negative*. See also *code numbers*.

Editing

In analytical terms, the succession of *shots* as they appear on the movie screen. In synthetic terms, the assembling and piecing together of *shots* by an *editor* according to the *script* or some predetermined idea.

CONTINUITY EDITING: A style of *editing* marked by emphasis on maintaining the continuous and seemingly uninterrupted flow of *action* in a story, as if this *action* were being observed by the audience as spectator.

DYNAMIC EDITING: A term used in film aesthetics to mean a type of *editing* which, by the juxtaposition of contrasting *shots* or *sequences*, generates ideas in the mind of the spectator which were not latent in any of the synthesizing elements of the film.

Editing room

A room equipped with a film *viewer*, a *moviola*, and the necessary accessories used in film *editing*. See *moviola* and *viewer*.

Editor

The person who is responsible for assembling the individual *shots* or *scenes* of a film into a coherent *continuity* in accordance with the *shooting script* and the *director's* annotations made during the shooting, and conforming to the *producer's* concepts of final filmic presentation. The *editor* progresses gradually from an *assembly* to a *rough cut* and thence to a *fine cut*, finally deputing the preparation of music and *sound effects tracks* to a *sound editor*. The *editor's* style will differ greatly according to the nature of his material, from *dynamic editing* in a *documentary* to *continuity editing* in a more conventional story film.

Executive screening

An *executive screening* is held when the *workprint* of a film is ready for review and approval by production executives. It is at this screening that last-minute changes may be suggested.

Exteriors

Outdoor *scenes*. Simulated outdoor *scenes* may be shot inside a studio, such as the exteriors of a home or other building, a courtyard, or a sidewalk café, when there is a not too extensive area to be covered in the *shots*.

Fade

An *optical effect* occupying a single *shot*, in which the *shot* gradually disappears into blackness (fade-out) or appears out of blackness (fade-in).

Fast motion

To accelerate action on the screen, the *film* is run through the *camera* at a slower rate of speed than normal, resulting in *action* appearing faster than normal when the *film* is projected at the standard rate; commonly called "undercranking." See also *slow motion*.

Film, Motion picture

Motion picture *film* is a thin, flexible ribbon of transparent material having perforations along one or both edges and coated with a sensitized emulsion capable of producing photographic images when it is exposed through the *lens* of the *camera* and developed in the laboratory.

Film library

A large collection of a great variety of *stock footage* maintained by a studio to draw upon when *stock footage* of some event, action, or atmospheric and background scenes can be used to provide authenticity, or in the interest of economy when new shooting would be expensive, inconvenient, or impossible. Many *film libraries* contain *stock footage* of great historical value. Library *stock footage* is correlated by means of a more or less elaborate cross-index card system. See also *stock footage, stock searcher,* and *stock shots*.

Fine cut

The version of the *workprint* of a film which follows the *rough cut* stage in the film's progress toward completion. At each successive stage the editing is refined and unnecessary or unwanted footage eliminated.

Fishpole

A long and lightweight pole from which a microphone can be suspended, the whole being swung round to provide the best pickup of *sound*. *Fishpoles* are often used by small and medium-size *production units* on *location*, where the size and weight of a *boom* would prove inconvenient. See also *boom, microphone*.

Flipover wipe
A kind of *wipe* in which the image appears to turn over, revealing another image on the "back," the axis of rotation being either vertical or horizontal. An *optical effect;* see also *shot*.

Follow shots
Shots in which the *camera* moves around following the *action* of the scene. Also called *dollying* and *trucking shots;* see *shot*.

Frame
The individual *picture* on a strip of *film*.

Gaffer
In studio parlance, the chief electrician who is responsible, under the *first cameraman*, for the lighting of *sets*.

Gobo
A wooden screen, painted black and so placed that it diverts the light from one or more studio lamps, thus preventing it from entering the *camera lens;* also used to create shadow effects in consonance with the mood of the scene being photographed. Gobos are usually mounted on adjustable stands, and are of many shapes and sizes. See also *diffusers* and *scrim*.

Grip
The person who, on the studio *set*, manipulates the *dolly* for *dollying shots*, and has charge of minor adjustments and repairs to *props*, camera tracks, and the like.

Insert
A *close up* on some object such as a letter, newspaper, map, or book to be *cut* into the main *scene* when the picture is *edited*.

Iris in; iris out
A type of *fade* or *optical effect*. In *irising in*, the image begins to appear in the center of the black field and rapidly expands in an enlarging circle until the blackness disappears and the full image fills the screen. In *irising out*, the image is rapidly obliterated as the blackness closes in a diminishing circle until the screen is completely black.

Jump cut
If a section is taken out of the middle of a *shot*, and the *film* re-

spliced across the gap, a *jump cut* is said to result. When the *shot* is motionless, this can be a useful device for eliminating dead footage.

Key light
The main light used for the illumination of a subject.
HIGH-KEY LIGHTING: A lighting technique in which the *key light* forms a very large proportion of the total illumination of the *set*, resulting in a low lighting contrast and an effect of general brilliance in the *scene*. It is used for bright mood pictures, comedies, and musicals.
LOW-KEY LIGHTING: A lighting technique in which the *key light* forms, in comparison with *high-key lighting*, a lower proportion of illumination. The result is that many objects are allowed to fall into semi-darkness or even total blackness, thus throwing others into correspondingly stronger relief. *Low-key lighting* is used for drama, mystery, and suspense.

Lap dissolve
See *dissolve*.

Lens, long- and short-focus
LONG-FOCUS LENS: A relative term describing lenses of longer focal length than normal, and consequently giving greater than normal magnification. See also *telephoto lens*.
SHORT-FOCUS LENS: A relative term describing lenses of shorter focal length than normal, consequently giving lower than normal magnification and a wider field of view. Also called *wide-angle lens*.

Level
A term used in *sound recording*. The *level* or volume at which *sound* or voice can be recorded most satisfactorily.

Limbo
A *limbo scene* is shot against a neutral or blacked-out background, and includes only the principal object or objects to be photographed, with minimal furniture or *props*. See *cameo shot*.

Lining up
The process by which a *cameraman* and the *director* line up a *scene* either by looking through the *camera viewfinder* or through the *camera lens*. *Parallax* adjustments are made before the actual shooting so that the exact image can be observed through the *viewfinder* as is observed through the *lens*. Reflex *cameras* such as the Arriflex and relatively new models of other professional *cameras* eliminate the

parallax problem, by allowing the camera operator to observe through the taking *lens* while shooting. See *parallax.*

Live recording
Recording of actual sounds in the physical world, as contrasted with *re-recording.*

Live sound
Dialogue and *sound* recorded at the time of shooting.

Location
Any place, other than the studio or studio lot, of a film producing organization, where one of its *production units* is shooting pictures.

Loop
A continuous band of film which passes through a projector or film reproducer in order to repeat a piece of *action* or *sound* over and over again. Loops are used for instructional purposes, as guide *tracks* in *dubbing,* and as convenient vehicles for continuous *sound effects* in *re-recording.*

Magnastripe
A 35 mm magnetic film on which *sound* is *recorded* for use by the film *editor* during the *editing* process.

Master positive
A *positive film* with special photographic characteristics making it suitable for acting as a master from which a series of *dupe negatives* can be printed with minimum loss of quality.

Matched dissolve
The *matched dissolve* is an *optical device* used for a smooth transition in time or mood from one *action* to an identical or closely related *action.* See Scenes 34, 35, and 36 in shooting script of *The Making of a Champion* and the explanatory note.

Mixer
The sound man on the set or on location who records the *live sound track;* also records narration *track.*

Mixer, re-recording
The senior member of a sound-recording crew, who is in charge of the balance and control of the dialogue, music, or *sound effects* to be *re-recorded.*

Mixing
The process of combining a number of separate *sound tracks* into a single *track.* See *mixer, re-recording.*

Montage
   A series of brief *scenes* used to quickly establish a mood or a dramatic setting, or as a dramatized time bridge. If no *dissolves* are used between individual *shots*, it is referred to as a *cutting montage*.

Mount, camera
   A *camera mount* is a gyroscopic mount, or a free-head, or a wheel-head mount to which the *camera* is affixed to permit *panning* and *tilting*.

Moviola
   The trade name for a certain type of motor-driven film-viewing machine used in *film editing*.

Music library
   A collection of a wide variety of music *sound tracks* maintained by a studio for repeated use. They are catalogued according to the type, nature, and mood of the music recorded on each *track*.

Negative
   The term "negative" is used to designate any of the following: (a) the *raw stock* specifically designed for negative images; (b) the negative image; (c) negative *raw stock* which has been exposed but has not been processed; (d) *film* bearing a negative image which has been processed.

Negative cutting
   The cutting of the original *negative* to match the final edited *positive print frame* by *frame* by an individual called a *negative cutter*.

Night filter
   Night filters are red filters used over the *lens* of the *camera* to give a night effect to *scenes* shot in daylight when black-and-white *film* is used. When color *film* is shot, a blue filter is generally used.

Optical effects
   Dissolves, fades, wipes, and the like. *Optical effects* are held to a minimum in modern theatrical and nontheatrical films when visual or verbal transitions are more effective.

Original
   A generic film term applied either to a filmed *scene* (whether visible or audible or both), or to the first recording of that *scene*. Since film processes are marked by sequential modification or degradation of a *scene*, the concept of an *original* is of great importance in setting up standards of comparison.

Outline

An *outline* is a brief presentation of the principal features of the idea of a film, in which the film maker's intended approach to his subject is roughly sketched. See *cutting outline*.

Out of sync

When the *sound* is not synchronized with an actor's lip movements.

Out takes

Rejected *shots* (or *takes* of a single *shot*) which do not find a place in the completed version of a film.

Overlap

In dialogue *editing*, the extension of a dialogue *sound track* over a *shot* to which it does not belong, usually a *reaction shot* of the person being addressed on the overlapping *sound track*. Also, the use of multiple-dialogue *tracks* which are overlapped to avoid cutting close to modulations.

Pan: Panning

Movement of the *camera* in a horizontal plane.

Parallax

Cameras with a *viewfinder* mounted several inches to the side of the *lens* pose the problem of *parallax*. Webster's Dictionary defines *parallax* as "The apparent displacement (or difference in apparent direction) of an object, as seen from two different points." As applied to motion picture photography, the image to be photographed, when observed through the *viewfinder*, may seem to be in a somewhat different position than when it is observed through the *lens* of the *camera* when the *camera* is first set up to begin shooting. To overcome this apparent difference in position, since the *camera lens* is in a fixed position and the *viewfinder* is in a movable position, the *viewfinder* must be adjusted by moving it to the left or right so that exactly the same image is seen through the *viewfinder* as through the *lens*, whether the camera is *panning, tilting,* or *dollying*. See also *lining up* and *viewfinder*.

Parallel

A platform which can be set up in the studio or on *location* to raise the *camera* and crew above the ground for *high angle shots*.

Picture (Picture image)

The visual image or likeness of an object recorded photographically on *film*.

Playback

(1) An expression used to denote immediate reproduction of a recording. The term "instantaneous" is sometimes applied to *playback,* so that there shall be no doubt of the immediacy of reproduction.

(2) Shooting to *playback:* A method of filming singing and other types of musical action in which the music is recorded first (called prescoring) and afterwards played back through loudspeakers on the *sound stage,* thus enabling the singers or dancers to perform to the music while being filmed with an unsilenced *camera* under imperfect acoustic conditions. This *action* is afterwards synchronized with the original recording made under substantially perfect acoustic conditions. See also *dubbing* and *re-recording.*

Positive print

Film bearing a positive image which has been processed.

Process projection

A composite studio technique whereby the actors, *sets,* and *props* in front of the *camera* are combined with a background which consists of a translucent screen on which a *picture* (moving or still) is projected from behind. Also called rear projection or *background projection.*

Producer

The person who carries ultimate responsibility for the original shaping and final outcome of a film.

Production

Production is the general term used to describe the processes involved in making all the original material that is the basis for the finished motion picture.

Production breakdown

Prior to actual *production,* a motion picture shooting *script* is "broken down" so that shooting may be scheduled in the most efficient and expeditious manner.

Production script

The approved final draft of the *shooting script,* with which it is synonymous. In theatrical films a *production* or *shooting script* is frequently called a *screenplay;* see "Blueprint for the Film" in Chapter 1. See also *screenplay.*

Production unit

A self-contained group consisting of *director,* camera crew, sound crew, electricians, actors, etc., which works on a sound *stage* or on *location* to shoot an assigned picture or section of a picture.

Property man

Also known as "Props." The individual who makes available and is in charge of the properties required on the *set* or on *location*.

Props

An abbreviation of "properties." The furnishings, fixtures, or objects and devices necessary to the *action* on a *set* or on *location*.

Raw stock

Film that has not been exposed or processed.

Recording, Live

A *recording* of an original sound, as distinguished from *re-recording*. Also called an original recording.

Reduction print

A 16 mm *positive* that has been reduced from 35 mm.

Reel (of film)

The standard unit of *film* measurement: the amount of *film* which will project for ten minutes (i.e., 900 feet of 35 mm *film* and 360 feet of 16 mm sound *film*). Standard *reels* are designed to hold these lengths of *film*, but will accommodate up to 1,000 feet of 35 mm *film* and 400 feet of 16 mm *film*.

Reflector

A reflecting surface, frequently silver in color, which is used to reflect light where it is needed. For *exteriors, reflectors* are often used to direct sunlight onto the actors or some other part of the *scene*. For interior lighting, reflectors are incorporated in lamps to reflect light coming from the back of the bulb.

Release print

A *composite print* made for general distribution and exhibition after the final trial *composite* or *sample print* has been approved.

Re-recording

Re-recording is the combining of the separate *sound tracks* of the narration and/or dialogue, music and *sound effects* onto a master *sound track* which is utilized in the final release print as a single *sound track*. See also *mixer, re-recording*.

Retake

The retaking or reshooting of a *scene* in which something has gone wrong.

Reverse angle

A *shot* of the same or similar action taken from a reverse or opposite angle.

Reverse motion

The shot of a diver, for example, ascending from a pool back up to the diving board.

Rolling title

A moving *title,* or foreword, that rolls up from the bottom of the screen. See also *title.*

Rough cut

The version of the *workprint* of a film which follows next after the *assembly* in the film's progress toward completion. See also *fine cut.*

Run through

A rehearsal.

Rushes

See *dailies.*

Sample print (Final trial composite)

A *composite print,* approved for release, in which all corrections found necessary in previous trial *composite prints* have been incorporated.

Scene

A *scene* is the smallest segment of a motion picture film in which a specific *action* is photographed. The one or more renderings (called *takes*) of an identical *scene* in the general sense, as delineated in a *script,* recorded in a *camera,* or rendered visible on the *film* itself. See also *shot.*

Score

The musical accompaniment or *score* for a film.

Screen direction

Proper and consistent *screen direction* is one of the "musts" in audiovisual production. It would be confusing to see a character in one *scene* moving from right to left and, in the next, moving from left to right. If a plane is shown flying from screen right to screen left and we cut to the interior of the cockpit, the pilot must be shown facing screen left. Sometimes *screen direction* should be indicated by the writer, as is done in the first part of *The Making of a Champion* (Chapter 4).

Screenplay

A term used in theatrical motion picture production, synonymous with *shooting script* and *production script*. It is the basis of a cinematic dramatization of a story, delineating situation, *scene, sequence,* characterization, dialogue, *sets,* and stage directions.

Scrim

A screen made of translucent material; its effect is partly to cut off, partly to diffuse the source of light near which it is placed. See *diffuser.*

Script

A common ready reference to a *production script, shooting script,* or *screenplay.*

Script clerk

The person responsible on a *set* or on *location* for keeping a record of all *scenes* and *takes* which are shot, recording technical notes on them, and putting all this information in a form useful to the film *editor.*

Segue

The musical transition from one *scene* to the following *scene.*

Sequence

A section of a film which is more or less complete in itself, and which sometimes begins and ends with a *fade.* However, sequences frequently end with *dissolves* or even *cuts,* which give a better flow of *action* than *fades.*

Set

An artificial construction which forms the setting or *scene* of a motion picture *shot* or series of *shots.*

Shooting outline

A *shooting outline* is used in the absence of a *shooting script.* It may be a sketchily written list of anticipated items, events, and *actions* to be shot by a camera crew, or a more thoroughly prepared *continuity.*

Shooting script

See *production script* and *screenplay.*

Shot

The individual *scene,* or "take" of a *scene,* the smallest segment on film (except an individual *frame*) of the *action* in a motion picture which is photographed from a single *camera angle,* or the photographing of a continuous and more prolonged *action* by a *dolly* or *boom (crane) shot. Shots* are characterized according to *camera angle* and the distance between *camera* and subject, but their common descriptions are necessarily relative to the object being photographed, whether it is a man or a mouse. A *close shot* of a man can be taken by the *camera* from a few feet away; a *close shot* of a mouse from inches away.

CLOSE SHOT: A *shot* of a human roughly encompasses his upper torso and head, from approximately the waist up.

CLOSE UP SHOT: A *close up* of a man shows only his head and shoulders.

DOLLY SHOT: A *shot* in which the *camera* moves bodily from one place to another on a special camera support such as a *dolly* or *boom*. Also called a *trucking* or tracking *shot*.

ESTABLISHING SHOT: *Long shots* which establish the location or environment of a *scene*.

EXTREME CLOSE UP SHOT: A *shot* closer than a *close up*. An *extreme close up* is often that of a human face filling the screen, featuring only the eyes and the mouth.

FULL SHOT: A complete overall view of an *action* taking place on an entire *set* or *location*, such as a mob scene or a *wide angle* view of the broad front of a battle scene.

HIGH ANGLE SHOT: A *shot* taken from an elevation which looks down on the subject or *action*. Also called *overhead shot*.

INSERT SHOT: A *close* or *extreme close up shot* of some object, usually a piece of printed matter, which is *cut* into a *scene* or *sequence* to help explain the *action*, or to more clearly orient the audience.

LONG SHOT: A *shot* in which the object of principal interest is, or appears to be, far removed from the *camera*. Sometimes synonymous with *full shot*.

LOW ANGLE SHOT: A *shot* which looks up to the subject, or *action*, often from ground level. Also called *low camera set-up*.

MEDIUM CLOSE SHOT: A *shot* intermediate in distance between a *close shot* and a *medium shot*.

MEDIUM LONG SHOT: A *shot* intermediate in distance between a *medium shot* and a *long shot*.

MEDIUM SHOT: A *shot* which shows a person at full figure, or full height, or views a *scene* at normal foreground distance.

MOVING SHOT: A *shot* taken by the *camera* from some moving vehicle such as an airplane, automobile, or boat.

PAN SHOT: A shot in which the *camera pans* horizontally across the scene.

PIT SHOT: A *shot* taken from a pit over which pass such objects and actions as charging horsemen or moving vehicles.

TILT SHOT: Tilting the *camera* on a vertical plane in contrast to *panning* on a horizontal plane.

TRUCK (TRUCKING) SHOT: A *shot* taken from a *camera* mounted on a motor vehicle (light truck), of a moving object or objects, such as a *shot* of racing horses as they race rather close toward and "into" the *camera* which travels ahead of them, maintaining a more or less fixed distance from them.

TWO SHOT: A *shot* containing two characters, usually a *close* or *medium close shot.* The term *three shot* has a corresponding meaning.

ZOOM SHOT: A *shot* taken with a *zoom lens.* See *Zoom, zooming.*

Single-system sound recording

A method by which the sound is originally recorded on the same *film* as the *visual.* (*Single system sound recording* has largely been replaced by the more advantageous *double system sound recording,* with the exception of certain types of newsreel coverage when the *sound* is recorded on the same *film* as the *picture image.*)

Slate board

A board placed in front of the *camera* at the beginning or end of each *take* of each *scene,* which identifies the *scene* and *take,* and gives the title of the motion picture, the *director,* and the *cameraman.*

Slow motion

Movement of the *film* through the *camera* at a faster speed than the standard rate, which results in the *action* appearing slower than normal when the *film* is projected at the standard rate. It is most frequently referred to as *high speed* photography.

Slug

A piece of blank leader inserted in a *picture* or *sound workprint* to replace damaged or missing footage, used during the *workprint* stage.

Soft focus

A photographic image that is not sharp; frequently used to obliterate the harsh lines of aging.

Sound camera

A *camera* designed for sound shooting (i.e., *picture* and concurrent *sound*), and therefore silenced so as not to produce camera noise. The term is also applied to the recording camera in which the *sound image* is transferred to *film.*

Sound effects

All sounds, other than synchronized voices, narration, and music, which may be recorded on the *sound track* of a film. Prior to *re-recording,* these effects usually occupy a separate *sound track* or *tracks* called *sound effects track(s).*

Sound image

A *sound image* is a photographically obtained *sound track* or sound record.

Sound track

A narrow band, along one side of a sound *film*, which carries the sound record. It can be optical or magnetic. In some cases, several such bands may be used.

Sound truck

A mobile conveyance fitted up with a sound-recording channel. It usually carries drums on which microphone and other cables are wound, and a battery system rendering it independent of external power supplies. Recently, *sound trucks* are being replaced by more compact, self-contained quarter-inch synchronous magnetic recorders.

Special effects

A generic term for trick effects which are artificially constructed, as a rule in a studio separate from the main shooting *stages*.

Speed

The correct *speed* at which a film mechanism is designed to run. The cry "Speed!" means that a *sound* or *picture camera* has reached synchronous speed. It is the signal for the director to call *"Action!"*

Splice or splicing

The joining together of two pieces of *film*, end to end, in such a way that they form one continuous piece of *film*. The joining so produced is called a *splice*.

Split screen

A process used to show *actions* that are occurring simultaneously at different locations, for example: an actor in New York is seen talking on the telephone to another actor in San Francisco.

Sprocket

A wheel carrying regularly spaced teeth of the correct pitch and separation to engage with film perforations and to propel the *film* through various types of mechanism while maintaining proper *synchronism*.

Stage

The studio in which shooting takes place is called a *stage*. If it is designed for sound shooting, it is called a *sound stage*.

Stock footage

The material in a *film library* which consists of *shots* such as es-

tablishing shots, historical material, and footage of other general application, which is likely to be used on many *productions* over a period of time.

Stock searcher

One who searches *film libraries,* depositories, and archives, and views *stock footage* for *scenes* and *sequences* of a specific nature from which he may select suitable footage.

Stock shots

Shots which are kept in stock for general studio use. They record historical events, famous places, and in general whatever it would be impractical to shoot for each *production.*

Story board

In the preparation of an *animation* film, and sometimes of other types of film, it is often convenient to make sketches of key incidents in the *action,* which are then arranged in order on a board called a *story board* and suitably captioned.

Straight cut

Cutting from one scene to another without the use of an *optical effect.*

Subtitles

See *title.*

Swish pan

A type of *panning shot* in which the *camera* is swung very rapidly from left to right or from right to left, the resulting *film* producing a blurred effect when viewed. It is used as a quick transition from one location to another, more quickly accomplished than with an *optical effect,* and far less subtle.

Synchronism

Synchronism is the close relation between the *picture* and *sound films* with respect either to the physical location on the *film* or *films,* or to the time at which corresponding *picture* and *sound* are seen and heard. The term is generally abbreviated to "sync"; a film is said to be "in" or *"out of sync."*

Synopsis

1) A short or preliminary version of the *script* of a film.

2) A brief summary of a completed film, often intended to catalogue its contents for a *film library.*

Take

Each performance of a piece of *action* in front of a *camera* which is exposing *film* is called a *take;* the successive *takes* of a *scene* are numbered from one upward and recorded by photographing a numbered *slate board.*

Telephoto lens
A *lens* which makes it possible to take a *close shot* of *action* that is occurring at a distance. See also *lens, long-focus.*

Teleprompter
A device used off *scene* which projects lines printed in large type to enable an actor or live narrator to read lines on camera.

Tilt shot
Pivotal movement of the *camera* on a vertical plane, contrasted with *panning shot* on a horizontal plane.

Title
Any written material which appears on a *film* and is not a part of an *original scene* is called a *title.*
CREDIT TITLES: The *titles* which enumerate the actors in a film and the technicians who made it.
CREEPER TITLE: A *title,* often carrying the names of the cast of a film, which creeps slowly round on a large unseen drum in front of the *camera.* Sometimes called *roll-up title.*
END TITLES: The *title(s)* which bring the film to an end.
MAIN TITLE: The *title* which appears at the beginning of a film, the *title* card carrying the name of the film itself.
PAN TITLE: A *title,* often carrying the names of the cast of a film, which is *panned* slowly past the *camera lens* in a flat plane. Sometimes called a *creeper title.*
STRIP TITLES: Superimposed *titles* placed near the bottom of the *frame,* usually to translate dialogue from a foreign language into the language of the audience.
SUBTITLES: *Titles* appearing in the main body of a film, to make a comment, explain or summarize, or to present the dialogue or commentary in a silent film.
SUPERIMPOSED TITLE: Any *title* which is superimposed on an actual *shot,* and not on an artificial background.

Tracks
A useful generic term for the bands of *sound* and *picture film* which play an important and complicated part in all processes of film making. The term is used most often in *cutting* and *re-recording.*

Treatment
A more or less detailed preparation of a story or idea in film form,

which has not yet been clothed in the technical terms which convert it into a *script*.

Tripod

A simple type of three-legged *camera* support, often used to hold *field cameras*. See also *camera, motion picture*.

Trucking shot

A *shot* made while the *camera* is moving along with the *action* or object being photographed. See also *dollying*.

Unit

See *production unit*.

Unit manager

The person in business control of a *production unit* on *location*.

Universal leader

A standardized length of *film* at the beginning of *release prints*, which is replacing the *Academy leader*. It contains identification and threading information for the projectionist. The *Universal leader* was devised and developed by the Society of Motion Picture and Television Engineers, Inc. (SMPTE).

Video

The *visual* content as distinct from the *audio* or *sound*. A term more familiar to TV than to motion pictures.

Viewer

A simple viewing device which enables *film* to be seen with the proper intermittency without the complication of a *moviola*. Since the one working spindle of the *viewer* revolves continuously, not intermittently, the device may be mounted between two rewinds, and the *film* pulled through at any desired speed.

Viewfinder

An optical device forming part of a *camera*, or attached to it, which provides an image (usually magnified) approximating that which is formed by the lens on the *film*. The more modern reflex *viewfinder* allows the *camera* operator to see the *exact image* that is being recorded on the *film* as it is being recorded, providing an instant visual check on focus, framing, and lighting. See also *parallax*.

Visuals

The *picture images* of which a film is composed are often called *visuals* in technical discussion to direct attention to the *picture* as contrasted with the *sound* elements of a film.

Voice over (VO)

The voice of an off-screen actor or narrator that is heard over a *scene*.

Wide-angle lens

See *lens, short-focus*.

"Wild" recording

Any *sound recording* which is not made synchronously with a *picture* record is called a *wild recording*. *Sound effects* and random voices are usually recorded "wild," narration and music sometimes so. Also called "non-sync."

Wipe

An *optical effect* between two succeeding *shots* on the screen in which the second *shot* appears and *wipes* the first off the screen along a visible line, which may run from side to side or top to bottom, or in any one of a number of patterns, such as a diagonal *wipe*.

Workprint, Picture

A *picture workprint* is a *positive print* which usually consists of intercut picture daily prints, picture library prints, prints of *dissolves, montages, titles,* etc., and has *synchronism* constantly maintained with the corresponding sound *workprint*.

Zoom, zooming

A *zoom shot* is made with a *zoom lens*, a *lens* of variable magnification properties that allows a continuous movement from a *wide angle shot* to a *close shot* without moving the *camera*. The same effect can be accomplished in reverse, from a *close shot* to a *wide angle shot*. The *zoom shot* can be accomplished either manually or by a motorized *zoom lens*. See *shot, zoom*.

The typefaces used in this book are 10/12 Caledonia for text, 9/11 Clarinda (Typewriter) for extracts, and 14 pt., 18 pt., and 30 pt. Trade Gothic Bold for display. The text was composed by Linofilm and the book was printed on a Mann Offset Perfector Press, on 60# Warren's Publishers' Eggshell Wove Text paper. The binding cloth is Columbia Colonial Linen.